Smart Business and Digital Transformation

Beginning in the mid-2010s, the Fourth Industrial Revolution has seen remarkable changes in information technology that have blurred the boundaries between the physical, digital and biological worlds. Industry 4.0 has enabled so-called smart factories in which computer systems equipped with machine learning algorithms can learn and control robotics with minimal need for human input. While smart technology has enabled many manufacturing businesses to increase efficiency and cut costs, many others are still struggling with implementing it.

This book aims to help students, practitioners and industry leaders to become change agents and take their first steps on the path of transformation. *Smart Business and Digital Transformation* addresses the challenge of becoming "smart" from three different perspectives: smart factory, smart industry and smart environment. Covering technologies including the Internet of Things (IoT), cloud, artificial intelligence (AI), mobility, 5G and big data analytics, the book shows how enterprises can take advantage of them and ultimately beat the competition. The book considers the importance of operational processes, business models and organisational culture. The contributing authors and editors, based at Corvinus University, present a multi-dimensional picture of Industry 4.0 which is both diverse in its voices and unified in its vision. *Smart Business and Digital Transformation* meets the growing demand for a textbook that not only presents the latest concepts and theories but is also practical for planning, managing and implementing digital transformation in practice.

The chapters include case studies to demonstrate the practical applications, and each chapter ends with review and discussion questions to develop students' skills and competencies. Students of business and digital transformation on advanced undergraduate and MBA courses will find it an indispensable guide to a vibrant and challenging topic.

Sándor Gyula Nagy, PhD, is Full Professor and the Director of the Research Centre for Supplier and Industrial Development, Corvinus University of Budapest, Hungary.

Tamás Stukovszky, PhD, is research fellow at the Research Centre for Supplier and Industrial Development of the Corvinus University of Budapest, Hungary.

Business and Digital Transformation

Digital technologies are transforming societies across the globe, the effects of which are yet to be fully understood. In the business world, technological disruption brings an array of challenges and opportunities for organizations, management and the workplace.

This series of textbooks provides a student-centred library to analyse, explore and critique the evolutionary effects of technology on the business world. Each book in the series takes the perspective of a key business discipline and examines the transformational potential of digital technology, aided by real world cases and examples.

With contributions from expert scholars across the globe, the books in this series enable critical thinking students to excel in their studies of the new digital business environment.

For more information about this series, please visit www.routledge.com/Routledge-New-Directions-in-Public-Relations--Communication-Research/book-series/BAD

Smart Business and Digital Transformation

An Industry 4.0 Perspective

Edited by Sándor Gyula Nagy and Tamás Stukovszky

LONDON AND NEW YORK

Designed cover image: © Getty Images

First published 2023
by Routledge
4 Park Square, Milton Park, Abingdon, Oxon OX14 4RN

and by Routledge
605 Third Avenue, New York, NY 10158

Routledge is an imprint of the Taylor & Francis Group, an informa business

British Library Cataloguing-in-Publication Data
A catalogue record for this book is available from the British Library

Library of Congress Cataloging-in-Publication Data
Names: Nagy, Sándor Gyula, 1980- editor. | Stukovszky, Tamás, author.
Title: Smart business and digital transformation: an industry 4.0 perspective / edited by Sándor Gyula Nagy and Tamás Stukovszky.
Description: Abingdon, Oxon; New York, NY: Routledge, 2023.
Identifiers: LCCN 2023001447 (print) | LCCN 2023001448 (ebook) | ISBN 9781032486956 (hardback) | ISBN 9781032486932 (paperback) | ISBN 9781003390312 (ebook)
Subjects: LCSH: Management–Technological innovations. | Strategic planning. | Organizational effectiveness. | Organizational change. | Industry 4.0.
Classification: LCC HD58.8 .S59 2023 (print) | LCC HD58.8 (ebook) | DDC 658.4/06–dc23/eng/20230120
LC record available at https://lccn.loc.gov/2023001447
LC ebook record available at https://lccn.loc.gov/2023001448

ISBN: 9781032486956 (hbk)
ISBN: 9781032486932 (pbk)
ISBN: 9781003390312 (ebk)

DOI: 10.4324/9781003390312

Typeset in Bembo
by Deanta Global Publishing Services, Chennai, India

Contents

Figures

Tables

Contributors

Sándor Ászity is a lecturer in Corvinus University and consultant of a lead automotive company. He worked for more than 30 years at almost every level of the automotive supply chain. He is currently working in full time in automotive supplier development and he is a senior research fellow of Research Centre for Supplier and Industrial Development of the Corvinus University of Budapest.

Bettina Boncz is a PhD candidate at Corvinus University of Budapest in the Doctoral School of Economics, Business and Informatics (EBI). She graduated at Corvinus University of Budapest (degree in leadership and management) with a CEMS double degree in international management in 2019. She received an EMBA degree from IMD Lausanne in 2021. Her research area is how artificial intelligence is transforming the labor market, economy and business.

Ilona Cserháti is an associate professor at the Corvinus University of Budapest in Hungary. She led the main direction on Social Innovation in the project "Sustainable, Intelligent and Inclusive Regional and City Models" co-funded by the European Union in 2017–2020. She is a member of the Statistical Science Subcommittee of the Hungarian Academy of Sciences and the Board of the Economic Modelling Society.

Máté Csukás is a PhD candidate in Strategic Management and project manager for FIER Automotive & Mobility, responsible for the European Alternative Fuel Observatory initiative. His research focuses on smart city development and sustainable electromobility in the CEE region.

Emil Evin (prof., CSc.) is the Head of the Department of Automotive Production at the Faculty of Mechanical Engineering of Košice. His scientific activity is oriented in the field of predicting the manufacturability of body parts. He published in top journals, such as *Metals*, *Materials*, *Lubricants* about strategy zero defect.

András Gábor (PhD, Dr. habil) is an Associate Professor at Corvinus University of Budapest. He has more than 40 years of experience in IT education and led 40+ EU-funded research projects in the past three decades. He co-authored several research papers, books, and book chapters about intelligent technologies, AI, e-governance, higher education, and smart farming.

Andrea Gelei (PhD) is Full Professor at Corvinus University of Budapest, Institute of Operations and Decisions Sciences, Department of Supply Chain Management. She received scholarships from the Mannheim Universität, the Harvard Business School and the Massachusetts Institute of Technology. Her main fields are Supply Chain

Management, Logistics and Operations Management involving Industry 4.0 solutions. She serves as the Vice President of the Committee of Business Administration at the Hungarian Academy of Sciences.

Orsolya Heidenwolf is a PhD candidate at Corvinus University of Budapest. She has received the Corvinus Research Excellence award and published in journals, such as *Sustainability* and *Hungarian Science* about construction industry digital transformation, and Construction 4.0.

Lilla Hortoványi (PhD, Dr. habil) holds a senior fellow researcher position at Mathias Corvinus Collegium. She has 15+ years of management experience in MNEs and led research projects on the social and economic impacts of technological progress. She co-authored several research papers, books, and book chapters about strategy and entrepreneurship.

Dora Horvath (PhD) is an assistant professor at Corvinus University of Budapest. She published in top international journals such as *MIT Sloan Management Review*, *International Journal of Production Research*, *Technological Forecasting & Social Change*, and *Renewable and Sustainable Energy Reviews*. Her main areas of expertise are strategy, business model innovation, and digital transformation.

Barbara Jenes (PhD) is an associate professor at John von Neumann University, her research area is place marketing, place branding and country brand equity measurement. She has 15+ years of management experience and worked as Head of Strategy at several advertising agencies. Her field of expertise is brand building, marketing and communication strategy.

Andrea Kő (PhD, Dr. habil) is a Professor and Director of the Institute of Data Analytics and Information Systems of the Corvinus University of Budapest. She has published more than 180 scientific papers in journals, books, and conferences in the fields of digitalization, artificial intelligence, semantic technologies, and applications of ICT.

Tibor Kovács (PhD) is an associate professor at Corvinus University of Budapest. He has 25+ years of management experience in the process industry and led several projects ranging from capital investment, process, and organisational development. He is researching and subjects lecturing related to business analytics focusing on performance management, machine learning and industry 4.0.

Sándor Gyula Nagy (prof.) is currently Full Professor at Corvinus University of Budapest. His main fields of research are Latin-America, the process of global, regional and European integration and the development of the SME sector. He is author of several books, book chapters and academic papers written in Hungarian, English, and Spanish.

Dušan Sabadka (PhD, Ing.) works as an assistant professor at the Faculty of Mechanical Engineering of Technical University in Košice. At the Department of Automobile Production he deals with the area of automobile production process management and innovations. He is the co-author of scientific and professional publications and articles in foreign magazines.

Tamás Stukovszky (PhD) is the Business Development and Strategic Director of N7 Holding in Hungary, researcher at Corvinus University of Budapest. His main reasearch fields are: innovation, automotive industry, SME sector, defence industry, supplier development, and sport economy.

Roland Z. Szabó (PhD, Dr. habil) is an associate professor at Széchenyi István University. He has received several Best Paper Awards and published in top journals, such as *Technological Forecasting & Social Change*, Cities, *International Journal of Production Research*, and *Technology in Society* about strategy, digital transformation, and Industry 4.0.

Zoltán Szabó (PhD) is an associate professor at Corvinus University of Budapest. He has 25+ years of academic experience in the field of Information Management and Business Information Systems. He participated in several EU funded R&D projects focusing on digital transformation, e-government, smart farming, semantic process management, IT service management and enterprise architecture management.

Foreword

New digital technologies have brought about a significant change in both work and private life in a short time. Experts agree that these changes will radically transform our best practices in organisation and leadership.

This challenge requires a serious commitment from everyone, so it is not easy to tick it off with a delegation of technical experts. This requires a new level of strategic commitment with technological capabilities, a new level of collaboration, a new leadership model and often a new organisational culture.

Carefully structured chapters introduce the reader to various aspects of digital transformation, helping them discover what it takes to prepare an organisation for today's most pressing challenges and reap the full benefits of digital tools and data. For example, the book allows readers to review the practice of traditional and data-driven decision-making in business, understand how data-driven operation can affect an industry and organisational success and how to employ digital solutions and machine learning effectively.

Consequently, this book is not just for students. It is also a very valuable read for practitioners and managers, as most are not digital natives, nor are they technology experts. Leadership circumstances are changing significantly, so today's decisions are about "how" to prepare the organisations they lead for tomorrow's competition and to stimulate growth. This book will help the reader acquire the knowledge and skills needed to build and operate agile, resilient and sustainable organisations for digital transformation.

László Palkovics
Former Minister of Technology and Industry of Hungary

Introduction

The Fourth Industrial Revolution marks the revolutionary changes in information technology that are blurring the boundaries between the physical, digital and biological worlds.

The main driver of the Fourth Industrial Revolution has been the development of business data processing, no surprise that manufacturing went through a profound transformation. Thanks to revolutionary innovations in information and communication technologies, today the concept of a smart factory is the reality that offers a shorter product life cycle and extreme mass customisation cost effectively. Additional benefits have emerged, such as better performance, quality, controllability and transparency in manufacturing processes. Industry 4.0 has enabled so-called smart factories in which robotics is remotely connected to computer systems equipped with machine learning algorithms that can learn and control robotics without the need for little human input. Becoming smart is not an option, but the key to future competitiveness.

Great experts, domestic and international, urge businesses, policymakers and society at large to embrace digital transformation and view it as an opportunity to grow. Some, mostly visionary manufacturers, have started the journey toward implementing smart factories, but many others are struggling with it. With this book, our mission is to help practitioners and leaders, as well as students, to become change agents and step on the path of transformation. It must be a collective effort, our future demands it.

This is so because the Fourth Industrial Revolution has had a profound impact not only on the way we produce and sell products and services but also on the way we live and work. It transforms and connects everything. In conditions of restricted resources and growing globalisation, the world faces an unprecedented number of social problems and challenges. By understanding the interdependencies between technological innovations and social needs, we can develop and diffuse novel solutions in ways not previously possible. The stake here is not only the future competitiveness of businesses, regions and nations but also the achievement of social well-being and a sustainable and inclusive society with the help of advanced technology. Consequently, the book – *Smart Industrial Development* – aims to guide all our dear readers on how to embrace the innovations the Fourth Industrial Revolution presents, with the right set of mentality to move things forward to meet the requirements of the future.

The present book addresses the challenge of becoming "smart" from three different perspectives

In the first part of the book, the smart factory is introduced to readers from the system of connected assets with varying levels of intelligent functionality, ranging from simple sensing and actuating to control, optimisation and fully autonomous operation thanks to the advancements in IoE, artificial intelligence and machine learning. In addition, the driving force and barriers of Industry 4.0, as well as its impacts on the value chain, daily operation, breakthrough innovation and continuous improvement efforts, are all from the perspective of a manufacturing firm.

The second part is about smart businesses. Today businesses must cope with the blurring of boundaries between traditional industries. All businesses, including those in health care, agriculture, industry and manufacturing, are now digital businesses. To stay ahead of the competition, they must compete with unprecedented business velocity and agility, which demands novel business models that challenge existing industry conventions. In this section, we introduce the reader to the transformation that business functions or sectors are undergoing. In particular, we discuss the transformation of business models and the supply chains as well as the fintech revolution.

Finally, the third perspective is from a bird's-eye view discussing the transformation in urban environments, both the opportunities and the challenges technology hold for addressing the problems we globally face today. As with any innovation, it is crucial whether the local ecosystem can embrace it and whether it nurtures the innovation that facilitates further innovations.

The Editors

Part I

Smart factory

1 Definitions and principles of Industry 4.0

Zsolt Roland Szabó, Lilla Hortoványi and Sándor Ászity

The Industrial Revolution is a series of events initiated by technological changes that led to more advanced forms of production. Not only new ways of working were introduced by also new ways of living that have fundamentally transformed the entire society. The First Industrial Revolution began with the invention of the steam engine, which made possible the transition from a farming and feudal mode of production to new, industrial manufacturing thanks to the use of coal as the main energy. This was followed by the Second Industrial Revolution, when electricity opened up mass production. In the Third Industrial Revolution, information technology was introduced to automate production.

The chapter introduces the concepts of the Fourth Industrial Revolution, digital transformation and Industry 4.0 (further referred to as I4.0), along with their driving and inhibiting factors.

1.1 The Fourth Industrial Revolution

The concept of I4.0 was introduced in 2011 (Buhr, 2015). I4.0 refers to the integration of information and communication technologies in an industrial environment (Günther Schuh et al., 2014; Xu et al., 2018). Roblek et al. (2016) identified five key elements of I4.0:

1. digitisation, optimisation and personalisation of production
2. automation and adaptation
3. human–machine cooperation
4. value–added services and warehousing and
5. automatic data exchange and communication

Zezulka et al. (2016) further identified three interrelated factors connected to I4.0: (1) digitisation and network integration, (2) digitisation of products and services, and (3) new market models. In digitisation, traditional products are replaced by digital products or at least digital features are added (Prem, 2015). Digitalisation goes beyond products; it affects the business model, organisation, management systems and entire value chain processes (Bleicher & Stanley, 2016). Digital transformation refers to the integration and exploitation of digital technologies to increase productivity and social welfare (Table 1.1).

The I4.0 technologies enable the tracking and control of equipment, products and services by collecting large amounts of data, embedding them in integrated systems and analysing them through virtual models, thus enhancing decision-making processes (Tortorella et

DOI: 10.4324/9781003390312-2

al., 2020). By using the Internet of Things, cyber-physical systems and cloud computing, among other things, companies can achieve previously inaccessible levels of operational performance (high variability at high speed) and profitability (Rosin & Forget, 2019).

The manufacturing value-added – measured in % of the GDP – reached a plateau over the last years, because the industrial sector is facing many challenges. Examples include the ageing of the working population, the pressure to minimise environmental impacts as well as the demand to provide timely responses to ever-changing customer demands. Experts claim that I4.0 can be the answer to these problems. I4.0 brings new digital technologies that solve issues and reduce pressures. By way of illustration, innovative alternative energy sources or innovative production methods shorten the time to market the products. Experts also claim that I4.0 may lead to an intelligent and transdisciplinary world in which smart factories represent the connection between digital and physical production networks (Lucato et al., 2019).

The smart factory is built from a network of data-driven, sensor-equipped and spatially dispersed manufacturing resources with varying levels of intelligent functionality, ranging from simple sensing and actuating to controlling and fully autonomous operation capable of learning and changing behaviours in response to new situations (Amaral et al., 2019). Within industrial environments, today some devices are connected, but many are not (Beudert et al., 2015).

Table 1.2 summarises the key digital technology levers and their business impacts.

Table 1.1 From digitisation to digital transformation (based on Bleicher & Stanley, 2016)

Digitisation	Digitalisation	Digital transformation
Digital data, efficiency	Digital process/product design, business opportunities	Exploitation, emerging business ecosystems, new business opportunities

Table 1.2 The attributes of a smart factory

Key digital technology levers	Implementation	Business impact
Connectivity	The use of Industrial IoT to collect data from equipment and sensors to improve factory performance	• Remote monitoring • Stock reduction • Energy savings
Intelligent automation	The use of robots, cobots and drones to eliminate repetitive tasks; and the use of machine vision and simulation with augmented or virtual reality to improve quality	• Reduction of fixed costs • Flexible production • Higher quality • Scrap reduction • Remote assistance
Cloud-scale data management	The use of predictive analytics and artificial intelligence to enable the made-to-order (or mass-customisation) capabilities	• Real-time decision support • Rapid escalation • Minimisation of downtime

Smart factories leverage digital technologies to significantly improve their productivity and operational efficiency First, thanks to the meaningful data collected by the sensors and equipment, high-level knowledge is derived from raw sensing data using advanced data mining and machine learning techniques. Based on that knowledge, the manufacturing process can be further improved even in real time, making the manufacturing processes safer, more efficient and more environmentally friendly.

Second, the use of advanced robotics not only improves the productivity of labour but also can detect anomalies, discrepancies and fluctuations in quality that would be problematic for humans to notice. Traditional quality assurance methods, such as product inspection after manufacturing, were not only time-consuming but also inefficient at finding the source of variations, which occurred throughout the production process (Bhuiyan & Baghel, 2005).

Third, the smart factory makes it possible to produce a wide range of products with custom features for a highly seasonal demand (made-to-market). Finally, cloud-scale data management enables the operation to run based on predictive decision-making. For example, the replacement components arrive before a piece of equipment needs maintenance. The anticipatory maintenance allows the operator to reduce the costs of unplanned shutdowns because the indirect costs of unplanned machine downtimes can be considerably high.

1.2 The impact of I4.0 on the value chain

It is not surprising then that I4.0 is attracting many businesses – regardless of their size – because it promises a high level of operational effectiveness and productivity due to the high level of automation. This is an attractive opportunity; however, the implementation calls for reshaping the existing value creation process and new value streams (Lucato et al., 2019).

In practice, however, digitalisation is still often associated with digitisation activities, such as the optimisation of internal workflows, the improvement of business processes or data exchange with either customers or suppliers (Sandkuhl et al., 2019). This implies that the gain in efficiency – even if it is significant – is isolated (Schumacher et al., 2016).

To understand the full potential of I4.0, we need to clarify the concept of the value chain. The most common method to identify the value creation process of a company is known as the **value chain analysis** and serves to determine the extent to which an activity contributes to delivering value to customers. According to Porter (2001), there are value activities that are physically and technologically distinct activities a firm performs and these are the building blocks by which a firm creates a product or service valuable to its buyers. These activities are also called **primary activities** (outbound and inflow logistics, production, trade and marketing, customer management and after-sales service). Porter recognised that not every activity contributes directly to value creation. For example, every value activity employs inputs, human labour and some form of technology; hence, they indirectly contribute to the value and, as such, these are **support activities** (such as enterprise infrastructure, human resource management, technology development, procurement, etc.). For more detailed information about the value chain, see Chapters 9 and 11 for the supply chain's role.

In contrast to digitisation, digital transformation is altering the entire value chain and, hence, gains and benefits are amplified. The I4.0 connects not only the equipment and resources of one smart factory but rather the entire chain. The tight integration enables connectivity and the exchange of information throughout the value chain, which can facilitate enhanced cooperation and systematic learning at all levels (Tortorella et al., 2020). Accordingly, it is manifested by **horizontal integration** (all members of the entire value chain, including suppliers and customers); **vertical integration** (where people, machinery and resources are communicating with one another through cyber-physical systems); as well as **end-to-end engineering** (enables the production of modular and interchangeable manufacturing systems for the production of highly customised and smart products and services).

Horizontal integration enables late adjustments or amendments in orders. Vertical integration enables the real-time adjustment of production by the efficient use of materials, energy and human resources resulting in potentially zero waste. For example, when the amount of raw material is low, the systems can automatically order from the supplier at the best price.

Thus, when it is fully implemented, digital transformation results in a value chain of interconnected and integrated factories, where the machines and products connected to the network become capable of intelligent and partly autonomous operation, which requires only minimal manual intervention.

Case illustration

Magyar Suzuki Corporation has recently implemented its ambitious smart factory project having three main pillars:

1. "Magyar Suzuki's supply chain involves around 240 suppliers delivering more than 4,500 types of parts to the Esztergom factory" (*Budapest Business Journal* [BBJ], 2018) The implementation of the complete electronic tracking of inputs, parts as well as products, is a significant step towards digital production control.
2. Its manufacturing was transformed into a connected network of welding robots, with 770 robots working currently throughout the production line and their operation is aided by smart systems.
3. It built an innovative supplier network with Hungarian partners to develop the next generation of vehicle prototypes from innovative, recyclable raw materials. With the incorporation of a lighter polymer in Suzuki models, Magyar Suzuki will further increase safety, contribute to the preservation of the environment and reduce the fuel consumption of its vehicles. The new prototypes must be less in weight, have lower fuel consumption and have a lower environmental impact but higher safety standards (BBJ, 2018).

In summary, although there is no universally accepted definition of I4.0 (Butt, 2020), experts agree that there are six design principles that can support companies in identifying I4.0 scenarios. These design principles are presented in Table 1.3.

These design principles are the building blocks of digital transformation. Some experts even argue that these principles are indispensable prerequisites and, hence, businesses must incorporate them into their implementation plan, otherwise they risk realising all the advantages promised by the I4.0 transition (Ghobakhloo & Iranmanesh, 2021).

Table 1.3 Design principles that help managers to plan their organisation's digital transformation

Design principle	Brief description
Interoperability	The ability of systems and workforce to communicate, exchange data, and coordinate activities
Virtualisation	Monitoring of physical processes by either one virtual resource from multiple physical resources or multiple virtual resources from one physical resource
Decentralisation	The transition towards system components
Real-time capability	Collation and processing of data in real time that allows informed and timely decision-making
Service orientation	Ability to use big data analytics to obtain a predictive analysis that can help in better understanding customer needs
Modularity	The ability of businesses to flexibly adapt to changing requirements and industry needs

Nevertheless, today prevailing business practices often fail to address this challenge and run the risk of losing control over their value creation. Usually, decision-making processes are slow and are often based on intuitive feelings rather than on hard data, while product development is done without a comprehensive understanding of the customer's needs (Schuh et al., 2017).

It is worth noting that there is a lack of readiness among companies towards the implementation of I4.0 and, consequently, many attempts fail (Szabó et al., 2020). When it comes to implementation, managers and leaders are facing the reality that switching to I4.0 involves highly complex, multiple-level transformations to which there are no available standard and proven approaches yet (Butt, 2020). The next section explains the most important barriers that inhibit the digital transformation of companies.

1.3 Driving forces and barriers of I4.0

Currently, the most important barrier to the spread of digital transformation and Industry 4.0 is the human factor. Managers are also not ready to move to a significantly more efficient, but significantly different operating model, and even middle management is explicitly resistant to change, fearing its role. Top managers need to lead the transformation of the management structure, including the transformation of the role of middle management (Szabó et al., 2019). Besides, acting top managers face many barriers and driving forces of I4.0 as listed in Table 1.4.

Overall, I4.0 is immensely resource intensive and complex. Businesses usually lack the necessary competencies to succeed in the transformation and, hence, the probability of failure is high. Leaders need to recognise that for a successful transformation, they must pre-equip the organisation with the necessary skills, such as change management and strategic planning. They are advised to assess in advance the maturity of their company's digital readiness to better understand whether the necessary competencies and resources are available.

Table 1.4 Driving forces and barriers of Industry 4.0 (based on Szabó et al., 2020, pp. 6–7)

Driving force	Barrier
Human resources	
• Increasing labour shortages • Reducing human work • Allocating the workforce to other areas(higher added value) • Demanded by employees (to remain an attractive employer) • Handling labour market challenges	• Lack of necessary competencies within the company • Lack of skilled workforce • Longer learning times (employee training) • Lack of abilities within the company
Financial resources and profitability	
• Attempt to decrease costs • Reducing costs • Realising financial benefits • Increase of ROA • Reducing expenditures	• Lack of financial resources • Return and profitability • Limited availability of financial resources
Market conditions and competitors	**Management reality**
• Market competition • Follow market trends • Pressure from competitors • Improving the market position • Overcoming competitors	
Management expectations	• Lack of managers with appropriate skills, competencies and experience • Lack of conscious planning: defining goals resources
• Need for higher control for the top management • Continuous monitoring of company performance • Real-time performance measurement • Compliance with management expectations	
Productivity and efficiency	**Organisational factors**
• Reducing the error rate • Improving lead times (compliance with market conditions) • Efficiency improvement • Ensuring reliable operation • Fewer stoppages in production	• Inadequate organisational structure • Resistance by employees • Inadequate process organisation • Resistance from middle management
Customer satisfaction	**Technological and process integration, cooperation**
• Demanded by customers/partners • Improving customer satisfaction • Demand for quality improvement • Compliance with customer needs • Flexibility improvement	• Lack of willingness to cooperate (at the supply chain level) • Lack of appropriate, common thinking • Lack of an integrated communication protocol • Lack of standards: technology and processes

Review questions

1. What are digitisation, digitalisation, digital transformation and Industry 4.0?
2. When planning a digital transformation, what are the design principles the company must start with?
3. Explain what the difference is between vertical and horizontal integration required by I4.0!
4. What are the driving forces of I4.0?
5. What are the barriers to I4.0?

Discussion questions

1. The implementation of a smart factory is challenging. Why is it critical for businesses to face it, rather than just ignoring it by continuing to do business as usual?
2. Please explain why it is not enough to digitise. In contrast, why is digital transformation associated with greater gains?
3. Management can be both a driver and a barrier to digital transformation. How is this possible?

Bibliography

Amaral, A., Jorge, D., & Peças, P. (2019). Small medium enterprises and industry 4.0: Current models' ineptitude and the proposal of a methodology to successfully implement industry 4.0 in small medium enterprises. *Procedia Manufacturing, 41*, 1103–1110. https://doi.org/10.1016/j.promfg.2019.10.039

Beudert, B. R., Juergensen, L., & Weiland, J. (2015). Understanding smart machines: How they will shape the future. *Schneider Electric*, 1–13.

Bhuiyan, N., & Baghel, A. (2005). An overview of continuous improvement: From the past to the present. *Management Decision, 43*(5), 761–771. https://doi.org/10.1108/00251740510597761

Bleicher, J., & Stanley, H. (2016). Digitization as a catalyst for business model innovation is a three-step approach to facilitating economic success. *Journal of Business Management, 12*, 62–71.

Budapest Business Journal [BBJ], 2018. https://bbj.hu/business/tech/telco/magyar-suzuki-s-esztergom-facility-to-become-a-smart-factory

Buhr, D. (2015). Social innovation policy for industry 4.0. *Good Society –Social Democracy # 2017 Plus*, 1–24.

Butt, J. (2020). A strategic roadmap for the manufacturing industry to implement industry 4.0. *Designs, 4*(11). https://doi.org/10.3390/designs4020011

Ghobakhloo, M., & Iranmanesh, M. (2021). Digital transformation success under Industry 4.0: A strategic guideline for manufacturing SMEs. *Journal of Manufacturing Technology Management*, (ahead-of-print). https://doi.org/10.1108/JMTM-11-2020-0455

Lucato, W. C., Pacchini, A. P. T., Facchini, F., & Mummolo, G. (2019). Model to evaluate the Industry 4.0 readiness degree in Industrial Companies. *IFAC PapersOnLine, 52*(13), 1808–1813.

Porter, M. E. (2001). The value chain and competitive advantage. In *Understanding business processes* (pp. 50–66). Open University.

Prem, E. (2015). A digital transformation business model for innovation. *The ISPIM Innovation Summit, 11*. Retrieved from https://www.researchgate.net/publication/284682831

Roblek, V., Meško, M., & Krapež, A. (2016). A complex view of industry 4.0. *SAGE Open, 6*(2), 1–11. https://doi.org/10.1177/2158244016653987

Rosin, F., Forget, P., Lamouri, S., & Pellerin, R. (2020). Impacts of Industry 4.0 technologies on lean principles. *International Journal of Production Research, 58*(6), 1644–1661. https://doi.org/10.1080/00207543.2019.1672902

Sandkuhl, K., Shilov, N., & Smirnov, A. (2019). Facilitating digital transformation by multi-aspect ontologies: Approach and application steps. *IFAC Papers Online, 52*(13), 1609–1614.

Schuh, G., Anderl, R., Gausemeier, J., ten Hompel, M., & Wahlster, W. (2017). *Industry 4.0 maturity index. Managing the digital transformation of companies.* Retrieved from https://boundarysys.com/wp-content/uploads/2021/03/Acatech_Maturity_Index_2020-IAN.pdf

Schuh, G., Potente, T., Wesch-Potente, C., Weber, A. R., & Prote, J. P. (2014). Collaboration mechanisms to increase productivity in the context of industrie 4.0. *Procedia CIRP, 19*(C), 51–56. https://doi.org/10.1016/j.procir.2014.05.016

Schumacher, A., Erol, S., & Sihn, W. (2016). A maturity model for assessing Industry 4.0 readiness and maturity of manufacturing enterprises. *Procedia CIRP, 52*, 161–166. https://doi.org/10.1016/j.procir.2016.07.040

Szabó, Z. R., Horváth, D., & Hortoványi, L. (2019). Hálózati tanulás az ipar 4.0 korában. *Közgazdasági Szemle, 66*(1), 72–94. Retrieved from https://doi.org/10.18414/KSZ.2019.1.72

Szabó, Z. R., Vuksanović Herceg, I., Hanák, R., Hortovanyi, L., Romanová, A., Mocan, M., & Djuričin, D. (2020). Industry 4.0 implementation in B2B companies: Cross-country empirical evidence on digital transformation in the CEE region. *Sustainability, 12*(22), 9538.

Tortorella, G. L., Vergara, C., Mac, A., Garza-Reyes, J. A., & Sawhney, R. (2020). Organizational learning paths based upon industry 4.0 adoption: An empirical study with Brazilian manufacturers. *International Journal of Production Economics, 219*, 284–294. https://doi.org/10.1016/j.ijpe.2019.06.023

Xu, M., David, J. M., & Kim, S. H. (2018). The fourth industrial revolution: Opportunities and challenges. *International Journal of Financial Research, 9*(2), 90–95.

Zezulka, F., Marcon, P., Vesely, I., & Sajdl, O. (2016). Industry 4.0 – An Introduction in the phenomenon. *IFAC-PapersOnLine, 49*(25), 8–12. https://doi.org/10.1016/j.ifacol.2016.

2 The concept of continuous and smart improvement

Zsolt Roland Szabó and Lilla Hortoványi

Increased competition and accelerating innovation are forcing businesses to improve their efficiency and productivity by all possible means, including the continuous improvement of their activities.

The Throughput Inc. provides an excellent illustration of why it is necessary for every aspect of life to think about continuous improvements. Consider the simple task of watering one plant for a week. This task seems quite simple to accomplish. But what if there are 50 plants? And what if plants should be watered twice a day for one full week? This might need some planning and coordination to sequence the plants and plan the quantity of water needed for each pot. The more complicated processes get, the higher the possibility for inefficiencies to set in. These inefficiencies can waste time, cost money and duplicate labour, which can, in turn, impact the total profits. Continuous improvement aims to eliminate these inefficiencies by improving planning and optimising operations, hence, directly reducing waste and duplications (Source: https://throughput .world/blog/lean-continuous-improvement/).

The chapter discusses how organisations can achieve continuous improvements by solving contemporary challenges. Several fundamental strategic models and methods are also introduced to highlight the practice.

2.1 Striving for perfection

Bhuiyan and Baghel (2005) defined continuous improvement (CI) as an **organisational culture** that aims to achieve sustained improvement by the elimination of waste in all systems and processes of the organisation as well as the better and more consistent quality of products or services. The primary responsibility for improving a process belongs to those who work in that process. Hence, improvement activities should be integrated into the regular work of individual employees (Berger, 1997). All business processes can and should be monitored to find ways of minimising problems, waste and variations as well as to improve quality. Thus, CI involves everyone working together to make evolutionary (also called incremental) improvements without necessarily making huge capital investments (Bhuiyan & Baghel, 2005).

Over the decades, several CI methodologies have developed; lean manufacturing, six sigma and the balanced scorecard are the most well-known examples (Bhuiyan & Baghel, 2005). While these individual CI methodologies are proven to improve organisational operations in many aspects, they are also found to be ineffective at solving all issues at once. To overcome the weaknesses of individual programs, organisations have recently begun to merge different methodologies and apply them together, resulting in a combined and comprehensive CI programme (Bhuiyan & Baghel, 2005).

DOI: 10.4324/9781003390312-3

The means of CI, nevertheless, vary (Berger, 1997). In the manufacturing industry, CI activities primarily focus on the simplification of production processes, increase in quality and elimination of waste. In service industries and the public sector, CI also targets the simplification of processes with the improvement of customer service through greater empowerment of individual employees and, correspondingly, less bureaucracy.

Within an organisation, continuous improvement can take place at three different levels: management, group and individual levels (Bhuiyan & Baghel, 2005). At the management level, CI is a drive for achieving a unique and sustainable competitive advantage if it is incorporated into the long-term strategic plan (Jha et al., 1996). This is so because it is almost impossible to copy CI practices of competitors (Bessant & Caffyn, 1997). At the group level, CI primarily drives continuous problem identification and problem-solving. Finally, on the individual level, it means improving daily tasks. To maximise the benefits of the CI program, organisations must be able to achieve continuous improvement at all three levels (Bhuiyan & Baghel, 2005).

CI comes from the company's strategic thinking and management practices and is implemented through projects and day-to-day management. The continuous practice of CI can also result in larger changes, but real breakthroughs require more than that, which is detailed in the following parts of the chapter.

2.2 Long-term strategic planning and thinking

Strategic thinking refers to the advantage-seeking behaviour of a company or an individual. To overcome the competitors, you need a superior strategy. "Strategy" can refer to a plan, a ploy, a pattern, a perspective or a position (Mintzberg, 1994). Strategic management is the cycle of planning – implementation – monitoring – feedback. Strategic tools help strategic management practices.

"Classical" strategic models and methods are based on a well-structured analysis process, during which it is necessary to explore the opportunities, threats, resources and capabilities inherent in the external and internal environment of the company.

The company's macro (external) environment: Political, Economic, Social, Technological, Environmental, Legal (PESTEL) analysis

The operation of companies is determined by external environmental factors, which, although unaffected, are changing opportunities and threats for the company and its competitors. If a company responds more slowly to opportunities or threats than its competitors, it puts the company at a competitive disadvantage. Therefore, it is important to identify the right trends.

The importance of changes in the external environment was recognised by management researchers decades ago. The PEST model developed for practising managers has proven to be a useful tool. The model is simple enough, and, yet, it can be rich enough to inform corporate strategies.

The PEST model includes four basic environmental factors: Political, Economic, Social and Technological components. In addition to the description of the individual factors, the main goal is to identify the most important changes and trends that hide opportunities and dangers for companies.

The model was applied successfully and the range of factors involved in the study expanded. The PEST model was complemented by the Legal and the Ecological environment, resulting in the **PESTEL model**.

The **Political environment** refers to the assessment of political stability, transparency, the extent of corruption, the role of interest groups in political decision-making and the role of professional consultations in political decision-making.

The **Economic environment** refers to the assessment of the economic growth rate, inflation, interest rates, GDP development, exchange rate policy, employment and unemployment development and income levels

The **Social environment** assesses the demographic processes, lifestyle changes, social inequalities, social mobility and consumption patterns.

The **Technological environment** estimates the impacts of emerging cutting-edge technologies, the rate of innovation investment and the development of patents as well as the ageing rate of technologies.

The **Ecological environment** assesses the level of the development of natural resources, the development of circular farming and the extent of other measures related to climate change and clean technologies.

The **Legal environment** judges the development of legal certainty, the enforcement of property laws, consumer protection laws, competition laws and employment laws.

The company's meso (external) environment: Porter's 5(+1) forces

The operation of companies is also determined by industrial environmental factors. Porter's "Competitive Strategy," published in 1980, identified empirical studies of many industry segments that also influence the profitability of an industry segment, also known as the **Porter 5(+1) forces model**. In 1980, Porter published the so-called Competitive Strategy, which identified empirical studies on many industry segments, which also influence the profitability of industry segments. Competitive Strategy is also known as Porter's 5(+1) forces model. These factors include:

Direct competitive environment, competition within the industry segment: In the case of several competitors, the profitability of the industry is lower. Special market structures, for example, when competitors cooperate (coopetition) are considered exceptions to these factors.

The threat of new entrants: If the industry segment is protected and entry barriers are high, the threat of new entrants is low; consequently, the profitability of the industry segment is high. Conversely, if entry barriers are low, profitability is low.

Bargaining power of customers: If there are several customers, their bargaining power is typically lower, which can lead to higher profitability. In the case of customer-supplier cooperation, higher profitability can be achieved and, thus, it is necessary to examine the bargaining power of customers as well.

Bargaining power of suppliers: In the case of several suppliers, the bargaining power of suppliers is typically lower, and higher profitability can be achieved. If customer-supplier cooperation is present, higher profitability can be achieved, which makes it necessary to examine the bargaining power of suppliers.

The threat of substitute products: If the products/services of the industry segment can be easily substituted, the profitability of the industry segment is low. If it is difficult to substitute its products/services, the profitability of the industry segment is high.

Contribution of complementary products to profitability: Higher profitability can be achieved for several complementary products.

The company's internal environment: Porter's 5(+1) forces

The operation of companies is fundamentally determined by their enduring goals. The corporate mission defines what the organisation's fundamental goal is (e.g., "fighting climate change"), while the vision includes the most important goal for the next well-defined period (e.g., "reducing CO_2 emissions that cause climate change globally by 20% by 2030"). Another example is that a corporation's mission (i.e., its fundamental goal) is to help mobility, while its vision (i.e., its short-term goal) is to achieve a 30% market share in the electric vehicle market by 2030.

The company's mission and vision can be further broken down into strategic actions and plans. However, doing so requires the integration of the company's internal capabilities and the changes in the external environment.

A useful method for mapping internal endowments is value chain analysis (Figure 2.1), which helps to understand the company's value-added activities. Complementing this with Valuable, Rare, Inimitable, Organised (VRIO) analysis (Figure 2.2), the income-generating capacity of corporate resources can also be identified. The income-generating capacity of corporate resources can be identified with the combination of value chain analysis and VRIO analysis (Figure 2.2).

The essence of the value chain model is that we need to determine the value added to each activity.

It is important to emphasise that in this model the primary activity is the one for which the buyer pays. Support activities help primary activities. However, primary and support activities represent only a small fraction of the value perceived by customers nowadays. In fact, the goal of any activity is to increase organisational efficiency so that the business

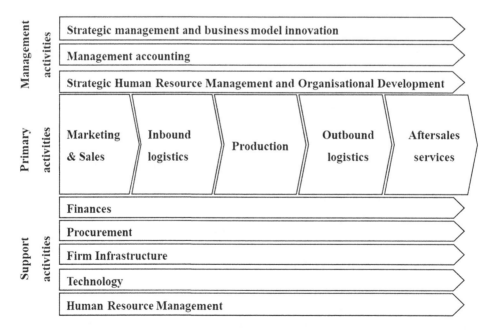

Figure 2.1 Contemporary value chain model (Szabó & Vida, 2009, p. 29)

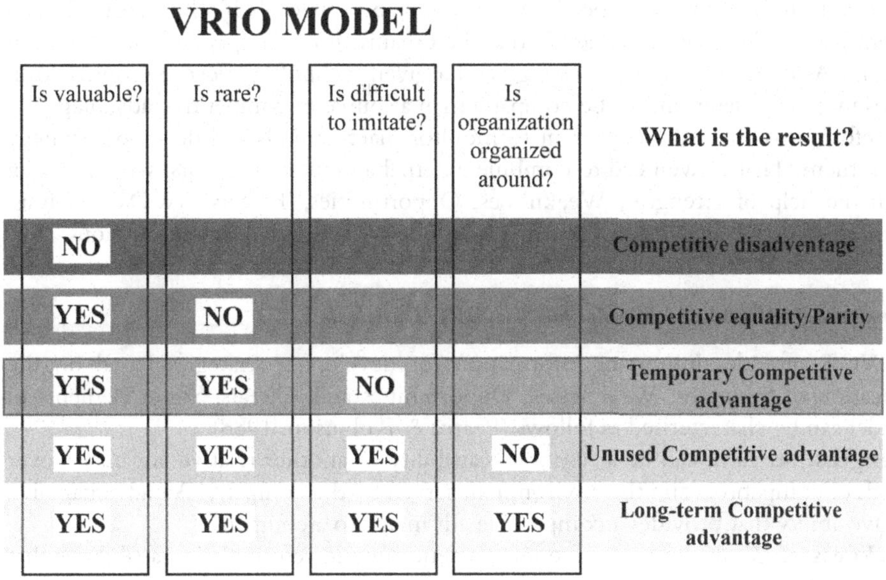

VRIO MODEL

Is valuable?	Is rare?	Is difficult to imitate?	Is organization organized around?	**What is the result?**
NO				Competitive disadvantage
YES	**NO**			Competitive equality/Parity
YES	**YES**	**NO**		Temporary Competitive advantage
YES	**YES**	**YES**	**NO**	Unused Competitive advantage
YES	**YES**	**YES**	**YES**	Long-term Competitive advantage

Figure 2.2 VRIO analysis (based on Managmentmania, n.d)

can deliver as much value as possible at the lowest possible cost. So, the value chain helps managers see how to create even more value for customers while keeping costs at a reasonable level.

This is well evidenced by the global optimisation trend that characterises today's management thinking. According to global optimisation trends, developed countries typically retain management, marketing and research and development activities, while other activities are outsourced to less-developed countries. It is also a trap from which it is difficult to move towards higher value-added activities. However, global optimisation is absolutely necessary for competitiveness. Business model innovation (a novel way of strategic analysis and strategy-making) has evolved into one of the most important, most valuable activities today.

Each activity requires resources (and capabilities; hereafter uniformly resources). The value of each resource (and ability) can be identified using the VRIO analysis, which identifies how valuable, rare and imperfectly imitable it is and the extent to which the organisation helps to exploit that resource (and capability).

The VRIO analysis can be used to identify resources (and capabilities) that lead to sustained and above-average performance. If a resource is not valuable enough, it does not provide the company with adequate competitiveness and profitability in the given environment. If valuable, but not rare, many other organisations can possess it, which means that a lasting competitive advantage cannot be built on such a resource. If a resource is valuable, rare and cannot be copied, then it is worth building an organisation around it and exploiting that resource (capability).

It is important to note that in the digital age, it is often necessary to reevaluate our resources (and capabilities). What used to be valuable and rare can become worthless and even a deterrent obligation overnight.

For example, when a production line tied to a particular technology is still novel and innovative, it can be a significant benefit to the company, especially if other resources (and capabilities) are in line with it, meaning that the organisation can operate under the right conditions. As external conditions change and a given technology becomes outdated, it becomes more of a deterrent to the company than a source of competitive advantage.

Therefore, it is especially important to monitor macro-trends and develop a strategy based on them. That is, we need to combine external and internal factors, which we can do with the help of Strengths, Weaknesses, Opportunities, Threats (SWOT) analysis. Based on the SWOT analysis, it is possible to define well-founded strategic actions.

Joint analysis of external and internal factors: SWOT analysis

The SWOT provides important information for developing strategies based on the identification of Strengths, Weaknesses, Opportunities and Threats. Some elements of the model can be characterised as follows (Pearce & Robinson, 1988).

Strengths: Strength can be a resource, capability or another relative advantage over the needs of competitors and the environment served by the company. An advantage is a distinctive ability that provides a competitive advantage to a company.

Weaknesses: Weakness is a constraint or deficiency in resources or capabilities that significantly limits a high level of performance. Buildings, financial resources, leadership skills, marketing skills and brand image can be a source of weak points, for example.

Opportunities: Opportunity is a fundamentally favourable situation in the company environment. Major trends in the environment can be a major source of opportunity. Previously overlooked market segments, changes in competition or regulatory conditions, technological changes and improved customer and supplier relationships can all illustrate a company's opportunities.

Threats*:* A threat is a fundamental adverse situation in the company's environment and can harm the company's current or future position. Examples include the emergence of a new competitor, a slowdown in market growth or an unfavourable technological change.

As can be seen from the above description, the strengths and weaknesses refer to the internal characteristics and capabilities of the company, while the opportunities and threats are used to assess and judge the environment (Table 2.1).

The models and methods presented in the previous subsections can be integrated into the SWOT analysis. Techniques for analysing the internal environment are used to identify strengths and weaknesses. Internal factors and endowments are basically micro-factors interpreted at the corporate level and refer to the past and the present.

Table 2.1 SWOT analysis dimensions

	Positive	*Negative*
Internal factors **The past or present situation** **microenvironment**	Strengths	Weaknesses
External factors **Present or future situation** **mezzo or macro-environment**	Opportunities	Threats

Table 2.2 SWOT-based strategy creation

	Strengths	*Weaknesses*
Opportunities	Formulate (intensive growth) strategies to help you seize opportunities by using your strengths	Formulate (adaptive/entrepreneurial) strategies to help you seize opportunities by overcoming weaknesses
Threats	Formulate (resource-based) strategies to help avoid threats by using strengths	Formulate (defensive) strategies to minimise vulnerabilities and avoid threats

External environment analysis tools help identify opportunities and threats. In the case of external factors, in addition to understanding the static current situation, the understanding of future expected states, trends, changes, and larger movements will provide the real input for the SWOT-based strategy creation (Table 2.2).

The SWOT analysis is subjective: we can get different results based on different assumptions, but this does not mean that the SWOT analysis does not have an internal set of rules and that important strategic conclusions cannot be drawn from it.

The factor that significantly determines subjectivity is whom we compare and benchmark when examining internal factors. The evaluation of external factors is significantly determined by the company's basic goals and the perception of the leader.

2.3 Project management

Organisations usually systematically realise their strategic objectives by launching projects (Jung & Wang, 2006). Projects, not departments, become the unit of control to avoid all the pitfalls of bureaucracy (Kwak et al., 2015). In practice, the project organisation provides a framework and a structure for carrying out continuous improvement activities.

The critical difference between continuous improvement projects (CIP) and standard projects is that instead of providing independent and individual solutions, the CIP emphasises improving the entire system in question or the entire value stream.

Hence CI occurs at the group level when dedicated members of an organisation work together for improving performance by continuously implementing small changes in their work processes (Sundqvist, 2019). All processes and resources within this system or the entire value stream are interdependent. The composition and structure of the CIP team are the keys to improving the system in a comprehensive and targeted way because these people must be knowledgeable about both the improvement approach and the processes to be advanced. They must understand the cause-effect relationships of organisational resources, processes and capabilities. Ideally, a cross-functional team composed of the same people who normally work with these processes on a daily basis ensures the successful implementation of CI (Lodgaard et al., 2016).

Former research pointed out that more and more businesses are investing in automation; however, managers often fail to recognise that automation and state-of-the-art technology alone cannot solve operational inefficiencies (e.g., Berman, 2012; Gerbert et al., 2015; Müller et al., 2018). Even before investing, problems need to be explored and processes improved. This implies that CIP is an essential and critical component of all automation and digital investments (Berger, 1997).

A "Continuous Improvement Project" has four prerequisites:

1. Defined material and information flows
2. Defined and applied standards
3. Decoupling of processes
4. Clearly defined roles and responsibilities

CIP provides a prioritised list of actions and identifies a longitudinal path of future development (Kwak et al., 2015). Establishing this clarity creates the necessary transparency and reveals any deviations from a target condition. Furthermore, this clarity also allows for establishing the relationship between the cause of a deviation and the effect of a measure aimed at eliminating it. We call a system that meets these criteria an "Improvable System." When CIP is incorporated into the strategy, the organisational commitment is found to be stronger and dedicated resources are more likely to be available for the execution of CIP (Jha et al., 1996).

The success of the CI project greatly depends on the expertise of organisational members at lower levels (Sangwa & Sangwan, 2020). However, it does matter who contributes to CI teams. Primarily employees who know the whole process and understand each activity's interdependencies are critical from different levels and with different backgrounds. It is also important that CIP members are aware of CI goals, they comprehend the extent to which CI will result in the change of the existing standards and they are still committed to it (Hirzel et al., 2017). Some scholars, for example, highlighted that CI in essence means continuously raising the bar, which can translate into higher workplace stress (Boje & Winsor, 1993).

Finally, the success of CIP demands an atmosphere for rewarding participation, where team members can openly communicate about problems and potentials for development. Employees who feel empowered by their co-workers and managers can take an active role in solving problems and promote the CI philosophy in their day-to-day work (Angell and Corbett, 2009).

This requires the careful hiring of people who fit well in such an organisational culture. A team can only offer creativity when it is **intrinsically motivated** to do so (Urick et al., 2017). The involvement of organisational members in CI still seems risky for many managers. Many factors militate against its widespread practice, including the fear of uncontrolled change, disbelief in the ability of employees to contribute and lack of skills as well as inappropriate organisational structures to support CI, among many other factors (Bessant & Caffyn, 1997).

Case illustration

Amazon is one of the fastest-growing companies worldwide. The company dominates the eCommerce market space and also claims leadership in several other industries such as warehousing, distribution, appliance installation, grocery retail, Internet and web services and so many other fields. Today Amazon's operations – the way they fulfil, ship, track and deliver orders – are world class. But they did not start that way.

As a technology company, Amazon initially had the belief that most issues could be resolved with technology, so it was not systematically engaging frontline workers in the process of continuous improvement. Thus, the company was trying to automate almost everything, with varying success. The automation designed for books did not work for new types of goods, such as shoes. When the shoebox reached the flip mechanism in the automated machine that was supposed to collect the shoes and bring them to the packing line, they went flying out of the box. Hence, Amazon had to reinvent its automation.

First, Amazon began to measure and collect data from every task and process. Manual data collection can be not only difficult but also inaccurate. The data themselves are often of questionable quality, skewed by bias or cut short due to time and effort. Rather, Amazon installed sensors and readers across its conveyor system that automatically scan a package's barcode as it moves through the value chain. First and foremost, this helped the tracking of the whereabouts of specific packages at any given time in the warehouse and also gave real-time insight to managers about the status and state of critical items. This knowledge is not only relevant to increase the quality and the speed of service but also to minimise mistakes as well as to understand the bottlenecks and key issues to be improved.

The company's commitment to CIP embodies a sense of understanding that all have a role to play. At Amazon, kaizen consists of front-line workers, engineers and some managers, people who are not afraid to ask questions: This is a problem, how do we fix it? They have no preconceptions or action biases, so they are open to new answers. They are free to use their creativity. Moreover, they are empowered to act. This approach is not foolproof but at Amazon, people are willing to be "fool" in order to do something new. The kaizen team should be judged on results that will be meaningful for the company in the long term. As a result, Amazon's every process, every customer experience and every function has an improvement plan and a roadmap (Onetto, 2014; Rossman, 2018).

CIPs usually follow a step–by–step approach:

1. Identification of customer needs (business requirements: required value stream in terms of quality, cost, delivery and sustainability)
2. Analysis of current state (or "As is" aka Value Stream Mapping – VSM)
3. Value gap analysis (business requirements that cannot be met with the company's current offering/value stream)
4. Definition of target conditions (process sequence and related responsibilities, monitoring Key Performance Indicators (KPIs), process stability criteria – KPIs intervention limits)
5. Setting the vision for a future state (or "To be") definition (Value Stream Design – VSD)
6. Rapid improvement workshops (RIWs; execution of CIPs)

A rapid improvement workshop usually lasts for 5 to 10 working days, and its main goal is to implement an idea for improvement. It targets inefficiencies and risks and the outputs of a RIW are measurable operational impacts delivered. A RIW also builds local capabilities for CI and promotes cultural change. A RIW often results in 30–50% improvement and requires a minimum amount of capital. The best RIW team is a cross-functional team from the shop floor to management.

Prerequisites for an effective RIW team member (Imai, 1986):

- Keep an open mind to change
- Maintain a positive attitude
- Never leave in silent disagreement

- Create a blameless environment
- Practice mutual respect every day
- Treat others as you want to be treated
- One person – one voice – no position or rank
- There is no such thing as a dumb question
- Understand the process and just do it

2.4 Daily management

Given that there is an organisational will to develop continuous improvement, the question is how it can be sustained and ensured that the workforce continually practices it in their day-to-day conduct (Bessant & Caffyn, 1997).

Fredrick Taylor, an industrial engineer in the 1900s, suggested a methodology to leverage the tools and methods of modern science to manage a system of production more efficiently (Stoller, 2015). Taylor's main idea included the reorganisation of industrial systems around tasks, setting quantifiable and measurable goals and rewarding the workforce upon completion. Taylor believed that the right person with the right tools should be assigned to a task to perform it correctly and productively. On the collective level, a system of synchronised tasks makes up a production process. The output of the process should be communicated with a predefined goal. If the worker succeeds in doing their task right, and within the specified time limit, they must be rewarded for their effort (Stoller, 2015).

Taylor's logic is the foundation of continuous improvement, which also demands the existence of **standards** regarding how tasks are to be done and standards to which performance can be measured and ultimately improved. Because the kaizen system of continual improvement requires a programme of standards that are measurable and reproducible, work tasks become meticulously regulated and enforced in a manner that is indistinguishable from scientific management (Boje & Winsor, 1993). CI, however, is beyond Taylorism, because it allows standards to be flexible: they can change as employees discover a better way to perform a function.

Continuous improvement is based on the employees who work in the workshop, and it is primarily their job to find solutions to improve the production process. CI recognises that the best improvements are based on a team's collective creativity when solving problems (Urick et al., 2017). CI imposes full ownership on the workers, which improves work ethic and employee engagement. Employees feel valued because they are asked for their opinions, which, in turn, improves the trust and cooperation between the shop floor workers and the management team. In addition, employees are far more willing to accommodate substantial increases in workloads and responsibilities if these are the consequence of their suggestions (Imai, 1986). Finally, if their suggestions are actually implemented, it will increase their sense of pride. It is this commitment that sustains continuous improvement efforts over the long run.

According to Caffyn (1999), CI comprises a set of ten generic CI behaviours that are seen as fundamentals in organisations of all types and sizes:

1. Employees are aware of the organisation's commitment to CI; the vision and the goals are clearly stated
2. Each CI team sets up its development priorities following these goals

3. Enabling mechanisms operate to encourage individuals' participation (e.g., training, teamwork) and mastering the necessary skills
4. Ongoing evaluation ensures that the organisation's structure, systems and procedures, and the approach and mechanism used to develop the CI, continuously reinforce and support each other
5. Managers at all levels actively support the launch and implementation of CI projects; they act as a catalyst for change
6. The identification of problems is inward-looking because defining what problems exist can be the source of the problem itself in its own right
7. CI projects involve employees from multilevels with diverse backgrounds and organisational units
8. An open atmosphere ensures that everyone understands that the act of questioning is not a sign of mistrust or an invasion of privacy, but is a valuable opportunity for learning
9. People are taught how to think about their behaviour in new and more effective ways, helping them to break down defences that hinder learning (no embarrassment or threat)
10. CI is a part of the shared, organisational cultural values

Case illustration

Like many other organisations, Amazon also struggled to create "standard works." The underlying problem was that tasks, in general, are very vague; it is up to the worker to figure out how to perform them. CI projects were the solutions, as team members had to take a detailed look at their assigned tasks. They quickly realised that what was happening in reality was quite different from what was written down, and it was riddled with abnormalities. Therefore, the teams' task was to track all abnormalities and offer solutions that eliminate them. For example, stowing products account for about 20% of the costs at Amazon; hence, it is a critical activity for productivity improvement. The challenge was to set standards because stowing a small book does not take the same time as stowing a computer screen. The kaizen team spent time recording the staff as they stow different products and came up with suggestions to define three types of carts with products for each type and agreed on the standard time to stow those products. But the improvement did not end there. The team kept on revisiting the process and worked on the further reduction of stowing time. According to an executive, the kaizen team should be judged on long-term results.

Another example is the empowerment of customer service agents, who usually have no real authority to intervene in product matters. At Amazon, when a service agent gets a phone call from a customer explaining that there is a problem with the product they have just received, and if the agent judges it as a repetitive defect, then the customer service agent is allowed to "stop the line," which means taking the product off the website until the defect is corrected. Customers can see products pulled for quality issues on the website in real time.

This has created incredible energy and motivated Amazon's frontline people to do great work for customers. Besides, statistics show that frontline people's assessments are almost always correct: 98% of the time. Amazon proves that people on the front line can be trusted to help improve services and productivity (Onetto, 2014).

2.5 Breakthrough development

Innovation can take many forms: capturing a share of the market with new products, increasing profitability through reducing internal costs, creating successful partnerships with customers based on innovative service, developing novel processes, etc. Most innovation is not a "breakthrough" but rather a process of systematic elaboration and development of original ideas. Studies of successful innovative organisations highlight the importance of systematic learning, the high levels of incremental problem-solving and the consolidation of knowledge as the core of their success (Bessant & Caffyn, 1997). Continuous small and incremental kaizen activities over some time lead to large improvements (Sangwa & Sangwan, 2020).

Nevertheless, breakthrough innovations usually have a missing element in their evolution where disparate technologies and unanticipated needs are brought together all at once (Mascitelli, 2000). In competitive, technology-intensive global markets innovations that are unique, original, and unexpected tend to provide a much greater competitive advantage than innovations that are predictable and incremental (Lynn et al., 1996). It enables firms to capture either temporary monopoly profits or a significant increase in market share (Mascitelli, 2000).

Conventional market analysis techniques cannot guide the development of breakthrough innovations. Breakthrough innovations are facilitated by the testing of potential markets with the prototypes of the products, which enable companies to draw consequences based on the tests, adjust the products and test them again (Lynn et al., 1996). Consequently, the first step in the testing and learning process is, in effect, to experiment— to introduce an early version of the product to a plausible initial market. Building a product iteratively based on the needs of early customers could lead to reduced market risks, such as expensive product launches and failures (Lenarduzzi & Taibi, 2016).

This early version, called the minimum viable product, is the version of a new product that allows the firm to collect the maximum amount of validated information about customers with the least effort (Ries, 2009). The starting point of this learning process is a detailed and in-depth understanding of the consumer, and their varying needs and requirements (Prahalad, 2012). The **customer journey**, the process of acquiring and using the product or service from the perspective of the customer, is mapped (Halvorsrud et al., 2016) because breakthrough innovations must challenge the existing product concept as well as the "go to market" strategy.

The **validated learning** methodology is proven to be effective to minimise the risks and expenses of breakthrough innovations. Validated learning is also based on the "lean" philosophy of management because it is an incremental, step-by-step but highly rigorous method for developing the right product or service that customers want and will pay for. It is incremental because the breakthrough innovation is the outcome of the iterations of the initial minimum viable product. As is suggested, validated learning involves the analysis of the customer journey as well as the measurement of how customers respond, and the collection of actionable metrics upon which the firm can decide whether to pivot or persevere (Ries, 2011).

In this sense, managing breakthrough innovations as a lean process has its origin in the foundation of the continuous improvement theory established by Deming (1986). Specifically, the reduction of waste by creating minimum prototypes of functionalities in products, the consideration of customer feedback to evolve, working with improvement cycles and the continuous evolution of the product need to be mentioned (Bortolini et al., 2018).

Finally, innovation is not about a product but about developing an appropriate ecosystem that enables a new business system to function. The question is not whether a product can be built, but whether it should be built. Unless there is a sustainable business around the set of products and services, innovation may fail.

2.6 The future of continuous improvement with IoT technologies

Many experts claim that the Internet of Things (IoT) technologies is the next evolutionary step in productivity improvement. As we discussed earlier, continuous improvement results in the fine-tuning of an activity (or process) to reduce or even eliminate errors and waste. Without unnecessary and time-consuming activities, production will be more efficient and faster.

IoT technologies, such as artificial intelligence (AI) or machine learning, can boost CIP efforts because they provide immediate feedback about the critical points in the manufacturing process. However, installing IoTs does not mean that models and algorithms work smoothly forever. Even when we trust data from a specific device, devices may behave differently in different conditions. In the case of IoT, it is especially true that analytical models require continuous monitoring and, if needed, the recalibration of the models. Consequently, IoT-driven continuous improvement stimulates continuous learning.

In summary, IoT enables the organisation to better connect its people and machines improving information flow between the entities, which results in the optimisation of manufacturing processes. But how exactly does IoT enable continuous improvement? According to Ajit Jaokar (kdnuggets.com), the goal of IoT analytics is to analyse the data as close to the event as possible because manufacturing needs real-time intervention. IoT-driven analytics are trying to find out what happened now as opposed to what happened in the past. Typically, data arising from sensors are in a time series format and are often geo-tagged. Moreover, there are two forms of analytics for IoT: time series and spatial analytics. Time series analytics provide insights when anomalies are detected. Spatial analytics, in contrast, provide new insights by looking at historical trends, streaming and combining data from multiple events and sensors. Nevertheless, IoT devices create a large amount of (usually spare) data with a temporal element. Hence, the application of IoT analytics is a game changer for continuous improvement projects.

Case illustration

Even though ships carried an estimated 9.6 billion tons of cargo in 2013, accounting for 80% of global trade by volume and more than 70% of global trade by value, the fragmented nature of the supply chain, from production to warehouse to shore to ship, has made it difficult for producers and transporters to effectively monitor their cargo between ports. In addition, the inherently isolated nature of ships at sea presented a unique set of logistical challenges for the maritime industry as it seeks to deliver goods on time and in proper condition and to ensure the safety and wellness of crews. IoT technologies solved the dual challenges of supply chain fragmentation and maritime-vessel isolation with a unified platform that links vessels onto the same network, allowing revolutionary data sharing within the organisational ecosystem. Sensors monitor everything from vessel location and speed to the status and temperature of refrigerated cargo containers, giving shipping companies and producers real-time data analysis of potential dangers and inefficiencies or else information about the conditions of the goods. Thus, shipping companies can achieve an unprecedented level of efficiency improvement from warehouse to customer (Aig, n.d.).

Review questions

1. Please explain the key attributes of continuous improvement projects.
2. What is an improvable system?
3. What are the critical aspects organisations must pay attention to when composing a continuous improvement/rapid improvement team?
4. What are the differences between Taylor's standards and standards of CI?
5. Why is it difficult to copy an organisational culture of continuous improvement?
6. How can managers minimise the risks and expenses of breakthrough innovations?
7. What are the factors in the PESTEL model?
8. What are the forces in Porter's 5(+1) model?
9. Explain the steps of performing a VRIO analysis. Explain the steps of performing a SWOT analysis.

Discussion questions

1. Why is it critical to involve those organisational members in CIP who normally work with the processes to be improved?
2. Explain how I4.0 impacts the value chain. Which functions are likely to be under massive transformation?
3. Explain what "Bias to Action" means at Amazon.
4. Based on the Amazon case study, please reflect on the empowerment of frontline workers. Why do some managers consider it risky? Why do customer service agents at Amazon feel respected and motivated to provide better service?
5. What is common to validated learning and continuous improvement philosophies?
6. Explain how the analysis of the customer journey can contribute to breakthrough innovations.
7. Many experts use the PESTEL model to collect input for Porter's 5(+1) model. Please try to think about your favourite company. Can you perform these analyses?

Bibliography

Angell, L.C. and Corbett, L.M. (2009). The quest for business excellence: Evidence from New Zealand's award winners. *International Journal of Operations & Production Management, 29*(2), 170–199. https://doi.org/10.1108/01443570910932048

Berger, A. (1997). Continuous improvement and kaizen: Standardization and organizational designs. *Journal of Integrated Manufacturing Systems, 8*(2), 110–117.

Berman, S. J. (2012). Digital transformation: Opportunities to create new business models. *Strategy and Leadership, 40*(2), 16–24. https://doi.org/10.1108/10878571211209314

Bessant, J., & Caffyn, S. (1997). High-involvement innovation through continuous improvement. *International Journal of Technology Management, 14*(1), 7–28. https://doi.org/10.1504/IJTM.1997.001705

Bhuiyan, N., & Baghel, A. (2005). An overview of continuous improvement: From the past to the present. *Management Decision, 43*(5), 761–771. https://doi.org/10.1108/00251740510597761

Boje, D. M., & Winsor, R. D. (1993). The resurrection of Taylorism: Total quality management's hidden agenda. *Journal of Organizational Change Management, 6*(4), 57–70. https://doi.org/10.1108/09534819310042740

Bortolini, R. F., Nogueira Cortimiglia, M., Danilevicz, A. de M. F., & Ghezzi, A. (2018). Lean startup: A comprehensive historical review. *Management Decision.* https://doi.org/10.1108/MD-07-2017-0663

Caffyn, S. (1999). Development of a continuous improvement self-assessment tools. *International Journal of Operations and Production Management, 19*(11), 1138–1153.

Deming, W. E. (1986). *Out of the crisis.* MIT Press.

Gerbert, P., Gauger, C., & Steinhäuser, S. (2015). *The double game of the digital strategy* (p. 6). BCG Perspectives.

Halvorsrud, R., Kvale, K., & Følstad, A. (2016). Improving service quality through customer journey analysis. *Journal of Service Theory and Practice, 26*(6), 840–867. https://doi.org/10.1108/JSTP-05-2015-0111

Hirzel, A. K., Leyer, M., & Moormann, J. (2017). The role of employee empowerment in the implementation of continuous improvement: Evidence from a case study of a financial services provider. *International Journal of Operations and Production Management, 37*(10), 1563–1579. https://doi.org/10.1108/IJOPM-12-2015-0780

Imai, M. (1986). *Kaizen.* Random House Business Division.

Jha, S., Michela, J., & Noori, H. (1996). The dynamics of continuous improvement: Aligning organizational attributes and activities for quality and productivity. *International Journal of Quality Science, 1*(1), 19–47.

Jung, J. Y., & Wang, Y. J. (2006). Relationship between total quality management (TQM) and continuous improvement of international project management (CIIPM). *Technovation, 26*(5–6), 716–722. https://doi.org/10.1016/j.technovation.2006.01.003

Kwak, Y. H., Sadatsafavi, H., Walewski, J., & Williams, N. L. (2015). Evolution of project based organization: A case study. *International Journal of Project Management, 33*(8), 1652–1664. https://doi.org/10.1016/j.ijproman.2015.05.004

Lenarduzzi, V., & Taibi, D. (2016). MVP explained: A systematic mapping study on the definitions of minimal viable product. *The 42th Euromicro Conference on Software Engineering and Advanced Applications (SEAA),* 112–119.

Lodgaard, E., Ingvaldsen, J. A., Aschehoug, S., & Gamme, I. (2016). Barriers to continuous improvement: Perceptions of top managers, middle managers and workers. *Procedia CIRP, 41,* 1119–1124.

Lynn, G. S., Morone, J. G., & Paulson, A. S. (1996). Marketing and discontinuous innovation: The probe and learn process. *California Management Review, 38*(3), 8–37.

Managementmania. (n.d.). *VRIO analysis.* Retrieved from https://managementmania.com/en/vrio-analysis

Mascitelli, R. (2000). From experience: Harnessing tacit knowledge to achieve. *Journal of Product Innovation Management, 17*(3), 179–193.

Mintzberg, H. (1994). *The rise and fall of strategic planning: Reconceiving roles for planning, plans, planners.* Free Press.

Müller, J. M., Buliga, O., & Voigt, K. (2018). Fortune favors the prepared: How SMEs approach business model innovations in industry 4.0. *Technological Forecasting and Social Change, 132*(September 2017), 2–17. https://doi.org/10.1016/j.techfore.2017.12.019

Onetto, M. (2014). *When Toyota met e-commerce: Lean at Amazon.* Retrieved from https://www.mckinsey.com/business-functions/operations/our-insights/when-toyota-met-e-commerce-lean-at-amazon#

Pearce, J. A., & Robinson, R. B. (1988). *Strategic management: Strategy formulation and implementation.* Irwin.

Porter, M. E. (1980). *Competitive strategy.* Free Press.

Prahalad, C. K. (2012). Bottom of the pyramid as a source of breakthrough innovations. *Journal of Product Innovation Management, 29*(1), 6–12. https://doi.org/10.1111/j.1540-5885.2011.00874.x

Ries, E. (2009). *Minimum viable product: A guide*. Retrieved from http://www.startuplessonslearned.com /2009/08/minimum-viable-product-guide.html

Ries, E. (2011). The lean startup: How constant innovation creates radically successful businesses. In *The lean startup*. Retrieved from http://theleanstartup.com/principles

Rossman, J. (2018). *Building your digital strategy: The Amazon way*. Retrieved from https://theleadersh ipnetwork.com/article/building-your-digital-strategy-the-amazon-way

Sangwa, N. R., & Sangwan, K. S. (2020). Continuous Kaizen implementation to improve leanness: A case study of Indian automotive assembly line. In *Enhancing future skills and entrepreneurship* (pp. 51–69). Springer.

Stoller, A. (2015). To cite this article: Aaron Stoller (2015) Taylorism and the logic of learning outcomes. *Journal of Curriculum Studies, 47*(3), 317–333. https://doi.org/10.1080/00220272.2015.1018328

Sundqvist, E. (2019). The role of project managers as improvement agents in project-based organizations. *Project Management Journal, 50*(3), 376–390. https://doi.org/10.1177/8756972819832784

Szabó, Z. R., & Vida, G. (2009). Szolgáltató központok Magyarországon. *Vezetéstudomány, 40*(4), 28–42.

Urick, M. J., Adams, D. E., & Smith, T. (2017). Taylorism and operational excellence improving on the "One Best Way". *Journal of Leadership and Management, 9*(10), 17–21.

3 The layers of I4.0 systems

Sándor Ászity and Lilla Hortoványi

In Chapter 1, we clarified that digitisation is very different from digital transformation. In this chapter, we further explore the path of digital transformation. We reveal why and how the Internet of Things (IoT) transforms the way we live and work, the way products are manufactured and, ultimately the evolution of the production process.

The Web (www) was invented by Sir Tim Berners-Lee in 1989 when he was trying to find a new way for scientists to share data from their experiments, but no one had thought to use the Internet to achieve this (Google Arts, 2019). Three main ingredients make up the World Wide Web: The URL (uniform resource locator), which is the addressing scheme to find a document; the HTTP (hypertext transfer protocol), which connects computers; and the HTML (Hypertext Markup Language), which formats pages containing hypertext links. Now let's discover where these inventions have led us.

3.1 The Internet and the Things

The Internet was born gradually as many talented people worked on each other's breakthrough inventions. The Internet is a huge network of connected computers, which was subsequently made available to everyone through any computer with the World Wide Web. The Web, in fact, is just one of many other protocols using the Internet (Want et al., 2015); however, it happens to be by far the most popular (Gillies & Cailliau, 2000).

With the advent of the Internet and the Web, computers were connected for the first time. Subsequently, the invention of wireless communication solutions, such as Wi-Fi and other radio frequency solutions, made it possible to connect physical things to the low-cost Internet, creating added value by combining the physical world and the digital world (Cyber-Physical System). The improvement of data transfer speed and network coverage made it possible to connect various industrial, service and public administration processes, thus creating smart cities, smart agriculture or smart homes, which is discussed in Section III in more detail.

The Internet of Things (IoT) refers to the emerging trend of augmenting physical objects and devices with sensing, computing and communication capabilities, connecting them to form a network and making use of the collective effect of the networked objects, which are usually mobile (Guo et al., 2013). According to the definition of the European Parliament, the Internet of Things (IoT) refers to a distributed network connecting physical objects that are capable of sensing or acting on their environment and able to communicate with each other, other machines or computers (www.europarl.europa.eu).

DOI: 10.4324/9781003390312-4

The data these devices report can be collected and analysed to reveal insights and suggest actions that lead to cost savings, increase efficiency or improve products and services.

At an operational level, IoT sensor data can be used to regulate the flow of materials, products and information on the shop floor with minimum human intervention. At strategic levels, the real value of the IoT comes from using data to inform decision-making in ways that make it more responsive and immediate than it is possible by the human workforce (Lin & Madden, 2015).

The **Internet of everything** is the next stage, which refers to the intelligent connection of people, processes, data and things. The Internet of everything (IoE) describes a world where billions of objects have sensors all connected over public or private networks delivering the right information to the right person (or machine) allowing intelligent decision-making (Figure 3.1).

The first pillar of IoE is the data, which continues to be its foundation. However, data are generated not only by machines but also by people in this case. For example, wearable devices already collect a tremendous amount of data. Moreover, these connected devices can make themselves recognisable to others so that they can communicate in real time with one another within and between different sectors via

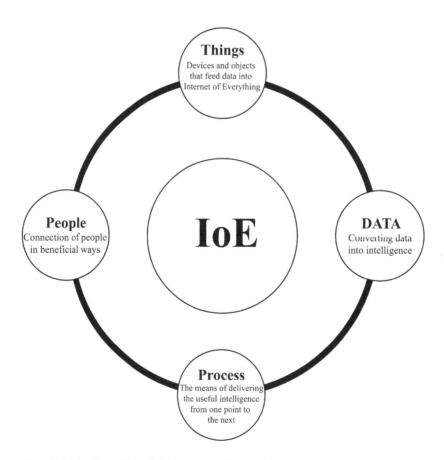

Figure 3.1 The four pillars of the Internet of Everything

the Internet. Businesses with the right analytical tools can take advantage of the data collected from these devices in the form of actionable information and better decisions. Nevertheless, the data are not only analysed for identifying problems but also for identifying innovation opportunities. The second pillar is the "things", which are the devices large and small, complex and simple that both feed the data into the Internet of everything and, in many cases, act upon the data to drive operations and create value. The third pillar is the process that must be in place to deliver the right information to the right person (or machine) at the right time. The fourth pillar is the ultimate goal of IoE, which is to connect people in a more relevant and valuable way, the creation of virtual communities and ecosystems.

Case illustration

In health care, IoT sparked the wide use of wirelessly connected devices such as glucometers and heart rate and blood pressure monitors. These wearables supply an enormous amount of data on the person's physiological systems: cardiovascular, digestive, endocrine, immune, muscular, nervous, renal, reproductive, respiratory or skeletal systems. By combining and analysing this data, IoE enables doctors and patients to monitor health conditions and vitals, track medications and track post-operation recovery to determine the most accurate diagnostics and care. In addition, the community of pharma companies, scientists and doctors from various disciplines, etc. get access to these medical sensor data and electronic medical records, which allow them to spot trends and patterns and come up with more targeted medications for patients who share common features. Consequently, IoE also accelerates the process of drug discovery and improved treatments (Laurie, 2021).

It is important to note that IoE fosters communication not only between machine-to-machine (M2M) but also between machine-to-people, people-to-machine, machine-to-objects and people-to-objects, generating tens of millions of real-time data.

Data are widely acknowledged to be today's most valuable asset. Since information is knowledge, data are money. However, the biggest challenge around big data is finding people to transform data into value. Moreover, to turn data into money, it is not enough to employ data scientists; rather, business and IT professionals must work together. Bridging the communication gap between data scientists and business decision-makers is the number one management challenge today. They both need to work together to understand what data needs to be collected in line with their business strategy and how that data can be turned into insights and actions. Moreover, digital transformation (i.e., the introduction of new technologies) must be preceded by significant organisational innovation, and it requires significant preparation and planning (Szabó et al., 2019).

Many researchers have pointed out that digitalisation accelerates industry competition and that businesses can survive in the long run only if they take action and step on the journey of digital transformation (Hetesi & Révész, 2017; Hortoványi et al., 2020).

Raising awareness

In 2020 Danny Pehar, a member of the Forbes Technology Council, warned readers that our data are our currency in the digital age. Yet we wilfully give our data away online without a second thought, for example, when we blindly click on terms and conditions of free apps without considering what it might mean to our data. We should remember that our data are very valuable to many "scary" people who may misuse our data. He argues that it is critical to educate people about cybercrime because it is incredibly lucrative for criminals.

Keeping this in mind, we must always remain careful about where we store our sensitive data and who we allow having access to that data. By considering our data as a currency, we will be able to keep it safer than most tend to do (Pehar, 2020).

3.2 The modular layers of digital technology

According to Yoo et al. (2010), we have witnessed three waves of digitalisation. The first wave was the conversion of analogue content and services into digital ones without fundamental changes in the industry structure. The second wave was the separation of devices, networks, services and contents, which were tightly coupled in the past. For example, voice service became completely independent of device and network, and the same quality voice service can be delivered through a fixed-line phone, a desktop computer or a mobile phone. The third wave of digitalisation has led to the emergence of novel products and services through the "mash-up" of different media across different product architectural boundaries. Devices, networks, services and content created for specific purposes are now being re-mixed. For example, users can both track and share their activities (Figure 3.2).

The device layer is further divided into a physical machinery layer (TV, PC, mobile phone, car, etc.) and a logical capability layer (operating system), which provides control of the hardware device. The network layer is similarly divided into a physical transport layer (including cables, radio spectrum, transmitters, etc.) and a logical transmission layer (including network standards, such as TCP/IP or P2P). The service layer contains the applications that directly interact with users as they create, manipulate, store and consume different content. With the service layer, users can listen to music, send and receive e-mails, read books, watch videos and receive navigation information. Finally, the content layer includes the actual data, such as texts, sounds, images and videos. The content layer can also contain meta-data, including ownership, copyright, encoding methods, content tags and geo-time stamps.

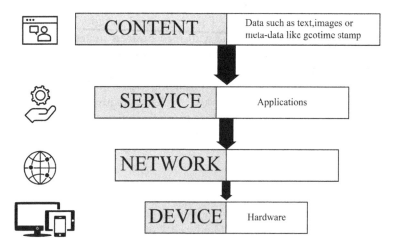

Figure 3.2 The four modular layers of the digital technology (based on Turber et al., 2014, p. 21)

There are two important implications. First, pure physical objects – like a piece of furniture or a pair of running shoes – can be equipped with these four layers of digital technology. Small and powerful computing devices today are often embedded into previously non-digital artefacts: a small RFID chip can be inserted into a pair of running shoes. This digitally enabled shoe collects data during running (such as pace, location and biometrics). Once captured, such information can be shared through one's social network services, like Facebook or Twitter, or can be mashed up with other media, such as Google Earth or Flickr photo services. Digitalisation is already making a way to transform all types of products. Second, these four layers can be de-coupled, which means that multiple stakeholders can contribute by generating values to the various layers simultaneously (Turber et al., 2014). It is important to note, that the digitalisation of physical products also means that these products adopt all characteristics of digital technology: they become programmable, addressable, sensible, communicable, memorable,[1] traceable[2] and associable.[3]

3.3 The evolution of manufacturing

The Reference Architectural Model, also known as RAMI 4.0, is a three-dimensional framework for developing future products deploying Industry 4.0 in a structured manner. Brecher and his co-authors (2021) argue that RAMI 4.0 was the first model that unites the technological and economic views with practical suggestions for the implementation of digital transformation. The recognition, that focusing only on the technology itself may lead to failure, gave a new impetus to scholars, and many other maturity models were developed. Nevertheless, the key point here is that these frameworks emphasise the simultaneous focus on economic profitability and overall enterprise development and treat both as critical for succeeding.

Determining the technologies related to Industry 4.0 is a matter of intensive scientific discussion: more than 1,000 different technologies were identified. The choice of technologies must depend on the context in which it is intended to be used. Another factor influencing the implementation of Industry 4.0 technologies is their level of maturity. Apart from the first experimenting pioneers, companies in large numbers will implement them only when the benefits are clear, economically verified and technically proven (Szabó et al., 2020; Szabó & Hortoványi, 2021) (Figure 3.3).

The vertical axis of the figure is the measurement of the capability maturity of a business. The basic idea behind capability maturity is that higher stages of maturity indicate improved capabilities (Rapaccini et al., 2013), the more mature a capability gets, the closer the organisation is to the desired end-stage (Mettler, 2011). Consequently, the process of becoming mature indicates the consistency of building an infrastructure and corporate culture that supports the completion of digital transformation. Eventually, the organisation relies on explicitly defined, managed, measured and controlled I4.0-compliant processes, which are mature (Hortoványi et al., 2022).

In this model, there are 2+4 stages. The first two, **computerisation** and **connectivity**, constitute the threshold level, namely, the minimum requirement for starting the journey to digital transformation. In manufacturing, assets – if maintained frequently – are productive for 30 to 50 years, and many of them are manually operated. Not surprisingly, many businesses are reluctant to replace old machinery on the shop floor.

The third stage is **visibility**, which is about the installation of sensors. Sensors and actuators are critical for collecting data, which is an essential building block for later

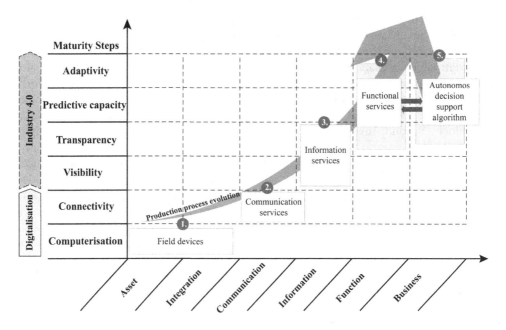

Figure 3.3 The production process evolution (based on Brecher et al., 2021, p. 2290)

stages. Real-time data enable the digital mapping of the production processes: equipment status and performance are both constantly monitored inside or outside the company.

The next stage is **transparency**. It refers to the purposeful analysis of data collected by the sensors to understand why something is happening and to make informed decisions. "Big data" can no longer be processed with traditional business analysis. Advanced applications, such as ERP or MES, are required.

Enterprise resource planning (ERP) is used to create and manage day-to-day operations, including production, material use, shipping and transportation. Therefore, ERP modules typically cover functions such as manufacturing, supply chain, order processing, inventory management, human resources and customer relationship management. It usually works within months, weeks and days. In contrast, the manufacturing execution system (MES) records the transformation of raw materials into finished goods. MES is needed to manage the manufacturing operation. Besides keeping records, it also notifies about exceptions. MES works in a time frame of days, shifts, hours and minutes.

Predictive capacity refers to an advanced level of data analysis. At this stage, data collected from the past will help predict the likelihood of future events. It provides scenarios. As a result, the management not only anticipates what will happen but can intervene in due time. By eliminating or reducing disturbances or design errors, operations will be more balanced.

The final stage is **adaptability**. Digitally fully transformed manufacturing means that certain decisions and interventions are made autonomously. The self-optimising operation is adapting itself to changing conditions, which reduces the reaction time compared to human interventions. As the business digitally transforms and matures stage by stage, the IT landscape moves from basic digitalisation through cross-functional connectivity enabling horizontal and vertical integration towards full digitalisation with the adaptability of systems (Li et al., 2019).

The horizontal axis, i.e., the device layer, represents the physical world. The next layer is the transition from the physical world to the information world. The communication layer refers to standard, Industry 4.0-compliant communication, which already uses a uniform data format. In the information layer, all data generated or modified by the device are consistently integrated. The functional layer provides a platform for the horizontal integration of the various functions of all devices. Finally, in the business layer, the services of the functional layer are coordinated, ensuring the integrity of the functions in the value chain.

The **cells of the matrix** enlist production evolution with highlights on information and communication technologies, which simultaneously ensure the functionality of the related RAMI 4.0 layers and the expected operating conditions at the given maturity stage.

In the model of Brecher et al. (2021), field devices are hardware components such as sensors, actuators, controllers (PLCs), etc., which also require appropriate automatic identification and data recording technology, such as radio frequency identification [RFID]), barcodes, magnetic strips, etc. The continuous data exchange between the installed field devices is ensured by communication service protocols. The prevailing data exchange protocols in the industrial sector are CAN, Modbus and Profibus, as well as machine-to-machine communication mechanisms, such as Open Platform Communications Unified Architecture (OPC UA) and Message Queuing Telemetry Transport (MQTT). Since the data come from a variety of devices in different formats, information services ensure that all data are mapped, integrated and stored. After establishing a coherent information management system, a runtime environment for system applications and technical functionality must be provided. For system state estimation, artificial intelligence is a great solution. Operation management systems, such as MES or ERP, can also be used for strategic decisions for both technical (e.g., predictive maintenance) and business (sales volumes, etc.) sights. Lastly, autonomous decision support algorithms are also assigned to the functional layer because the reason for this is that the business layer is not associated with specific solutions; it works with the information provided in the functional layer instead. However, this information is used by a self-optimising production system.

Raising awareness

At some of the world's most successful enterprises – e.g., Google, Netflix, Amazon, Alibaba and Facebook – decisions are frequently made by autonomous algorithms instead of talented managers. Executives agree that empowering autonomous decision support algorithms is now as organisationally important as empowering people. However, there are still large organisations with self-interests behind the machines. Without clear lines of authority and accountability, the dual use of human and artificial intelligence must be maintained. We can learn to trust autonomous systems only if we can compare the outcomes. The benefits and drawbacks of each decision-making system can be revealed only by hybrid decision-making (Schrage, 2017; Bergmann, 2017).

Review questions

1. Explain the difference between IoT and IoE.
2. Explain what the four modular layers of digital technologies are.

3. When planning the digital transformation, what is the first step managers must start with in terms of investing in technology?
4. Explain why it is important to evaluate technology in the context within which it is intended to be used.
5. Why is it important to assess the digital capability maturity stage of a business? What do we mean by "digitally matured business"?

Discussion questions

1. What do experts mean by designating data as today's currency? Why is it critical to keep our data secured?
2. Please explain what the shared fundamentals are in the evolution of manufacturing and the evolution of production processes.
3. Why do some experts urge maintaining dual or hybrid decision-making? Why do they have concerns about AI?

Notes

1 Memorability refers to the ability to record and store information that was generated, sensed or communicated.
2 Traceability refers to the ability to chronologically identify, store and relate events and entities in time.
3 Associability refers to the ability to be related to and identified with other entities, such as places or people.

Bibliography

Bergmann, B. (2017). *Autonomous decision-making: Assessing the technology and its impacts on industry and society*. Retrieved from https://www.swissre.com/institute/conferences/autonomous-decision-making.html

Brecher, C., Müller, A., Dassen, Y., & Storms, S. (2021). Automation technology as a key component of the industry 4.0 production development path. *The International Journal of Advanced Manufacturing Technology, 117*(7–8), 2287–2295. https://doi.org/10.1007/s00170-021-07246-5

Gillies, J., & Cailliau, R. (2000). *How the web was born: The story of the world wide web*. Oxford University Press.

Google Arts & Culture (2019). *The world wide web: The invention that connected the world*. Retrieved from https://artsandculture.google.com/theme/the-world-wide-web-the-invention-that-connected-the-world/eAJS4WcKh7UBIQ

Guo, B., Zhang, D., Yu, Z., Liang, Y., Wang, Z., Zhou, X., Guo, B., Zhang, D., Yu, Z., Liang, Y., Wang, Z., Zhou, X., & Zhou, X. (2013). From the internet of things to embedded intelligence. *World Wide Web, 16*, 399–420. https://doi.org/10.1007/s11280-012-0188-y

Hetesi, E., & Révész, B. (2017). Milesz a személyes kapcsolatok sorsa az információstechnológia világában az üzleti piacokon? In M. Vilmányi & K. Kázár (Eds.), *Menedzsment innovációk az üzleti és a nonbusiness szférákban*, SZTE Gazdaságtudományi Kar, Szeged, (pp. 245–266).

Hortoványi, L., Morgan, R. E., Vuksanovic Herceg, I., Djuričin, D., Hanak, R., Horváth, D., Mocan, M. L., Romanová, A., & Szabó, R. Z. (2022). Assessment of digital maturity: The role of resources and capabilities in digital transformation in B2B firms. *International Journal of Production Research*.https://doi.org/10.1080/00207543.2022.2164087

Hortoványi, L., Szabó, Z. R., Nagy, S. G., & Stukovszky, T. (2020). A digitális transzformáció munkahelyekre gyakorolt hatásai – Felkészültek-e a hazai vállalatok a benne rejlő nagy lehetőségre (vagy a veszélyekre)? *Külgazdaság, 64*(3–4), 73–96.

Laurie, O. (2021). *How wearable devices empower healthcare providers.* Retrieved from https://medcitynews .com/2021/07/how-wearable-devices-empower-healthcare-providers/

Li, D., Fast-Berglund, Å., & Paulin, D. (2019). Current and future industry 4.0 capabilities for information and knowledge sharing. *The International Journal of Advanced Manufacturing Technology, 105*(9), 3951–3963.

Lin, A., & Madden, A. (2015). *Understanding the role of IoT technologies in supply ecosystems. ICEB 2015 Proceedings (Hong Kong, SAR China).* 69. https://aisel.aisnet.org/iceb2015/69

Mettler, T. (2011). Maturity assessment models: A design science research approach. *International Journal of Society Systems Science, 3*(1/2), 81–98.

Pehar, D. (2020). *In the digital age, our data is currency.* Retrieved from https://www.forbes.com/sites/ forbestechcouncil/2020/02/20/in-the-digital-age-our-data-is-currency/?sh=110568c37b0d

Rapaccini, M., Saccani, N., Pezzotta, G., Burger, T., & Ganz, W. (2013). Service development in product-service systems: A maturity model. *The Service Industries Journal, 33*, 300–319. https://doi .org/10.1080/02642069.2013.747513

Schrage, M. (2017). *4 models for using AI to make decisions.* Retrieved from https://hbr.org/2017/01/4 -models-for-using-ai-to-make-decisions

Szabó, R. Z., Vuksanović Herceg, I., Hanák, R., Hortovanyi, L., Romanová, A., Mocan, M., & Djuričin, D. (2020). Industry 4.0 implementation in B2B companies: Cross-country empirical evidence on digital transformation in the CEE region. *Sustainability, 12*(22), 9538.

Szabó, Z. R., & Hortoványi, L. (2021). Digitális transzformáció és Ipar 4.0: magyar, szerb, szlovák és román tapasztalatok. *Külgazdaság, 65*(5–6), 56–76.

Szabó, Z. R., Horváth, D., & Hortoványi, L. (2019). Hálózati tanulás az ipar 4.0 korában. *Közgazdasági Szemle, 66*(1), 72–94. Retrieved from https://doi.org/10.18414/KSZ.2019.1.72

Szabó, R. Z., Vuksanović Herceg, I., Hanák, R., Hortovanyi, L., Romanová, A., Mocan, M., & Djuričin, D. (2020). Industry 4.0 implementation in B2B companies: Cross-country empirical evidence on digital transformation in the CEE region. *Sustainability, 12*(22), 9538.

Turber, S., Vom Brocke, J., Gassmann, O., & Fleisch, E. (2014). Designing business models in the era of Internet of things: Towards a reference framework. *International Conference on Design Science Research in Information Systems, 8463*, 17–31. https://nest.com/thermostat/life-with-nest-thermostat/

Want, R., Schilit, B. N., & Jenson, S. (2015). Enabling the internet of things. *Computer, 48*(1), 28–35.

Yoo, Y., Lyytinen, K. J., Boland, R. J., & Berente, N. (2010). The next wave of digital innovation: Opportunities and challenges: A report on the research workshop "digital challenges in innovation research." *SSRN Electronic Journal.* https://doi.org/10.2139/SSRN.1622170

4 Connectivity and data sharing with stakeholders inside and outside the organisation

Lilla Hortoványi

The result of the Fourth Industrial Revolution is that vast but relevant information is now available in real time, and people, things and systems are connected in a dynamic, self-organising way not only within the company but also outside the company.

This chapter defines the main stakeholders of the company, why it is worth to co-create with them and how to connect and share data with them during this cooperation. As the previous chapters pointed out, the smart factory is at the heart of Industry 4.0, which fundamentally changes manufacturing. The future of manufacturing is a digitalised factory, where autonomous robots work along with humans, and embedded computers and networks monitor and control the physical processes, usually with feedback loops to reflect on and improve behaviour (Gabor et al., 2016; Lee, 2008). Essentially, not only complex physical works are performed better by advanced machines but also some mental tasks – formerly preserved for human minds – can better be dealt with by computers on-site (Gabor et al., 2016). Chen et al. (2020) argue that it is made possible by cyber-physical space-based production systems that collect real-world information, analyse the information and notify the corresponding physical system about the findings.

4.1 Why connect?

Traditionally, a company created value for its customers through a one-way and sequential process: the company created the concept, designed the product or the offering and then manufactured, stocked and marketed it. However, creating value is a dynamic process today; customers do not passively accept products made by producers. Instead, customers directly or indirectly help shape product development by acting as co-producer, and they can be involved in the entire value and service chain (Chien & Chen, 2009). The best examples of customer involvement are Dell Computers's build-to-order online store and H&M's millennial-centric brand Nyden, which uses social media and influencers to crowd-source its next collections.

Besides customers, suppliers are also recognised for their valuable partnerships. Owing to the shortened life cycle of products and services, the fierce competition and the ease of product imitation, there is ever-increasing pressure on companies to speed up their innovation process. Scholars have long recognised that suppliers can help the company to shorten the concept of the development process and improve quality as well as reduce cost (Chien & Chen, 2009). Integration with suppliers involves significant risk, time and financial resources from both parties and thus it requires trust between the parties. The firm needs assurances that the supplier possesses the capabilities needed, while the supplier, in turn, needs some assurance that there will be a continuation of the

DOI: 10.4324/9781003390312-5

relationship and enough business to make integration worthwhile (Koufteros et al., 2007). If successful, supplier integration provides the firm with access to a pool of competencies and resources possessed by its suppliers and co-suppliers. This access, in turn, enables the firm to minimise the risk of having mismatches among different components of its product and also to come up with innovative solutions needed to serve customers better (Zhang et al., 2016).

Consequently, Industry 4.0 has begun to transform the ability of companies to create value. Innovative companies create a **platform** where their employees work in teams with their customers and suppliers simultaneously to improve the production process, develop new applications of current technologies, components and materials or innovate the functionality and features of products and services.

The value-creating ability of a company is extensively addressed in the strategic management literature; however, we briefly summarise the key points.

Every firm is a collection of activities performed to create value for their customers because the ultimate goal of a firm is the creation of value for buyers that exceeds the costs of creation. Customers purchase the product or service because it satisfies a need, and yields utility.

Corporate value chains are typically linked to a larger value system, which is a network of suppliers and co-suppliers with an integrated business process to bring a product or service from its initial conception to production and sales. It encompasses a sequence of activities, where some are performed "cross-border," in the case of firms located in different countries. A value system may encompass both intra-firm and inter-firm transactions. This is exemplified by a multinational corporation working together with its subsidiaries and joint ventures, as well as with subcontractors, suppliers, service providers and strategic alliances. The literature often refers to it as a global value chain (GVC), where the "flagship" firm focuses on the core capability areas that are perceived as essential to preserve the competitive advantage, while all the other activities are outsourced to suppliers to reduce operating costs (Hernández et al., 2014).

Case illustration

Information-enabled collaboration helps companies to reduce costs across the entire value system. For example, Walmart outsources much of its inventory management to suppliers. This is an enormous activity, as the retail giant hit 1 billion in sales in 2019 with nearly 6,300 stores and more than 11,700 retail units operating in 28 different countries in addition to its e-Commerce space. Walmart, however, recognised the opportunity in digital transformation and pioneered the most advanced and efficient inventory management system that shows in real time what products are needed, how many products are needed and when these products are needed. Moreover, Walmart was the first to introduce **vendor-managed inventory**, which means that the suppliers are responsible for managing their inventory in Walmart warehouses (Nguyen, 2017).

Sometimes the words *value chain* and *supply chain* are used interchangeably but they are different, although both chains overlay the same network of companies. Both are made up of companies that interact to provide goods and services. When we talk about supply chains, however, we usually talk about a downstream flow of goods and supplies from the source to the customer. Value flows the other way. The customer is the source of value, and value flows from the customer, in the form of demand, to the supplier. Thus, the primary difference between a supply chain and a value chain is a fundamental shift in focus from the supply base to the customer. Supply chains focus upstream on integrating supplier and producer processes, improving efficiency and reducing waste; in contrast, value chains focus downstream on responding to demands by creating value in the eyes of the customer (Adiguzel & Zehir, 2016).

Figure 4.1 illustrates the value activities within the value system of the sports apparel industry.

At each value activity, the suppliers either provide the materials or inputs (e.g., synthetic fibres) or sub-assembly (e.g., cut or sew components, etc.). The chain of activities performed by the suppliers increases the overall value of the product. In the case of sports apparel, innovation and competitive advantage come from product design and marketing rather than manufacturing know-how, making it relatively easy for the leading flagship companies to outsource production while maintaining a dominant position in the value chain.

Since these suppliers do not have an established brand or distribution channel, they do not have direct access to end-users and, therefore, they are typically highly dependent on the flagship company. Thus, it is not surprising that the industry is dominated by a few powerful companies.

Stakeholder theory begins with the assumption that values are necessarily and explicitly a part of doing business, and managers and entrepreneurs must consider the legitimate interests of those groups and individuals who can affect (or be affected by) their activities (Freeman et al., 2004). A detailed list of company stakeholders is shown in Table 4.1.

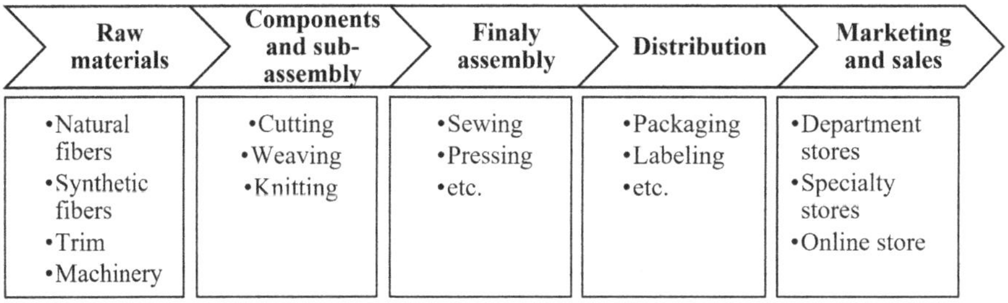

Raw materials	Components and sub-assembly	Finaly assembly	Distribution	Marketing and sales
•Natural fibers •Synthetic fibers •Trim •Machinery	•Cutting •Weaving •Knitting	•Sewing •Pressing •etc.	•Packaging •Labeling •etc.	•Department stores •Specialty stores •Online store

Figure 4.1 The illustration of sports apparel value system (based on Duke University, n.d.)

Table 4.1 Stakeholders of a company

Internal stakeholders	*External stakeholders*
Owners (Shareholders)	Customers
Employees	Suppliers
	Investors
	Creditors
	Media
	Communities (wider society)
	Government agencies
	Trade unions/Chamber of commerce/Industry associations

Consequently, stakeholder theory assumes that a company is responsible to a wide range of stakeholders, so it must define its strategic goals to meet the expectations and needs of all stakeholders: employees, managers, suppliers, customers, government, creditors and the wider society (Laczkó, 2010). A firm is stakeholder-oriented if it is sensitive and responsive to stakeholders' needs (Maignan et al., 1999).

The literature on how stakeholders influence organisational strategy argues that firms will pay attention to primary or influential stakeholders who can "affect" the firm because they control critical resources. By way of illustration, shareholders (the key stakeholders) have a direct say in the formation and approval of the corporate strategy through the corporate governance bodies representing them. The influence of investors, creditors, suppliers, customers and regulators can pressure firms to undertake certain practices (or discontinue others) by withholding important resources from the firm. Other stakeholders, such as local communities or environmental groups on whom the firm is not resource-dependent, can acquire power and exercise indirect influence via stakeholders who control the critical resources (Henriques & Sharma, 2005). For example, social media is a powerful resource nowadays in the hands of affected parties because they can exercise the power to either grant or withhold the legitimacy of an organisation and affect its reputation in the eye of other stakeholders.

The greater integration of the firm's activities with its stakeholders the more information sharing happens, which eventually may blur the organisational boundaries of the firm (Prajogo & Olhager, 2012).

The next sections address the drivers and challenges of connecting with three very influential stakeholder groups: customers, employees and suppliers.

4.2 Data and information sharing with suppliers and business partners

Sharing information between businesses is very complex, given that parties are independent but interdependent, which makes cooperation and coordination between them very complex.

According to BCG's global survey (D Küpper et al., 2020), nearly three-quarters of manufacturing managers worldwide consider sharing data with their suppliers in order to improve. The true masters of digitisation integrate suppliers into their operations: in fact, the organisational boundaries have begun to blur. In this **extended enterprise model**, sharing data not only improves existing applications of technology but also contributes to the joint development of applications that would not be possible otherwise.

The reward for exchanging data with external parties is estimated to be significant. First, by integrating end-to-end visibility into their value chains, manufacturers can react quickly to unexpected events and reduce inventory. Furthermore, sharing data allows manufacturers to synchronise and optimise connected production processes. Finally, by sharing data, participants in the value chain can determine the origin and quality of each component; thus, defective components are filtered out before their assembly. Needless to say, each of the components must have a unique identifier that is traceable throughout its manufacturing lifecycle to achieve this.

The car manufacturer giant Toyota facilitates inter-organisational knowledge transfers within its production network. The automotive industry consists of a network of suppliers who often produce as much as 70% of the value of a vehicle, while the vehicle's maker, the original equipment manufacturer, contributes only 30% of the value. Recognising this, Toyota built close collaboration with suppliers and worked together to improve component designs, enhance the quality of the parts and minimise waste (bcg.com).

Data-sharing collaborations fail primarily due to trust or technical reasons. Building trust between the parties is difficult as both companies pass on valuable and commercially sensitive data to the other party, which can make them vulnerable. Technical problems are usually due to the risk of data corruption and loss of availability and interoperability issues. It is therefore essential for successful cooperation that the parties concerned develop the logic of data sharing in advance, reach a mutually beneficial agreement and operate according to secure technologies and mutually agreed standards.

4.3 Connecting with customers

Today customers demand interactivity from their business counterparts, and the integration of traditional customer engagement activities, including processes, systems and technologies with emergent social media applications (Trainor et al., 2014). These technologies enable new forms of interactions between the firm and customers:

- **Sharing** and distributing digital content (e.g., coupons, texts, videos, images, etc.)
- **Communicating** with customers and mediating between them (e.g., blogs, discussion forums, etc.)
- **Building relationships** via online user communities

From the firm's point of view, customers are no longer passive takers; a customer is not only one out of a million others. Rather, customers can engage and share their content via social networks. By becoming active members in digital channels, customers can readily voice their concerns, report issues or seek help and publish positive and negative experiences with or without the permission of the company. Examples include blogs, discussion forums, user-created communities and user-generated content sites.

Many brands (including Nike, Lego, Heineken and Swatch) have recognised that personalisation is a critical factor in the intensified competition these days, and they invite customers to co-create future products. The firm that realises the power of these technologies can have access not only to valuable business intelligence on existing customers but can also gain insight about its **non-customers**. Non-customers are usually segmented into three groups: soon-to-be, resisting and unexplored. Using social media, firms can learn valuable information about why these people are not customers already, what barriers inhibit their purchase and how these barriers could be overcome by innovations.

For example, the swimwear company Arena learned from customer-to-customer interactions that the most common reason for novice swimmers to give up learning to swim was breathing. Poor breathing creates problems with executing strokes, making it harder to move forward in the water. This knowledge inspired Arena to develop the Freestyle Breather, a pair of plastic "fins" that can be attached to most marketed goggles. This innovation secures inhalation by protecting the mouth and nose from splashes and water drops and helps novices to continue swimming (hbr.org, n.d.).

Consequently, digital communication channels provide many benefits, for example:

- The firm better understands its customers and can provide timely responses to their needs.

- The customers who can participate in the firm's value chains either as co-designers or co-producers (by providing ideas, feedback or resources).
- The firm can collect business intelligence not only about its customers but also about its non-customers.

All of the above benefits are critical for serving customers better, faster and more efficiently in the digital age. However, Industry 4.0 not only means more customer–firm interactions over digital channels but it also has its challenges. Research has confirmed (Straker et al., 2015) that issues such as product quality, lack of availability, poor service and high prices are now transparent and instantly broadcasted by the customer often impacting a company's reputation, resulting in a loss of customers and revenue.

Therefore, executives must be aware that customer engagement today requires a solid foundation on which firms connect and interact with their customers.

4.4 Connecting with employees

The transformation of traditional workplaces into smart ones is an important step in the digital transformation of firms. The integration of workplace technologies like mobile, cloud, analytics and social tools into work is critical for long-term business performance.

By definition, the **digital workplace** enables any employee to complete a task, share information and work as a member of a team with other employees in the organisation and any partner organisation on a **location-independent** basis for all the parties concerned (Köffner, 2015).

Digital technologies can refer to the use of wireless, stand-alone devices (e.g., portable WiFi scanner, e-Reception Kiosk, etc.) as well as to a fully integrated work environment, where employees have the opportunity to utilise advanced information communication technology (such as video conferencing, smart sensors, etc.) embedded in artificial intelligence and social tools, which assist employees in performing their day-to-day activities more effectively and efficiently (Papagiannidis & Marikyan, 2020). By transforming the work setting into digital, firms gain compelling benefits.

First, there is evidence for a reduction in costs. For example, companies can save a significant amount of office space and rental expenses if employees work remotely from their homes one or two days a week. Flexible seating can be smoothly implemented with meeting room and desk booking applications; smart sensors detect changes in the physical environment and free up the room in case of a no-show. The hybrid work style – both on-site and off – requires connectivity. This is where communication and knowledge-sharing technologies play a crucial role. It requires a core platform that is integrated with other business information systems and services and can be accessed independently of location.

The second benefit is the increase in employee productivity. Businesses struggle to meet the varying needs of a multigenerational workforce. For example, millennial workers are found to be IT savvy and expect easy-to-use tools that help them to perform less repetitive and monotonous tasks and they are interested in more creative and engaging work. Digital office tools are found to break down functional barriers and encourage collaboration and enterprise-wide information sharing, as well as stimulate employee engagement (Attaran & Kirkland, 2019).

Besides the benefits, digital offices have their drawbacks. Information is growing at exponential rates. Employees are overwhelmed by emails. Filtering, reading and responding to these emails can take up to 20% of the time of a typical office worker. Being connected to their workplace 24/7, employees report that the work physically and psychologically intrudes into their family life. They tend to develop habits of being preoccupied with work when they are at home (Eddleston & Mulki, 2017), which can cause stress and burn-out. The organisations of the future will be the ones that foster the employee work–life balance.

When effectively planned and implemented, digital workplaces empower employees to work faster and communicate more easily – anytime, anywhere. Smart lighting systems that change and adjust to light patterns, or smart room temperature controls that adjust to the weather outside, not only reduce overheads but also all create a more enjoyable work experience and, as such, improve employee productivity and engagement.

In conclusion, digital transformation is not just about buying the right information and communication technology. It is about changing the way business and work are done. Hence, it requires a complete transformation of how the firm communicates and shares information with its internal and/or external stakeholders.

Review questions

1. Explain in your own words what the differences are between value chain, value system and supply chain.
2. Explain how customers, suppliers and investors can influence corporate strategy.
3. Spell out the advantages of the extended enterprise model. What benefits can the original equipment manufacturer reap?
4. Explain how a disappointed customer can harm the firm's reputation and long-term viability.
5. What are the most compelling benefits of transforming into a digital workplace?

Discussion questions

1. Walmart's vendor-managed inventory system benefitted the company because it took a load of work off Walmart itself, reduced the problems that came with managing inventory from multiple suppliers and nearly guaranteed items were in stock at all times. But what did suppliers gain? How could other industries learn from the Walmart example? What other functional areas could benefit from the co-creation with customers or suppliers?
2. Discuss how a local community can enforce sustainable environmental practices from a manufacturing firm. Who are the other affected stakeholders?
3. Elaborate on what companies can do to prevent unwanted data and knowledge spillover.
4. Digital transformation helps firms to learn about their non-customers. How can a firm collect such business intelligence about non-customers? How can the firm exploit this business intelligence?
5. How can corporate culture intervene if work interferes with employees' personal life?

Bibliography

Adiguzel, Z., & Zehir, C. (2016). A study of the effects of competitive strategies on stakeholders relationship management and stakeholder behavior. *Research Journal of Business and Management-RJBM, 3*(3). https://doi.org/10.17261/Pressacademia.2016321995

Attaran, M., & Kirkland, D. (2019). The need for digital workplace: Increasing workforce productivity in the information age. *International Journal of Enterprise Information Systems, 15*(1), 32. https://doi.org /10.4018/IJEIS.2019010101

Chen, G., Wang, P., Feng, B., Li, Y., & Liu, D. (2020). The framework design of smart factory in discrete manufacturing industry based on cyber-physical system. *International Journal of Computer Integrated Manufacturing, 33*(1), 79–101. Retrieved from https://doi.org/10.1080/0951192X.2019 .1699254

Chien, S.-H., & Chen, J.-J. (2009). Supplier involvement and customer involvement effect on new product development success in the financial service industry. *The Service Industries Journal, 30*(2), 185–201. https://doi.org/10.1080/02642060802116354

Duke University. (n.d.). Global value chain. Retrieved from https://sites.duke.edu/sociol342d_01d _s2017_team-7/2-global-value-chain/

Eddleston, K. A., & Mulki, J. (2017). Toward understanding remote workers' management of work–family boundaries: The complexity of workplace embeddedness. *Group & Organization Management, 42*(3), 346–387.

Freeman, R. E., Wicks, A. C., & Parmar, B. (2004). Stakeholder theory and "the corporate objective revisited". *Organization Science, 15*(3), 364–369.

Gabor, T., Belzner, L., Kiermeier, M., Beck, M. T., & Neitz, A. (2016). A simulation-based architecture for smart cyber-physical systems. *IEEE International Conference on Autonomic Computing (ICAC)* (pp. 374–379).

Henriques, I., & Sharma, S. (2005). Pathways of stakeholder influence in the Canadian forestry industry. *Business Strategy and the Environment, 14*(6), 384–398. https://doi.org/10.1002/bse.456

Hernández, R. A., Mario Martínez-Piva, J., & Mulder, N. (2014). *Economic development global value chains and world trade prospects and challenges for Latin America (No. 127).* Economic Commission for Latin America and the Caribbean (ECLAC).

Köffner, S. (2015). Designing the digital workplace of the future – What scholars recommend to practitioners. *International Conference on Information Systems (ICIS).*

Koufteros, X. A., Edwin Cheng, T. C., & Lai, K. H. (2007). "Black-box" and "gray-box" supplier integration in product development: Antecedents, consequences and the moderating role of firm size. *Journal of Operations Management, 25*(4), 847–870. https://doi.org/10.1016/j.jom.2006.10.009

Küpper, D., Okur, A., Betti, F., Bezamat, F., Fendri, M., & Fernandez, B. (2020). *How manufacturers can unlock value from data sharing.* Boston Consulting Group. Retrieved from https://www.bcg.com/ publications/2013/procurement-supply-chain-management-buyer-supplier-collaboration

Laczkó, M. (2010). A vállalat érintettjeinke szerepe a stratégiai menedzsmentben. In *Stratégiai Menedzsment,* Akadémiai Kiadó, Budapest (pp. 127–150).

Lee, E. A. (2008). *Cyber physical systems: Design challenges.* Retrieved from http://www.eecs.berkeley .edu/Pubs/TechRpts/2008/EECS-2008-8.html

Maignan, I., Ferrell, O. C., & Hult, G. T. M. (1999). Corporate citizenship: Cultural antecedents and business benefits. *Journal of the Academy of Marketing Science, 27*(4), 455–469.

Nguyen, T. T. H. (2017). Wal-Mart's successfully integrated supply chain and the necessity of establishing the Triple-A supply chain in the 21st century. *Journal of Economics and Management, 29*, 102–117.

Papagiannidis, S., & Marikyan, D. (2020). Smart offices: A productivity and well-being perspective. *International Journal of Information Management, 51*, 102027. https://doi.org/10.1016/j.ijinfomgt.2019 .10.012

Prajogo, D., & Olhager, J. (2012). Supplier involvement and customer involvement effect on new product development success in the financial service industry. *International Journal of Production Economics, 135*(1), 514–522. https://doi.org/10.1016/j.ijpe.2011.09.001

Skubana. (2020). *Walmart supply chain [2021]: Why it continues to dominate.* Retrieved from https://www .skubana.com/blog/walmart-leading-way

Straker, K., Wrigley, C., & Rosemann, M. (2015). Typologies and touchpoints: Designing multi-channel digital strategies. *Journal of Research in Interactive Marketing, 9*(2), 110–128. https://doi.org/10 .1108/JRIM-06-2014-0039

Trainor, K. J., Andzulis, J. M., Rapp, A., & Agnihotri, R. (2014). Social media technology usage and customer relationship performance: A capabilities-based examination of social CRM. *Journal of Business Research*, *67*(6), 1201–1208. https://doi.org/10.1016/j.jbusres.2013.05.002

Zhang, M., Zhao, X., Voss, C., & Zhu, G. (2016). Innovating through services, co-creation and supplier integration: Cases from China. *International Journal of Production Economics*, *171*, 289–300. https://doi.org/10.1016/j.ijpe.2015.09.02

5 Data mining, analysis and evaluation

Andrea Kő and Tibor Kovács

Data are generated continuously in our increasingly online world. Data growth statistics are surprising: on average, every human created at least 1.7 MB of data per second in 2020, for example (IDC Data Economy Trends, 2021; IDC Data Innovation Report, 2021). Everything generates data, including social media presence, sales, purchase, hire, communication and interaction. Some of these data are generated by the firm, some by customers and some by third parties. Given the proper attention, these data can often lead to powerful insights that allow businesses to serve their customers better and become more effective and productive.

There are several frameworks available for data analysis in the context of Industry 4.0. This chapter aims to provide an overview of translating data to useful information: data collection, transmission, storage, processing, visualisation and application, following the framework of the Manufacturing Data Life Cycle (MDLC; Tao et al., 2018). As part of MDLC, data analysis and data mining are discussed in more detail, as they play a key role in the Industry 4.0 environment. This section includes concepts and methods and it leads to some practical application scenarios.

5.1 Data characteristics

Data coming from various sources and in different forms is a key component of Industry 4.0 systems. The amount of data produced in manufacturing could be vast and remain useless if not processed and mapped into information that is understood by users. There is a wide range of manufactured data, including structured (e.g., databases), semi-structured (e.g., XML documents), or unstructured data (e.g., textual information from equipment and error logs; Gandomi & Haider, 2015). Due to the characteristics of big data, it is not feasible to expect humans to analyse it using traditional manufacturing tools; data analytics solutions provide more efficient means. Big data, namely, large amounts of multi-source, heterogeneous data, are characterised by the 5V: **Volume** (great volume), **Variety** (various modalities), **Velocity** (rapid generation), **Veracity** (inconsistency and uncertainty) and **Value** (huge value but very low density; Chen et al., 2014). Compared to traditional manufacturing, Industry 4.0 systems and smart manufacturing have an extreme focus on real-time data collection and conversion through physical and computational processes. Big data analytics (BDA) and business intelligence (BI) in smart manufacturing, (where big data refers to high-volume, high-velocity and high-variety sets of dynamic data that exceed the processing capabilities of traditional data management approaches) have received increasing attention because of their versatility and outstanding

DOI: 10.4324/9781003390312-6

role in improving overall business performance (Chen & Zhang, 2014). The Industry 4.0 initiative led many manufacturers to utilise data mining as a powerful approach to gain insights from data.

5.2 Data analysis framework

Data analytics refers to extracting useful information and knowledge from data as a support for the problem-solving process in business. Problem-solving in context means changing the (perceived) current situation to a desired one (Bartee, 1973). Bartee defines four basic steps of the problem-solving process: (1) **genesis**, the awareness that the problem exists; (2) **diagnosis**, the definition of the problem components and boundary conditions; (3) **analysis**, the reduction of the diagnosed elements to smaller components; and (4) **synthesis**, integrating the analysed parts into a solution. Both exploratory and confirmatory data analysis plays a key role in all four steps of the problem-solving process. Exploratory data analysis screens data to generate ideas, clues and hypotheses that are confirmed or refuted using confirmatory data analysis (de Mast & Kemper, 2009). Exploratory data analysis may be perceived more as art than as science (Good, 1983), where the process includes displaying and visualising the data, identifying salient features and interpreting these salient features (de Mast & Trip, 2007). Confirmatory data analysis is aimed at modelling and testing the relationships between dependent and independent variables, in which experimental design, hypothesis testing and model building: statistical techniques play a key role.

Gröger (2018) discusses the functional and non-functional core requirements related to the Bosch Industry 4.0 Analytics Platform. Functional core requirements are:

- The platform should support the whole range of structured and unstructured data sources
- The platform should support the whole range of analytical capabilities (e.g., descriptive, diagnostic, predictive and prescriptive analytics)
- The platform should address the whole range of target groups, (e.g., business users, business analysts or data scientists) that produce and consume analytical results

Capgemini introduced a widely accepted threefold taxonomy for business analytics in 2010, including descriptive, predictive and prescriptive analytics (Holsapple et al., 2014). Descriptive analytics addresses two main questions, namely what happened and what is happening in an organisation. It involves business reporting (OLAP reports), dashboards, business performance management, data warehousing technology, data marts, ETL (extract, transform, load), data quality solutions and visual analytics. Predictive analytics aims to forecast what will happen in the future, and why. It covers a group of methods that use historical data to predict a target variable in the future. This category of analysis includes the application of machine learning, data, web and text mining, for example. Prescriptive analytics is defined by questions of what business should be pursued and why. Typical technologies of this category are expert systems, simulations and decision support systems. The non-functional core requirements are:

- The platform should provide the standardisation of tools and governance concepts to ensure reusability and knowledge transfer
- The platform should provide scalability
- The platform should provide different deployment options)

The other framework, MDLC proposed by Tao et. al. (Tao et al., 2018) looks at data analytics as a holistic process from the sources of data to their business application (Figure 5.2). The following section relies on MDLC as a framework to discuss the individual elements of data analytics in more detail.

The comparison of these frameworks reveals similarities in structuring the phases of the data life cycle (Table 5.1).

The first phase in both frameworks is the investigation of typical data sources, followed by data collection and integration tasks. In the Bosch Industry 4.0 framework, data cleaning and the related ETL process are parts of the integration phase. In MDLC, the ETL process is a part of data collection and data cleaning is a part of the data processing phase. The third phase of the framework is dedicated to data processing and data analysis, covering the comprehensive investigation and evaluation of data by applying various data analytics techniques, such as reporting and dashboarding, smart data discovery of data mining or machine learning. Data visualisation is emphasised in MDLC, as it is designated as a separate phase. The last phase in MDLC is about possible and common industrial data applications, such as smart design, product quality control and fault prediction (see Figure 5.1). Gröger (Gröger, 2018) mentions only typical use cases in the Bosch Industry 4.0 framework. Regarding the last phase, Gröger (2018) draws attention to the clash of

Table 5.1 Differences and similarities of Bosch Industry 4.0 and MDLC phases

Bosch Industry 4.0 Analytics Platform phases	*MDLC phases*
1. data sources	1. data sources
2. data integration	2. data collection, data storage
3. analysis and optimisation	3. data processing, data visualisation
4. data consumers	4. data application

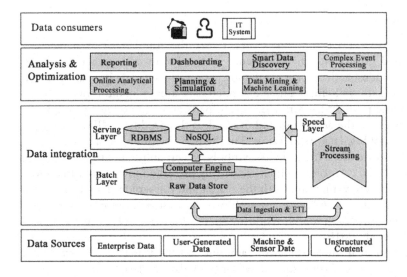

Figure 5.1 Conceptual architecture of the Bosch Industry 4.0 Analytics Platform (Gröger, 2018)

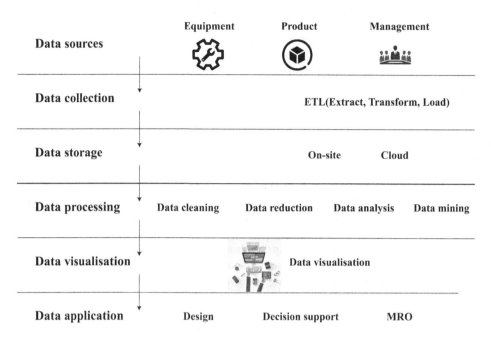

Figure 5.2 Manufacturing Data Life Cycle (based on Tao et al., 2018)

cultures between business domain specialists and data scientists, namely the difficulties in use case identification and definition, the slowly evolving data-driven culture and the inappropriate analytics results.

Because of the similarities between the Bosch Industry 4.0 and MDLC frameworks, the following sections discuss MDLC in more detail.

5.3 Data sources

The advent of Industry 4.0 technologies meant that the number of available data sources has increased greatly and the emergence of the Industrial Internet of Things (IIoT) delivered new sensors that collect real-time manufacturing data in quantities that were not possible to achieve before. These extended data sources could now cover the entire life cycle of the product from raw materials, parts and components through the manufacturing process to the actual use and disposal of the product. IoT technologies enable the collection of big data. As mentioned in the introduction, manufacturing data can be classified into structured (e.g., digits, symbols, tables) and semi-structured (e.g., JSON, XML documents) categories, which are usually presented in a well-defined format, with agreed rules, convenient for both the reader and the writer. The data is often tagged, or marked up, in a standardised way; however, unstructured data (e.g., logs, audio, videos, images) are often messy, requiring special knowledge for processing and interpretation (Tao et al., 2018).

With the evolution of manufacturing, the amount and the variety of collected data continued to increase. The foundations of automated data collection in the manufacturing process were laid during the "Information Age" (Tao et al., 2018) with the introduction of SCADA (supervisory control and data acquisition), MES (manufacturing execution system) and MIS (manufacturing information system). The communication protocols were, however, proprietary, and the interoperability of these systems was limited. Industry 4.0 technologies can eliminate these limitations and enable utilisation of data from much wider sources and in larger quantities.

Equipment data

Since the "Machine Age" the manufacturing equipment is fitted with sensors that monitor the production process and machine conditions. Conventional sensors like temperature probes, pressure gauges, movement and rotation sensors were extended with more complex ones, which help characterise and control the process and the equipment. Equipment logs generated during the production process could carry valuable information, which may be used to predict equipment failure or interpret abnormal behaviour. This equipment log data may come in the semi-structured format of XML messages; however, employing these data has certain challenges, as it contains a large amount of noise (data that are irrelevant to the goal of the analysis), which needs to be filtered out (Sipos et al., 2014). The way data are collected also changed significantly, moving towards the automated collection and storage of entirely digitised data. The so-called SCADA systems (Daneels & Salter, 1999) have a crucial role in industrial data collection. SCADA refers to "supervisory control and data acquisition", which includes software and hardware elements used in industrial organisations for several purposes. These operations consist of controlling industrial processes even at remote locations; monitoring, gathering and processing real-time data; interacting with devices such as sensors, and motors, and recording events into a log file.

The communication protocols of the SCADA-like systems, which collect data from industrial IoT (IIoT) sensors, are often proprietary; however, they frequently use the TCP/IP network and standard communication protocols (Jaloudi, 2019). These communication protocols primarily include advanced message queuing protocol (AMQP) ("ISO/IEC 19464. AMQP v1.0," 2016), message queuing and telemetry transport (MQTT) ("ISO/IEC 20922 MQTT v3.1.1," 2016), extensible messaging and presence protocol (XMPP) ("RFC 6120 (XMPP)," 2011) and JavaScript object notation (JSON) ("RFC 7159 (JSON)," 2014). The TCP/IP networks include Wi-Fi, Internet, Intranet and modern mobile networks. Communication infrastructure and protocols depend on the field of application, timing requirements and data transmission rates. In IIoT applications, MODBUS is often used as the application protocol (*MODBUS Application Protocol Specification V1.1b3*, 2012), which is an open de facto standard. It is based on a polling mechanism and follows the synchronous request-response pattern, as opposed to the asynchronous publish-subscribe pattern.

Product data

Industry 4.0 gives new opportunities to monitor and understand how products perform under real-world usage conditions. In the past, this was restricted to customer complaints or spot surveys. New technologies enable us to collect performance data in the context of specific usage situations (e.g., time, location, humidity or temperature). However, taking full advantage of these technologies requires customers to agree to the monitoring of their products; in exchange, they are given something valuable (e.g., insights about the operation). Furthermore, processing product performance data and acting upon emerging issues quickly as well as a culture that accepts the truth however bad it may be are all necessary elements (Ramaswamy, 2016).

Management data

Ample data are generated through the supply chain that has a direct link to the financial performance of the firm. These data are related, inter alia, to production planning, scheduling, order fulfilment and dispatch, materials and inventory management and human resources utilisation. Laboratory analysis results of raw materials, parts, intermediates and finished products (either performed in-house or outsourced), financial information, sales, marketing and customer service information also carry valuable information when optimising and improving the performance of the firm.

Public data

Data from open databases can be used to guarantee that the manufacturing process and the products comply with all government regulations and industry standards, and they are safe to all stakeholders. These data sets are related to intellectual property, civic infrastructure, scientific development, environmental protection and health care, and they are most often available as unstructured data: documents in various formats.

5.4 Data collection

Data may be collected at regular intervals or at predefined events, resulting in regular or irregular time series, which contain a key/value pair and a timestamp. If the timestamp is irrelevant, it could simply be called a data series. Time series from IoT devices are one of the main enablers of big data. These data could be enriched using RFID (radio frequency identification) or location-based technologies, supplying additional information about the context of the data. The ETL (extraction, transformation and loading) process is responsible for collecting the data from data sources and storing the data in a Data Warehouse (DW). If the data are collected from IoT sensors, different communication protocols (we detailed them in the data sources part) result in different payload, latency and the ability of synchronous–asynchronous (event-based) communication. The ETL process must be prepared to ensure that the data from heterogeneous sources are cleansed and transformed, reconciling possible semantic heterogeneities (e.g., synonyms and homonyms, different representations of semantically equivalent concepts). During the data acquisition process, signals are sampled and converted into digital numeric values. Data acquisition systems (DAS) usually convert analogue waveforms into digital values for processing. There are three components of data acquisition systems (Bolton, 2019):

- Sensors, to convert physical parameters to electrical signals
- Signal conditioning circuitry, to convert sensor signals into a form that can be converted to digital values
- Analogue-to-digital converters, to convert conditioned sensor signals to digital values

These components are often physically integrated into one device, which communicates with the control system using the protocols described above.

The control systems interpret electrical signals, and their role is crucial in the automation process. The three most widely used control systems are (Bolton, 2019):

- Supervisory control and data acquisition (SCADA), which applies human–machine interface displays (it was introduced in the Equipment data section)
- Programmable logic controllers (PLCs) are used when data management needs up to about 3,000 input/output (I/O) points
- Distributed control systems (DCSs) are employed when the I/O point count is greater than 3,000

Data acquisition depends on several factors, such as the type of industry and production, the automation level and the number of operations performed manually.

5.5 Data storage

Traditional manufacturing focused on structured data, i.e., management data (e.g., inventories, production plans, order fulfilments, financials, etc.) and equipment data of sensor values from SCADA systems that are often stored in Relational Database Management Systems (RDBMS). Data Warehouse (DW) schemas are used for integrating and consolidating this enterprise data. Industry 4.0 requires the adoption of big data technologies to fulfil the data collection, storage, processing and analysis needs of increased volume and variety. A possible implementation of these new requirements is the Data Analytics Architecture of Bosch (Santos et al., 2017).

According to this approach, the data storage layer should have multiple components for different contexts:

- NoSQL database for real-time data streams
- Hadoop Distributed File System (HDFS) as a staging area with a delimited period of use
- Big Data Warehouse (BDW) components save data from a historical perspective and are used through the SQL Query Engine component

In addition, this architecture consists of a layer for Security, Administration and Monitoring with components for (1) **Cluster Tuning and Monitoring**, which detects bottlenecks and improves performance; (2) **Metadata Management**, which defines and describes data ownership information, business definition, tables definition, data characterisation and the description of data status (active, archived or purged); (3) **Authorisation and Auditing**, which manages user authorisations and data access policy; (4) **Data Protection** and (5) **Authentication**.

Time series data are an especially important element of Industry 4.0 as IoT applications produce this type of data in big quantities, which require efficient storage and retrieval. Data from time series are merely measures or occurrences that are controlled, downsampled and indexed over a period. Examples could be server statistics, the tracking of system performance, network information, sensor information, occurrences, clicks and many other types of analytical data. The most significant aspects of choosing the right data storage system for time series data are scalability, the capacity to manage large quantities of data at an appropriate speed, versatile schema, convenience with a variety of analytical instruments, safety and cost (Nasar & Kausar, 2019). A time series database (TSDB; a time-stamped optimised database) can meet these requirements.

A further consideration when defining data storage strategies for a firm is whether it selects the cloudor on-premise data storage. While nowadays there are many advantages of cloud data storage, such as flexible up-front investment costs, reduced internal IT support requirements and efficient multi-tenant usage (scalability, recoverability, patching, security), on-premise data storage is still plausible in business, especially in the long run. On-premise data storage is less vulnerable to price increases, data leakage or external security threats (assuming internal security is mature). If an organisation has high confidence in the capacity of internal IT resources and their ability to deliver the necessary results, the on-premises cost structure can be expected to save money over the long term compared to the cloud. Nevertheless, an external cloud service can free IT resources for other priorities and the capital budget is also less impacted when a cloud subscription (expensed) is chosen over on-premise hardware and software license purchases (capitalised; Fisher, 2018).

5.6 Data processing

Data processing is a series of operations that transform raw data into more useful information and knowledge. Formalised and explicated information can be easily packed in a reusable form (Liew, 2007). Salopek and Dixon (2000) define knowledge as the meaningful links people make in their minds between information and its application in action in a specific setting. For example, when the company monitors the temperature of a bearing, to predict the failure of this part, data are the raw signal acquired from the sensor, while the information is the explicit temperature value stored in a structured format (e.g., values, measurement name, timestamp stored in Excel files). In this case, knowledge refers to the prediction of failure.

Data processing starts with data pre-processing, namely data cleaning and data reduction, which have a critical impact on the outcome. These are usually complex, non-trivial operations.

Data pre-processing: data cleaning, data reduction

It is crucial to clean data gathered from IoT devices. The possible issues include the malfunctioning of devices at some time intervals, the corruption or the loss of data as a result of noise or a defect in the communication mechanism. Veracious IoT data poses several challenges: the methods and algorithms for processing big data need to have high performance for real-time analytics, which can generate information before it becomes outdated; they have to be scalable and lightweight with low computation effort; they have to meet the requirements for accuracy, completeness, privacy and security (Liu et al., 2018). Thus, data cleaning involves the process of detecting and correcting corrupt or inaccurate records from the database, filling in missing values, smoothing noisy data, identifying or removing outliers and resolving inconsistencies. Data reduction is used to reduce the complexity of the data by feature selection, feature extraction and instance selection, transforming the massive volume of data into ordered, meaningful and simplified forms. García et al. (2016) summarise that the most influential data pre-processing algorithms cover missing values imputation, noise filtering, dimensionality reduction, instance reduction, discretisation and the treatment of data for imbalanced pre-processing.

Data analysis and data mining

Data analysis, especially data mining and machine learning, plays a key role in the Manufacturing Data Life Cycle (MDLC) framework. The term "data mining" is relatively new, but the idea behind it is not. It has its roots in statistical analysis and artificial intelligence from the 1980s. It has gained popularity in the business world as well, for the following reasons:

- More intense competition at a global scale
- The recognition of the value in data sources
- The availability of quality data on customers, vendors, transactions, web, etc.
- The consolidation and integration of data repositories into data warehouses
- An exponential increase in data processing and storage capabilities and a decrease in their cost
- A movement towards the conversion of information resources into a nonphysical form.

The application of data mining for analytical tasks has been increasing in manufacturing in recent years. The most widely used definition of data mining is that it is a non-trivial process of identifying valid, novel, potentially useful and ultimately understandable patterns in data stored in structured databases (Fayyad et al., 1996).

Pattern is a mathematical (numeric and/or symbolic) relationship among data items, such as association, prediction, cluster (segmentation) or sequential (time series) relationships. In this definition, the *process* refers to the fact that data mining has several, iterative steps. *Non-trivial* means that the process is not as straightforward as a simple query or the computation of predefined quantities. *Valid* indicates that the discovered patterns should hold the truth even on new data with acceptable certainty. *Novel* means that this pattern is not previously known, while *potentially useful* refers to the potential benefit that the discovered pattern provides for the user. *Ultimately understandable* means that the pattern should make business sense.

While several synonyms are used for data mining, such as knowledge extraction, pattern analysis, knowledge discovery, information harvesting, pattern searching and data dredging (Sharda et al., 2016), it is certain that data mining is an essential part of the knowledge discovery process (Fayyad et al., 1996).

Data mining is a complex process that requires the involvement of different people with various expertise. Data mining projects require a sound methodology and effective project management. The most well-known standardised data mining process model, which could help in understanding the interactions in this complex process, is the CRoss-Industry Standard Process for Data Mining (CRISP-DM). It was suggested by a European consortium of companies as a standardised methodology for data mining (Wirth & Hipp, 2000). Figures 5.3 and 5.4 illustrate the CRISP-DM process and its phases.

The main phases and tasks are summarised in Figure 5.4.

Another well-known data mining methodology is SEMMA from the SAS Institute (SASHelp Center: Introduction to SEMMA, n.d.). SEMMA is an acronym that stands for the processes of Sampling, Exploring, Modifying, Modelling and Assessing.

Data mining and statistics are similar domains in the sense that they both look for relationships in data sets. However, statistics start from a well-defined proposition and hypothesis, while data mining starts from a loosely defined discovery statement. Statistics

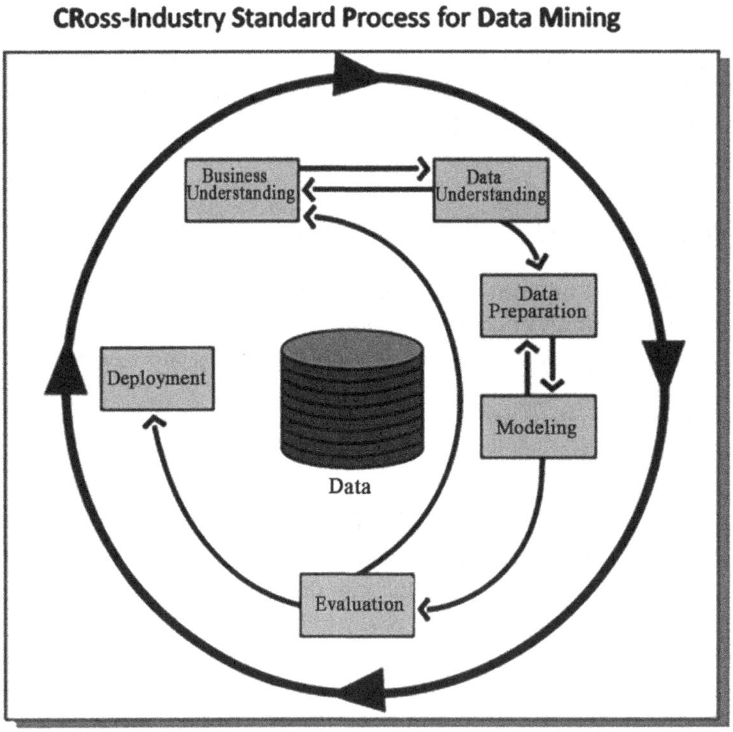
CRoss-Industry Standard Process for Data Mining
Business Understanding
Data Understanding
Data Preparation
Modeling
Evaluation
Deployment
Data

Figure 5.3 Phases of CRISP-DM (Wirth & Hipp, 2000)

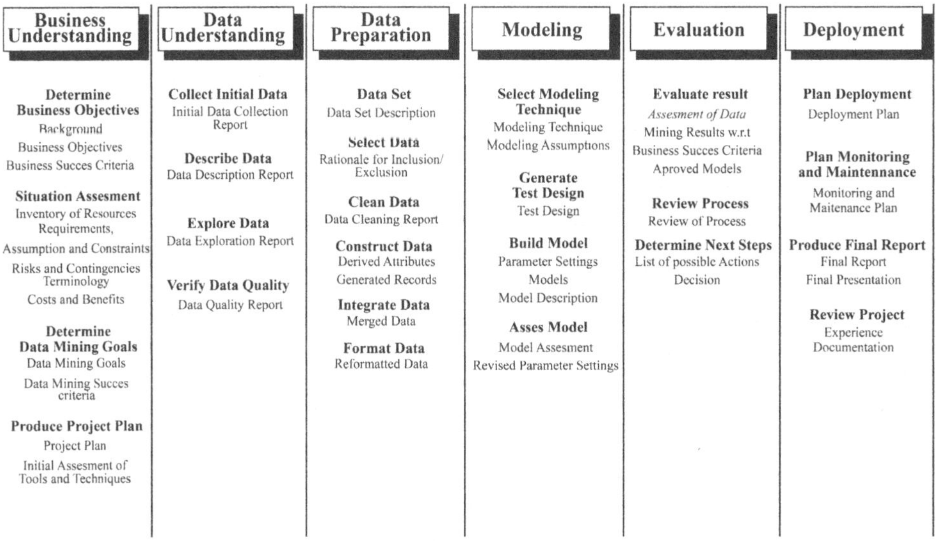
Business Understanding
Determine Business Objectives
Background
Business Objectives
Business Succes Criteria
Situation Assesment
Inventory of Resources Requirements,
Assumption and Constraints
Risks and Contingencies Terminology
Costs and Benefits
Determine Data Mining Goals
Data Mining Goals
Data Mining Succes criteria
Produce Project Plan
Project Plan
Initial Assesment of Tools and Techniques
Data Understanding
Collect Initial Data
Initial Data Collection Report
Describe Data
Data Description Report
Explore Data
Data Exploration Report
Verify Data Quality
Data Quality Report
Data Preparation
Data Set
Data Set Description
Select Data
Rationale for Inclusion/ Exclusion
Clean Data
Data Cleaning Report
Construct Data
Derived Attributes
Generated Records
Integrate Data
Merged Data
Format Data
Reformatted Data
Modeling
Select Modeling Technique
Modeling Technique
Modeling Assumptions
Generate Test Design
Test Design
Build Model
Parameter Settings
Models
Model Description
Asses Model
Model Assesment
Revised Parameter Settings
Evaluation
Evaluate result
Assesment of Data
Mining Results w.r.t
Business Succes Criteria
Aproved Models
Review Process
Review of Process
Determine Next Steps
List of possible Actions
Decision
Deployment
Plan Deployment
Deployment Plan
Plan Monitoring and Maintennance
Monitoring and Maitenance Plan
Produce Final Report
Final Report
Final Presentation
Review Project
Experience
Documentation

Figure 5.4 Phases and tasks in CRISP-DM (based on Chapman et al., n.d) usually utilise sample data, while data mining uses all existing data. Data mining relies on the biggest possible data set, while statistics might look for the right size of data.

Data mining and machine leaning have a lot in common. Machine learning is a branch of artificial intelligence, concerned with the design and development of algorithms that allow computers to evolve behaviours based on empirical data (Sharda et al., 2016). Machine learning (ML) is primarily concerned with the design and development of algorithms that allow computers to "learn" from historical data to discover new patterns in the data.

A large variety of machine learning methods are available to perform data mining processes, including classification, regression, clustering and association (Sharda et al., 2016). These methods are summarised in Figure 5.5.

Supervised learning refers to the machine learning method that maps an input to an output based on example input–output pairs (Russell & Norvig, 2010). Supervised learning aims to build a model that makes predictions based on the observations, referred to as training data. It infers a function from labelled training data consisting of a set of training examples (Mohri et al., 2012). Supervised learning methods are the most popular approaches in manufacturing. Application areas are widespread. For example, Support Vector Machine (SVM) (Yang & Trewn, 2004) is suitable for tool/ machine condition monitoring and fault diagnosis (Azadeh et al., 2013; Salahshoor et al., 2010). Quality monitoring in manufacturing is an additional promising field where SVMs were successfully applied (Ribeiro, 2005). Image recognition and time series forecasting are other domains where SVM optimisation is successfully used (Salahshoor et al., 2010).

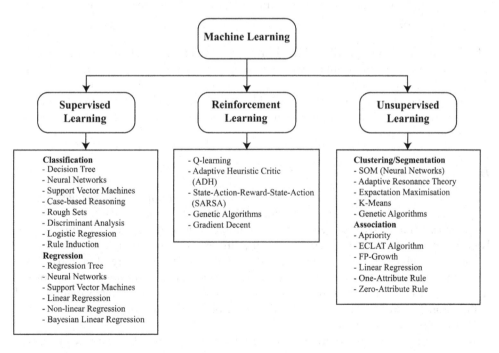

Figure 5.5 Machine learning methods (based on Sharda et al., 2016)

Unsupervised learning is a machine learning method that looks for previously undetected patterns in a data set with no pre-existing labels and with minimum human supervision (Russell & Norvig, 2010). Unsupervised learning methods can be applied to identify the outliers in manufacturing data, for example (Hansson et al., 2016). Reinforcement learning is defined as the provision of training information by the environment. The information on how well the system performed in the respective turn is provided by a numerical reinforcement signal (Wuest et al., 2016). Reinforcement learning is not common but there are growing examples of successful applications today (Doltsinis et al., 2012; Günther et al., 2014).

Machine learning applications are suitable to fulfil several manufacturing requirements (Wuest et al., 2016). The abilities of ML include:

- The identification of relevant patterns, intra- and inter-process relations, correlation and/or causality without special initial assumption or requirements
- Making predictions based on properties learned from the data
- Adapting to a changing environment with reasonable effort and cost
- Managing high-dimensional problems and data sets with reasonable effort

The main advantages of the application of ML in manufacturing are (Alpaydın, 2010; Guo et al., 2008; Monostori et al., 1998):

- The improvement of resource utilisation in certain manufacturing problems
- The production of powerful tools for continuous quality improvement
- The capability of handling high-dimensional problems and data
- The detection of certain patterns or regularities that describe relations
- The ability to learn from the dynamic environment and to adapt (in some cases) automatically

The aims of data mining and machine learning are different. While data mining focuses on extracting patterns and unknown properties on the data (e.g., discovering the items that are usually purchased together), machine learning focuses on developing prediction models, based on known properties learned from the training data (e.g., e-mail spam classification algorithms). Nonetheless, machine learning methods and models are applied in data mining.

Data visualisation

Data visualisation is aimed at helping to convey and communicate knowledge through graphical means, which was discovered during the data processing and data analysis phases. Data visualisation has the potential to assist humans in analysing and comprehending large volumes of data and to detect patterns, clusters and outliers that are not obvious using non-graphical forms of presentation (Lee et al., 2003). Therefore, data visualisation has many application fields, including data exploration and data mining, and supporting the deep and profound cognitive tasks of understanding causality, multi-variedness and comparison (Zachry & Thralls, 2004). The form of visualisation depends on the data as well as on the story to be communicated.

Visual displays of quantitative data must be aligned with the abilities of human perception and cognition, the ability to spot even subtle differences between objects in our field of vision, for example, differences between the contours and colours of leaves (Few, 2016). Because of the human abilities of visual perception, certain types of charts, like three-dimensional graphs, should be avoided as depth is not perceived directly but through a combination of other attributes, including area, blur, occlusion and stereoscopic vision. Some data visualisations make it easy to see and compare overall patterns among an entire set of values (e.g., line graph) and others make it easy to see and compare individual values (e.g., bar graph). Few (2017) proposes seven criteria to evaluate the effectiveness of visualisations using two dimensions: (1) The **Informative dimension** consists of Usefulness, Completeness, Perceptibility, Truthfulness and Intuitiveness, and (2) The **Emotive dimension** includes Aesthetics and Engagement.

Data application

The final step of the MDLC is to exploit the information and knowledge that is the result of the above-mentioned phases and to create business value from it. There are various areas where it could add value (Tao et al., 2018). First, in the product or process design phase, it reveals insights about customers, competitors and markets and helps better understanding product features and quality requirements. Second, it can support the control and improvement of the production process by leading to informed decisions concerning whether and how to adjust the manufacturing processes and equipment. Furthermore, it provides early warnings of quality defects and rapid diagnosis of root causes. Third, it can support MRO (maintenance, repair and operations) processes, including preventive maintenance, fault prediction and repair-replacement decisions.

Design - Selecting the optimal number of wire harness modules for the motorcar manufacturing case

An example of a smart design using data mining is the optimisation of the number of wire harness modules for motorcar manufacturing (da Cunha et al., 2010). A wire harness is a set of wires and connectors transmitting power and information in cars. Depending on the silhouette and the engine type, different sets of these elements are used, with a potential diversity is about 7 million different wire harnesses for a unique car model. Data mining was used to extract association rules for different demand configurations with an output variable describing the assembly time required when a specific set of modules was used. The minimum set of modules that satisfies the customer's expected mean assembly time were calculated and compared using four different strategies: (1) random selection, which does not consider information about the customer's behaviour; (2) pattern-based selection, which is based on extracted rules from customer data and constraints; (3) component-entropy selection, which is based on components' demand and constraints; and (4) pattern-entropy selection, which is based on component's demand, extracted rules and constraints. The specific example in the paper shows that the minimum number of modules required to satisfy customers' requirements for an assembly line could be reduced from 288 using the random method (or from 150 using pattern-based selection) to 24 using pattern-entropy selection. Therefore, using data mining methods can reduce the complexity of manufacturing, leading to improved economics and reliability of supply.

Decision support – Investment-casting process quality monitoring case

The Ravi investment-casting process exemplifies the decision support for product quality monitoring (Sata & Ravi, 2017). Investment casting is widely used for producing near-net shape industrial parts of ferrous and nonferrous alloys used in automobile, aerospace, biomedical and many other industries. Product quality monitoring and prediction are difficult, and defect analysis requires considerable experience and domain knowledge, coupled with in-depth scientific analysis. The method that they describe is using Bayesian inference to estimate the probability of defective items, supporting the decision-making process to prevent the occurrence of various defects. Shopfloor data of various process parameters and chemical compositions are collected with the specific defects that occurred during production. The computation of posterior probabilities was performed in three steps: pre-processing for categorising the input parameters in four ranges, the processing or computation of probabilities and the post-processing of results. The decision model based on these posterior probabilities is used subsequently to estimate the occurrence of specific defects and to understand the effect of various process parameters on product quality.

Maintenance, Repair and Operations (MRO) – Optimising the operations' scheduling and maintenance of pumps case

Finally, an example of MRO maintenance and operating cost optimisation is related to pump operation, as described by Zhang et al. (2015). Pumps transporting liquids are common industrial parts, responsible for significant energy consumption and maintenance costs. The proposed model optimises the scheduling operations and the maintenance of pumps to minimise energy consumption and maintenance costs while maintaining the desired hydraulic workload of pumps. The optimisation model considers different configurations of pump speeds, chamber levels and flow rates, resulting in different energy consumptions and maintenance costs. The model was not only able to find optimal configurations – based on historical data – but also led to additional benefits of smoothed process parameters.

Review questions

1. What are the main phases of the Manufacturing Data Life Cycle (MDLC)?
2. What are the main phases of the Bosch Industry 4.0 Analytics Platform?
3. Compare Manufacturing Data Life Cycle and Bosch Industry 4.0 Analytics Platform.
4. Discuss the functional and non-functional core requirements related to the Bosch Industry 4.0 Analytics Platform.
5. What is the difference between regular and irregular time series data sets?
6. Explain the advantages and disadvantages of cloud vs. on-premise data storage.
7. What are the main data mining methodologies? Detail their phases and tasks.

Discussion questions

1. What are the main steps in the Manufacturing Data Life Cycle? Explain them.
2. What do we refer to as data mining and machine learning? How do they relate to each other?

3. What are the challenges in terms of data collection and preparation in these cases?
4. Find recent cases of successful data mining applications in the field of car manufacturing, product quality monitoring and MRO.
5. What could the prerequisites of the real-world application be in product quality monitoring?
6. Describe the model that is used in MRO. What other data mining/machine learning models are appropriate in this case for this task?
7. Machine learning applications are suitable for the fulfilment of several manufacturing requirements. Why?
8. What are the main advantages of the application of ML in manufacturing?

Bibliography

Alpaydın, E. (2010). *Introduction to machine learning* (2nd ed.). MIT Press.

Azadeh, A., Saberi, M., Kazem, A., Ebrahimipour, V., Nourmohammadzadeh, A., & Saberi, Z. (2013). A flexible algorithm for fault diagnosis in a centrifugal pump with corrupted data and noise based on ANN and support vector machine with hyper-parameters optimization. *Applied Soft Computing*, *13*(3), 1478–1485. https://doi.org/10.1016/j.asoc.2012.06.020

Bartee, E. M. (1973). A holistic view of problem solving. *Management Science*, *20*(4), 439–448. Retrieved from https://www.jstor.org/stable/2629624

Bolton, B. E. (2019, November 26). *Eight data acquisition best practices*. Retrieved from https://www.controleng.com/articles/eight-data-acquisition-best-practices/

Chapman, P., Clinton, J., Kerber, R., Khabaza, T., Reinartz, T., Shearer, C., & Wirth, R. (n.d.). The CRISP-DM user guide. *Lyle.Smu.Edu*. Retrieved September 14, 2020, from https://lyle.smu.edu/~mhd/8331f03/crisp.pdf

Chen, C. L. P., & Zhang, C. Y. (2014). Data-intensive applications, challenges, techniques and technologies: A survey on big data. *Information Sciences*, *275*, 314–347. https://doi.org/10.1016/j.ins.2014.01.015

Chen, M., Mao, S., & Liu, Y. (2014). Big data: A survey. *Mobile Networks and Applications*, *19*(2), 171–209. https://doi.org/10.1007/s11036-013-0489-0

Daneels, A., & Salter, W. (1999). What is SCADA? *International conference on accelerator and large experimental physics control systems*.

de Mast, J., & Kemper, B. P. H. (2009). Principles of exploratory data analysis in problem solving: What can we learn from a well-known case? *Quality Engineering*, *21*(4), 366–375. https://doi.org/10.1080/08982110903188276

de Mast, J., & Trip, A. (2007). *Title exploratory data analysis in quality-improvement projects*. Retrieved from https://hdl.handle.net/11245/2.53536

Doltsinis, S., Ferreira, P., & Lohse, N. (2012). Reinforcement learning for production ramp-up: A Q-Batch learning approach. *2012 11th international conference on machine learning and applications* (pp. 610–615). https://doi.org/10.1109/ICMLA.2012.113

Fayyad, U., Piatetsky-Shapiro, G., & Smyth, P. (1996). From data mining to knowledge discovery in databases. *AI Magazine*, *17*(3), 37. https://doi.org/10.1609/aimag.v17i3.1230

Few, S. (2016). The visual perception of variation in data displays. *Visual Business Intelligence Newsletter*.

Few, S. (2017). Data visualization effectiveness profile. *Visual Business Intelligence Newsletter*.

Fisher, C. (2018). Cloud versus on-premise computing. *American Journal of Industrial and Business Management*, *8*(9), 1991–2006. https://doi.org/10.4236/ajibm.2018.89133

Gandomi, A., & Haider, M. (2015). Beyond the hype: Big data concepts, methods, and analytics. *International Journal of Information Management*, *35*(2), 137–144. https://doi.org/10.1016/j.ijinfomgt.2014.10.007

García, S., Luengo, J., & Herrera, F. (2016). Tutorial on practical tips of the most influential data preprocessing algorithms in data mining. *Knowledge-Based Systems*, *98*, 1–29. https://doi.org/10.1016/j.knosys.2015.12.006

Good, I. J. (1983). The philosophy of exploratory data analysis. *Philosophy of Science*, *50*(2), 283–295. Retrieved from https://www.jstor.com/stable/188015

Gröger, C. (2018). Building an industry 4.0 analytics platform. *Datenbank-Spektrum*, *18*(1), 5–14. https://doi.org/10.1007/s13222-018-0273-1

Günther, J., Pilarski, P. M., Helfrich, G., Shen, H., & Diepold, K. (2014). First steps towards an intelligent laser welding architecture using deep neural networks and reinforcement learning. *Procedia Technology*, *15*, 474–483. https://doi.org/10.1016/j.protcy.2014.09.007

Guo, X., Sun, L., Li, G., & Wang, S. (2008). A hybrid wavelet analysis and support vector machines in forecasting development of manufacturing. *Expert Systems with Applications*, *35*(1–2), 415–422. https://doi.org/10.1016/j.eswa.2007.07.052

Hansson, K., Yella, S., Dougherty, M., & Fleyeh, H. (2016). Machine learning algorithms in heavy process Manufacturing. *American Journal of Intelligent Systems*, *6*(1), 1–13. https://doi.org/10.5923/j.ajis.20160601.01

Holsapple, C., Lee-Post, A., & Pakath, R. (2014). A unified foundation for business analytics. *Decision Support Systems*, *64*, 130–141. https://doi.org/10.1016/j.dss.2014.05.013

IDC data economy trends 2021 – IDC data innovation report. (2021). Retrieved from https://www.statista.com/statistics/871513/worldwide-data-created/

ISO/IEC 19464. AMQP v1.0. (2016). *In information technology – Advanced Message Queuing Protocol (AMQP) v1.0 specification*. ISO/IEC. Retrieved from www.iso.org

ISO/IEC 20922 MQTT v3.1.1. (2016). *In information technology – Message Queuing Telemetry Transport (MQTT) v3.1.1*. ISO/IEC. www.iso.org

Jaloudi, S. (2019). Communication protocols of an industrial internet of things environment: A comparative study. *Future Internet*, *11*(3). https://doi.org/10.3390/fi11030066

Lee, M. D., Butavicius, M. A., & Reilly, R. E. (2003). Visualizations of binary data: A comparative evaluation. *International Journal of Human – Computer Studies*, *59*(5), 569–602. https://doi.org/10.1016/S1071-5819(03)00082-X

Liew, A. (2007). Understanding data, information, knowledge and their inter-relationships. *Journal of Knowledge Management Practice*, *8*(2), 1–16.

Liu, X., Tamminen, S., Su, X., Siirtola, P., Roning, J., Riekki, J., Kiljander, J., & Soininen, J.-P. (2018). Enhancing veracity of IoT generated big data in decision making. *2018 IEEE International Conference on Pervasive Computing and Communications Workshops (PerCom Workshops)* (pp. 149–154). https://doi.org/10.1109/PERCOMW.2018.8480371

MODBUS Application Protocol Specification V1.1b3. (2012). Modbus Organization, Inc. Retrieved from https://www.modbus.org

Mohri, M., Rostamizadeh, A., & A Talwalkar, A. (2012). *Foundations of machine learning* (2nd ed.). Cambridge, MA; London, England: MIT Press

Monostori, L., Hornyák, J., Egresits, C., & Viharos, Z. J. (1998). *Soft computing and hybrid AI approaches to intelligent manufacturing* (pp. 765–774). https://doi.org/10.1007/3-540-64574-8_463

Nasar, M., & Kausar, M. A. (2019). Suitability of influxdb database for IOT applications. *International Journal of Innovative Technology and Exploring Engineering*, *8*(10), 1850–1857. https://doi.org/10.35940/ijitee.J9225.0881019

Ramaswamy, S. (2016). Using IoT data to understand how your products perform. *Harvard Business Review, June*. (hbr.org)

RFC 6120 (XMPP). (2011). *In RFC 6120 – Extensible Messaging and Presence Protocol (XMPP)*. Internet Engineering Task Force (IETF). http://www.rfc-editor.org/info/rfc6120.

RFC 7159 (JSON). (2014). *In RFC 7159 – The JavaScript Object Notation (JSON) data interchange format*. Internet Engineering Task Force (IETF). http://www.rfc-editor.org/info/rfc7159.

Ribeiro, B. (2005). Support vector machines for quality monitoring in a plastic injection molding process. *IEEE Transactions on Systems, Man and Cybernetics, Part C (Applications and Reviews)*, *35*(3), 401–410. https://doi.org/10.1109/TSMCC.2004.843228

Russell, S., & Norvig, P. (2010). *Artificial intelligence: A modern approach (3rd ed.)*. Upper Saddle River, NJ: Prentice Hall

Salahshoor, K., Kordestani, M., & Khoshro, M. S. (2010). Fault detection and diagnosis of an industrial steam turbine using fusion of SVM (support vector machine) and ANFIS (adaptive neuro-fuzzy inference system) classifiers. *Energy, 35*(12), 5472–5482. https://doi.org/10.1016/j.energy.2010.06.001

Salopek, J. J., & Dixon, N. M. (2000). Common knowledge: How companies thrive by sharing what they know. *Training and Development, 54*(4), 63–64.

Santos, M. Y., Oliveira e Sá, J., Andrade, C., Vale Lima, F., Costa, E., Costa, C., Martinho, B., & Galvão, J. (2017). A big data system supporting Bosch Braga Industry 4.0 strategy. *International Journal of Information Management, 37*(6), 750–760. https://doi.org/10.1016/j.ijinfomgt.2017.07.012

SAS help center: Introduction to SEMMA. (n.d.). Retrieved September 14, 2020, from https://documentation.sas.com/?docsetId=emref&docsetTarget=n061bzurmej4j3n1jnj8bbjjm1a2.htm&docsetVersion=14.3&locale=en

Sata, A., & Ravi, B. (2017). Bayesian inference-based investment-casting defect analysis system for industrial application. *International Journal of Advanced Manufacturing Technology, 90*(9–12), 3301–3315. https://doi.org/10.1007/s00170-016-9614-0

Sharda, R., Delen, D., & Turban, E. (2016). *Business intelligence, analytics, and data science: A managerial perspective*. London, England: Pearson.

Sipos, R., Fradkin, D., Moerchen, F., & Wang, Z. (2014). Log-based predictive maintenance. *Proceedings of the ACM SIGKDD international conference on knowledge discovery and data mining* (pp. 1867–1876). https://doi.org/10.1145/2623330.2623340

Tao, F., Qi, Q., Liu, A., & Kusiak, A. (2018). Data-driven smart manufacturing. *Journal of Manufacturing Systems, 48*, 157–169. https://doi.org/10.1016/j.jmsy.2018.01.006

Wirth, R., & Hipp, J. (2000). CRISP-DM: Towards a standard process model for data mining. *Proceedings of the 4th international conference on the practical applications of knowledge discovery and data mining* (pp. 29–39).

Wuest, T., Weimer, D., Irgens, C., & Thoben, K. D. (2016). Machine learning in manufacturing: Advantages, challenges, and applications. *Production and Manufacturing Research, 4*(1), 23–45. https://doi.org/10.1080/21693277.2016.1192517

Yang, K., & Trewn, J. (2004). *Multivariate statistical methods in quality management*. McGraw Hill Professional.

Zachry, M., & Thralls, C. (2004). An interview with Edward R. Tufte. *Technical Communication Quarterly, 13*(4), 447–462. https://doi.org/10.1207/s15427625tcq1304_5

Zhang, Z., He, X., & Kusiak, A. (2015). Data-driven minimization of pump operating and maintenance cost. *Engineering Applications of Artificial Intelligence, 40*, 37–46. https://doi.org/10.1016/j.engappai.2015.01.003

6   Lean 4.0

*Emil Evin, Dušan Sabadka, Lilla Hortoványi,
Sándor Gyula Nagy and Tamás Stukovszky*

Lean management (LM) and I4.0 set similar goals for advocate organisations: both seek improvements in productivity and quality and both focus on the elimination of waste with increased responsiveness to customer needs. However, many practitioners regard these two concepts as contradictory. First, LM is usually considered a low-tech approach that excels at simplicity (Dickmann, 2008). Second, LM requires intense human involvement. In this chapter, we strive to resolve the contradiction and prove that these two approaches are synergistic with one another. We discuss Lean philosophy and some of its models, such as Six Sigma, the DMAIC (Defining–Measurement–Analysis– Improvement–Management) and the Kaizen methodologies. Finally, we elaborate on the burning question of whether Lean and Industry 4.0 are mutually exclusive concepts giving hard choices for manufacturers. We show that these two approaches cannot only coexist but mutually support each other.

6.1 Lean manufacturing

Emil Evin and Dušan Sabadka

Lean manufacturing (LM) has become almost a standard since it was first introduced by Toyota Production System during the 1950s. Lean manufacturing tools and techniques, such as just-in-time, cellular manufacturing, total productive maintenance (TPM) and many more, have been consistently applied by organisations all over the world striving to maintain competitiveness (Rohani & Zahraee, 2015).

Lean manufacturing (LM) aims at eliminating the value stream and reducing process variations, resulting in better quality and productivity and meeting customers' expectations (Pagliosa et al., 2019). LM is a socio-technical approach where corporate culture is the driving force of continuous improvement, committed to the continuous improvement of one's work.

Lean is an association of principles and methods that focus on identifying and eliminating activities that add no value to the end products or services. It starts with defining the value of the product/service as perceived by the customer, then continues by sorting out Value Added activity (VA) and Non-Value-Added activity (NVA).

To clearly define the value of a specific product or service from the end customer's perspective, organisations must work backwards to build the production process. To identify customers' value, it is important to answer the following questions. What do customers want? When and how do they want it? What combination of features, capabilities, availability and price will be preferred by them? The next step is to map how

DOI: 10.4324/9781003390312-7

this value is delivered to the customer. By mapping the value stream, the management can identify three types of activities: (a) those that add value; (b) those that do not add value but cannot be currently avoided; (c) and those that do not add value and are simply wastes and, hence, should be eliminated.

NVA is a waste because it uses resources and imposes costs without adding value to the product (Ohno, 1988) (see Figure 6.1).

1. *Motion excess*: any movement of the worker that is not directly related to the addition of value is unproductive
2. Waste stemming from *waiting* time: The most common sources of waste include machine failure, lack of material, lack of information, uneven production, etc. It is more difficult to detect this type of waste when the operator waits for the next product to appear for processing
3. Waste stemming from *overproduction* stems from the production of products in larger quantities than required by the customer. It arises from the rule either for higher utilisation of production capacities or to produce a certain quantity of finished products in case of emergency. This creates an unnecessary need to use storage space, thus increasing transport and administrative costs
4. Waste stemming from product *defects*: Re-creating parts is a huge source of excess spending
5. Waste generated by unnecessary conveyance operations: Production cannot be done without *transport*. Transportation is a part of the production process, but the movement of materials and products does not bring any value
6. Waste due to excess *inventory*: more stock than is necessary or ideal
7. Waste due to *overprocessing*: unnecessary processes, which have no value to the customer, increase the cost and reduce the effectiveness of production

Figure 6.2 shows typical waste both in production and in transportation.

Muda (waste), mura (unevenness) and muri (overburden) in production are illustrated in Figure 6.2.

Suppose that a firm needs to transport six tons of material to its customer and is considering its options. One is to pile all six tons on one truck and make a single trip. But this would be muri because it would overburden the truck (rated for only three tons), leading

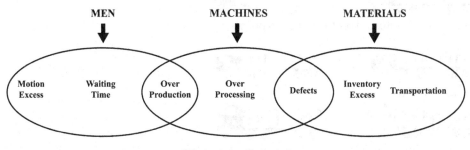

Figure 6.1 Seven areas to find NVA organisations (based on Čiarnienė & Vienažindienė, 2012)

to breakdowns, which also would lead to muda and mura. A second option is to make two trips, one with four tons and the other with two. But this would be mura because the unevenness of materials arriving at the customer would create jam-ups on the receiving dock followed by too little work. This option also would create muri, because on one trip the truck still is overburdened, and muda as well, because the uneven pace of work would cause the waste of waiting by the customer's receiving employees. A third option is to load two tons on the truck and make three trips. But this would be muda, even if not mura and muri because the truck would be only partially loaded on each trip (Figure 6.3).

Although waste is often related primarily to material flow, it is a problem in many other cases outside the material flow. Below is a list of examples of when we may encounter mura and when it can cause problems:

• Uneven customer demand
• Uneven production speed or change in production volumes

Figure 6.2 The three types of deviations or problems (based on Doanh, 2017a)

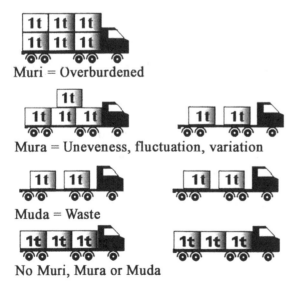

Figure 6.3 Typical wastes to be eliminated in transportation (based on Doanh, 2017a)

- Irregular work rhythm
- Untrained or careless staff
- Uneven workload distribution (Roser, 2015).

Waste needs to be detected and, if possible, eliminated and regularly double-checked to prevent unwanted recurrence:

- Map the processes
- Form a task force to identify which process steps were wasted
- Determine the annual costs
- Prioritise the actions to be introduced
- Re-engineer the processes, this time eliminating sources of waste (ISO, 2011; Ohno, 1988)

A simple illustration shows that muda, mura and muri are often related; therefore, eliminating one also eliminates the others. Finding an optimal solution in real-world Lean implementations is not always simple or feasible.

Returning to the concept of lean management, apart from the elimination of waste, another very important change is required. Companies should not push their products to customers, but let customers pull products or services in such a way that materials are not released and activities are not done until they are needed (Čiarnienė & Vienažindienė, 2012). The discipline of pull is established and enforced by using kanbans, which are physical or electronic mechanisms transmitting the need for parts and subassemblies from one point in the process to the preceding one.

In summary, there are five steps to implement lean thinking in a company: (1) define value from the perspective of the customer, (2) determine the value streams, (3) achieve flow, (4) schedule production using pull and (5) seek perfection through continuous improvement (Rohani & Zahraee, 2015).

Given the scope of this book, the so-called Deming cycle PDCA (Plan–Do–Check–Act), Kaizen, Six Sigma and DMAIC cycle methods are presented in the next section.

Deming PDCA cycle

The PDCA methodology aims to improve the overall performance of the organisation, meet customer requirements, manage risks and opportunities and build a stable basis for meeting its own goals and those of sustainable development.

- **P**lan – planning the intended improvement (intent)
- **D**o – implementation of the plan
- **C**heck – verification of the implementation result against the original intention
- **A**ct – modifications of the plan, as well as the actual implementation, based on verification and widespread implementation of practical improvements to improve customer satisfaction

Under the STN EN ISO 9001: 2015 standard, the PDCA process cycle is a method of gradual improvement of the quality of products, services, processes, applications and data, which takes the form of the repeated performance of the following activities (Figure 6.4).

The PDCA cycle can be applied to all processes and the quality management system as a whole. Figure 6.4 illustrates how Clauses 4 to 10 can be grouped in relation to the PDCA cycle. Figure 6.5 shows how parts 4 to 10 can be grouped in relation to the PDCA cycle (ABCI Consultants, 2021).

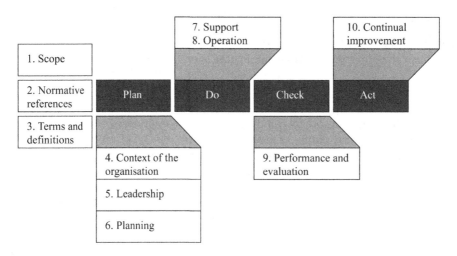

Figure 6.4 PDCA relationship to the ISO 9001.2015 clauses (based on ABCI Consultants, 2021)

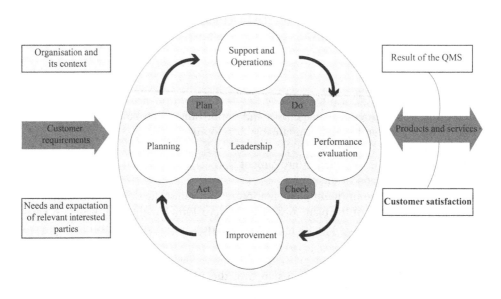

Figure 6.5 Process approach under STN EN ISO 9001 2015 in the PDCA cycle. (based on ABCI Consultants, 2021)

It is essential to determine right at the beginning of the cycle what aspect of the operation is targeted for improvement:

- The production process itself, resulting in products or services provided to customers
- The process of finding problems in the production process and proposing changes
- The process by which the production process moves from a certain level to a higher level
- The process in which the individual benefits of improvement activities are evaluated and subjected to improvement (Svozilová, 2011)

In this cycle of the system, the customer plays an important role not only in defining the requirements but also in the moment the product is handed over to it. Customer satisfaction is ensured through universal indicators (continuous process time, effective use of process time, total process costs, effective cost utilisation, process share of non-conformities, level of process capability, number of deviations registered in the process, etc.), indicators of production processes (workers' productivity, machine productivity, capital productivity, overall equipment efficiency, machine and process capability indices, the share of non-conforming products in the total output, average worker profitability, etc.), indicators of non-production processes (organisation's profit compared to the costs of design and development, user effect from the use of new products, the costs of finding eligible suppliers, the evaluation of suppliers, the speed of response to reported non-conformity by customers, the share of planned orders to completed orders, etc.), indicators of measuring deviations (delayed delivery of material and information inputs, tool defects, etc., incompetent employees, etc.), indicators of measuring process performance indices (measurement periods, current indicator values, indicator weights, etc.).

The PDCA cycle of continuous improvement affects the overall performance of the business and helps the organisation better respond to opportunities and threats. To fulfil this principle, the organisation must do the following:

- Systematically identify weaknesses (e.g., through audits and self-assessments)
- See weaknesses solely as opportunities for improvement
- Decide on improvement project assignments
- Plan improvement activities and free up adequate resources for process improvement
- Provide the necessary staff training in the application of improvement methods
- Systematically measure and monitor the effectiveness and efficiency of the implemented improvements (Nenadál, Noskievičová, Petříková, Plura, & Tošenovský, 2008)

Implementation of 5S

The 5S aims to ensure the control of the shop floor resulting in an efficient workplace organisation. In particular, it is a system for organising spaces so work can be performed efficiently, effectively and safely. Its origin is debated: some say that it was inspired by Henry Ford's CANDO (cleaning up, arranging, neatness, discipline and ongoing improvement); nevertheless, it requires top management's support to succeed (Bhoraniya, n.d.).

The 5S has expanded and can be found within total productive maintenance (TPM), the just-in-time (JIT) process and lean manufacturing today (Soumya & Shantha, 2015) (Figure 6.6).

Figure 6.6 Five S (based on Ghori, 2015)

The 5S helps to reduce non-value-adding time, increases productivity and improves quality. It was used in the design of efficient facilities (Chapman, 2005). 5S techniques were integrated with other lean tools to reduce change over time (Bevilacqua et al., 2015).

The 5S lean technique can be summarised as follows (Ramdass, 2015):

1. **Sort** (Seiri): The phenomenon of sort defines the proper arrangement of materials as well as tools. Things are sorted according to their needs. In the case of things, for example, it is relevant whether they are needed, when they are needed and how long they are needed. The main aim of sorting is to organise the work environment and get rid of junk. Another objective is to discard the items that are not needed on the shop floor

2. **Set in order** (Seiton): Set in order is the method by which the tools and materials are arranged in the appropriate order of the machine assembled. The arrangements are done in such a manner that the necessary tools are arranged by the order of their use. It helps to reduce the travelling distance as the searching time for things gets reduced. Also, labels, tapes, floor markings and signs are used to execute the set in order

3. **Shine** (Seiso): The literal meaning of shine is to do systematic cleaning. The main purpose of shine is not to show beauty but to serve a purpose. Cleanliness helps to make the environment healthy and better visibility results in higher-quality work. The other purpose of SHINE is to identify dirty areas and clean them

4. **Standardise** (Seiketsu): Following the creation of guidelines and setting them in order, the next step is standardising. The main purpose of it is to create best practices and ensure that the best practices are used by workers and members. By not having clear standards, there is no path to keep eye on the improvements. The standards are easy to understand and they are communicable

5. **Sustain** (Shitsuke): The prime aim of sustain is habit formation. The other objective is to sustain the activities, such as sorting and shining every day. Sustain improves inter-human relationships. Sustain teaches discipline and keeps the 5S process running

The 5S analysis was adopted as part of lean manufacturing, the Kaizen and Six Sigma methods.

The 5 × Whys quality improvement process helps to find the root cause of each problem and identify opportunities for improvement. The main activity of this analysis is to ask "why", until it reaches the root cause of the problem. There is no rule that the question "why" can be used only five times, but usually after five logically asked questions, it is possible to learn the answer:

Why did the problem occur?
Why was the problem (fault) not detected in time?
Why did the system allow it?

An example of a problem is: The vehicle will not start

First why? – The battery is dead
Second why? – The alternator is not functioning
Third why? – The alternator belt has broken
Fourth why? – The alternator belt was well beyond its useful service life and not replaced
Fifth why? – The vehicle was not maintained according to the recommended service
schedule (Spear, 2010)

The Kaizen method

When translated, Kaizen means improvement or perfecting. It applies to all activities, all levels and all employees. Translated literally," kai" refers to a change in everything that can be improved (every product, technological process, work activity, production system, service, etc.), while "zen" refers to the good, the better and the involvement of as many employees as possible, who actively and purposefully participate in continuous, gradual and daily improvement (Dirgo, 2005).

The starting point of Kaizen is to acknowledge the fact that every business has problems. In line with Kaizen, these problems are solved by creating a corporate culture in which everyone is free to admit these problems. Kaizen is an understanding of the fact that the leadership of any company must strive to meet customer needs if it wants to stay in the game and make a profit. It is a strategy of improvement, the driving force of which is customers' needs. It emphasises the production process. Kaizen leads to a way of thinking that focuses on the production process and management systems, which support and recognise human efforts to improve production processes (Imai, 2005).

Kaizen is an umbrella term that can include most of the techniques originally used by the Japanese, such as absolute quality control, quality control groups, automation, workplace discipline, kanban, just-in-time, just-in-sequence (JIS) new product development, management-employee cooperation, the system of improvement proposals and others (Kováčová, 2012; Košturiak & Frolík, 2006). Kaizen also refers to improving all processes in the value chain of business activities and, at the same time, reducing costs in the focus on customers. It is based on a mass initiative of employees supported by an effective motivation system. Kaizen is primarily employee-oriented because employees are the bearers and co-creators of the company's values. Improvement in Kaizen is a slow, gradual and not immediately visible process; its results are felt only after a long time. The application of the improvement cycle by the Kaizen method (Figure 6.7) allows:

- The elimination of redundancy, inefficiency, shortcomings and waste. The so-called 3M stands for three obstacles in Lean: muda (waste, losses, the opposite of added value), muri (excessive burden, overload) and mura (imbalance, deviations). Resolving these three interconnected areas leads to a smooth flow
- The maintenance of permanent orderliness at workplaces, discipline and initiative of employees – quality groups
- The achievement of the productive maintenance of the capital goods
- The achievement of absolute quality control – flawless production (zero)
- Autonomous cell workplaces
- Production without warehouses – JIT and JIS deliveries
- Standardisation, the optimisation of the machinery, etc.

The Kaizen Improvement Initiative is a refined and sophisticated system of work based on adherence to the following principles:

- Kaizen is a philosophy based on the openness of all employees

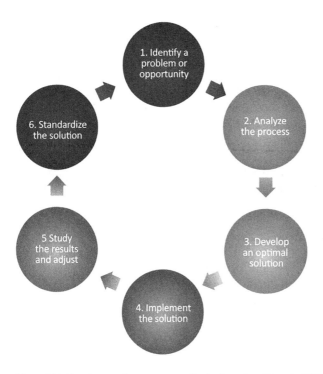

Figure 6.7 Continuous Improvement Cycle (based on Doanh, 2017b)

- Attention needs to be paid not only to significant and fundamental improvements but also to small changes that can move the company forward in small steps
- Create strong enough and active support from management because Kaizen is built on bottom-up activities, and it is otherwise unable to live
- Decisions need to be taken slowly after considering all options based on a broad consensus
- Preconditions for improved communication in production need to be created, for example by introducing production meetings, visits of managers in production, the introduction of information boards, company Key Performance Indicators (KPIs), updating data on the production quality, etc.
- Involve the Kaizen team in the immediate implementation of corrective measures as soon as the Kaizen action is ready
- Motivate employees – explain the goal, highlight the results and the positive impact on customer requirements. Always strive to see what will benefit the people in the production process, and what simplification will occur
- Incorporate continuous improvement into management meetings and report current problems in production, goals, restrictions, proposals and cooperation with the company's management (Svět productivity, 2012)

In the USA, the so-called Blitz Kaizen (Kaizen blitz, which is based on the principles of Kaizen) was developed in AME (Imai, 2005). However, it is different from Kaizen

- It involves the significant support of senior management, top-down direction, further improvement in teams, the members are from different sections and departments of the company and the Kaizen form, namely, short, striking, intense action. The duration of one Kaizen blitz event is usually two to eight working days when all team members focus solely on a given, management-approved area and Kaizen activity
- Manual work in the process of Kaizen implementation is done by all team members. Furthermore, a low budget is adhered to in the sense that small improvements are made right away, without the need for investment
- Because the improvement of the selected process must be implemented in a short time interval, there is no time to request investment and solutions feasibly applied in a matter of days are preferred

Activities in the company can be divided into maintenance and improvement activities. Top management is mainly engaged in improvement activities related to the strategic vision of the company. Production workers devote most of their working time to maintenance activities.

Six Sigma improvement methodology

The Six Sigma methodology is based on the principle of improving business processes by reducing their variability. The basis for achieving the stability of processes is to reduce the number of defects of the products and deviations from the required value of the product's monitored parameter.

Six Sigma is a systematic and extremely result-oriented methodology, which is based primarily on mathematical and statistical procedures. The most widely used guide to Six Sigma projects is the DMAIC improvement cycle. Through real improved quality requirements, it transforms the management philosophy and organisational culture. Its projects guarantee earlier or later benefits. The Six Sigma strength lies in the standard DMAIC improvement procedure (Figure 6.8). Table 6.1 shows an overview of the activities performed at each stage of the DMAIC cycle and the tools recommended at each stage.

DMAIC cycle

The DMAIC (Defining–Measurement–Analysis–Improvement–Management) model is used in the Six Sigma methodology as a standard improvement procedure. This model makes it possible to reduce the undesirable variability of business processes and thus helps to increase the stability of processes. This methodology was developed by Motorola and introduced in 1986 in the same company with the purpose of quality assessment based on the measurement of standard deviations of product metrics. The Six Sigma methodology was initially used only in production, but later also in the administrative and sales side of the company. It is a structured and highly quantitative approach to improving product quality through metrics of quality indicators. If the customer requirement is not clearly defined, the initial level of stability may be expressed by the ability to satisfy customer requirements to at least 90% or more.

Before setting quality metrics, attention needs to be paid to the meanings of "non-conformity-defect" and "non-conforming-defective". Any feature of the product or service that does not meet the customer's specifications is a non-conformity. Defective is the term used to qualify a product.

For example, if a car part is to have a length of 10 ± 0.5 cm, but its specific length is 8 cm, the product is defective and has one defect. If discrepancies in two dimensions were recorded, it has two defects.

The goal of Six Sigma is to achieve near perfection, namely, complete compliance with customer specifications. The statistical tools used in Six Sigma allow not only the qualitative elimination of errors perceptible to customers but also the reduction of variations in the process output over time, i.e., the quantification of the short-term and long-term process capability.

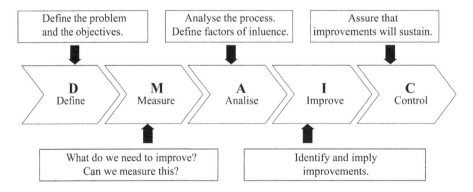

Figure 6.8 Concept of the DMAIC methodology (based on Hessing, 2014)

Table 6.1 Tools and activities are performed at different stages of the DMAIC cycle (based on Burieta, 2017)

Contents	Methods and tools
(Stage) Define: Defining the project, its scope and objectives.	
• What is important for the customer? • What is important for the company? • What are the main opportunities? • What are the key projects? • How do key projects work?	Audit, benchmarking, project charter Quality Function Deployment (QFD), value stream mapping, FMEA, Pareto analysis, cost and benefit calculation, key issues diagram – TOC, IPO Inputs Process, Outputs, SIPOC diagram, VOC Voice of Customer.
(Stage) Measure: Measure the current level of process performance.	
• How is process performance measured? • How should process performance be measured correctly? • What are the customer's requirements for individual process indicators? • What is the current process performance?	Pareto analysis, Ishikawa (1991) diagram, PF diagram, value flow map, FMEA, FPY process, process maps, Chi^2 test, risk tree, 7/7 quality tools, statistical tools, control diagrams, process imaging, process audits.
(Stage) Analysis: Problem analysis and the identification of the main causes	
• What are the interrelations between the process inputs and outputs? • What is the capability and speed of the process? • Identification of variance and bottlenecks. • Which sources of variance are under control? • Which sources of variance depend on suppliers? • Which variables affect process mean, its variance and process performance fundamentally? • Defining the main types of waste and their causes.	Ishikawa (1991) diagram, FMEA, fault tree, risk analysis, control diagrams, process capability, Cpk, Cp, Cpm, Reliability Analysis, Root Case Analysis, 5x Why? Systems engineering, value analysis, bottleneck analysis, brainstorming, simulation and regression analysis.
(Stage) Improve: Measures to improve the process and eliminate the causes of problems.	
• Generating and selecting ideas for improvement • Testing the proposals • Evaluating the proposals • Action plan for the proposed implementation • Proposal implementation	Brainstorming, planned experiment, modelling and simulation, Robust Design, Plan-Do-Check-Act (PDCA), Failure Mode and Effects Analysis (FMEA), G8D Total Productive Maintenance (TPM), Single Minute Exchange of Die (SMED), TOC, 5S, visualisation, pull control systems, Theory of Constraints (TOC), Kaizen, idea management, Contonius Improvement Process (KVP), Poka Yoke, workshops, work analysis and measurement.
(Stage) Control: Monitor and control the process and ensure continuous improvement.	
• Documentation of project results and benefits • Measures to maintain improvement • How has the process improved? • What has been saved or gained? • Rewarding the solvers	Statistical Process Control (SPC), control diagrams, time series, Base Station Controller (BSC), management by objectives, preventive planning, FMEA, visual management and process standardisation.

The process at the 6 SIGMA (± 6σ) level is considered to be a quality standard, which corresponds to 0.002 product defects per million opportunities. However, the tables often show 3.4 defects per million opportunities (Table 6.2).

Practical experience has shown that, in the long run, it is possible to consider the process as sufficiently centred at the shift of the average value of the set of measured data by ± 1.5σ (Figure 6.9). This shift by 1.5σ captures an estimate of the change in the average value of the indicator between short-term and long-term periods.

A shift of 1.5σ is a long-term capability at the level of 4.5σ (6σ − 1.5σ = 4.5σ) (Figure 6.9). If the unit contains more than one defect ($n_{CTQC} > 1$), this change is expressed in terms of the Defects per million opportunities (DPMO) ratio, i.e., the number of defects (D) in one million opportunities (n_{unit}) as follows:

$$DPMO = \frac{\text{total number of defect found in a sample}}{\text{sample size.number of defect opportunities per unit in the sample}} .1000000$$

$$= \frac{D}{n_{units}.n_{CTQC}} .1000000.$$

Table 6.2 DPMO to sigma-level relationship (based on Six Sigma Daily, 2013)

Six Sigma level without 1.5s shit	DPMO without 1.5s shit	Six Sigma level with 1.5s	DPMO with 1.5s shit	RTY yield for the first time (%)	Cost of poor quality (COPQ)
1	317 311	1	697 672	30.2328	Unacceptable
1.5	133 614	1.5	501 350	49.865	
2	45 500	2	308 770	69.123	
2.5	12 419	2.5	158 687	84.1313	
3	2 700	3	66 811	93.3189	25–35
3.5	465.35	3.5	22 750	97.725	
4	63.37	4	6 210	99.379	15–25
4.5	6.8	4.5	1 350	99.865	
5	0.574	5	232.67	99.9767	5–15
5.5	0.038	5.5	31.69	99.9968	
6	0.002	6	3.4	99.9997	

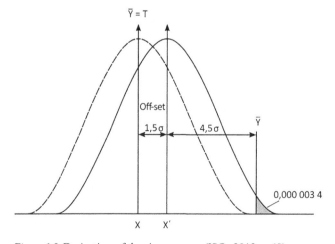

Figure 6.9 Derivation of the sigma scores (ISO, 2012, p.49)

Where D is the total number of defects found in a sample of defects or non-conformities (total number of defects found in the sample),

n is a sample size,

x_i is a variable value,

$\bar{x}$ is the sample arithmetic mean value of x_i,

Z_{value} Sigma score or value,

n_{CTQC} is a number of critical to quality characteristics,

n_{units} are the number of units surveyed or sample size (ISO, 2011).

This means that the process known as Six Sigma (6σ) has a specification limit set as 4.5 times the standard deviation (4.5σ) from the average value of the output quality indicator, which corresponds to 1,350 non-conforming products per million opportunities (Table 6.10).

Example: A total of 50,000 pizzas were delivered to order. However, upon delivery, it was found that in 35 cases, the delivery was returned for the following reasons:

- Late delivery in eight cases
- Cold pizza in 15 cases
- The type of pizza did not match the specification of the order in seven cases

$$DPU = \frac{35}{50000} = 0.0007\,\%$$

As three types of error were identified, the following relation was used to calculate the process capability:

$$DPMO = \frac{35}{50000.3}.1000000 = 210$$

In the above case study, this means that the value of DPMO = 210 from Tab. 1 corresponds to a sigma score of 5.17. DPU and DPMO indicators have been introduced because processes are constantly being improved and their level of performance is regularly improved to the extent that the use of % units (e.g., 0.001 5%) proved impractical.

Six Sigma is a statistical approach to continuous improvement, which allows companies to eliminate product deficiencies and push their processes to fit the defined limits so that the probability of producing a defective product is very small or zero ppm. The priority here is high customer satisfaction together with ensuring the profitability of the company.

It follows from the Taguchi Loss Function that the losses from poor quality increase quadratically with the distance from the target value of the characteristic parameter analysed in Figure 6.10 (Young et al., 2020). The cost of poor quality (COPQ) is associated with product repair, the delivery of defective materials, additional inspection, the handling of complaints, penalties, customer dissatisfaction (loss of favour), additional measurement, delayed product launch, legal disputes, etc. The cost of poor quality negatively affects the overall economic result of the company, its position in the market and its competitiveness.

The process in which all measurements of the output characteristics are within limits is considered to be capable. The process capability indices (PCI) indicate the extent to which a process can produce output that meets consistent requirements. It is determined by the comparison of the natural variability of the process with the customer or technical specifications (Futó & Baranová, 2012; Stapelberg, 2009; O'Connor & Kleyner, 2006; Benková, 2007).

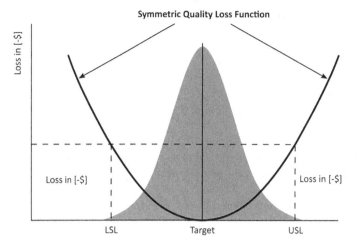

Figure 6.10 Taguchi loss function (Young et al., 2020)

The relation between the current process performance and specification limits can be quantified using the process capability indices (Sekerešová, 1995). Many procedures for determining capability indices from Cp, Cpk and Cpm to various robust indices are known from standards and the literature. The role of the Process Capability Indices (PCI) are to simply express the relation between the Target Value (T), the LSL and the USL (Lower/Upper Specification Limit), the actual process in terms of the mean $\bar{x}$ and the standard deviation σ of the values measured, concerning the selected quality characteristics of the process at hand. The target-T value and the mean $\bar{Y}$ value of the quality characteristic to be achieved should converge as much as possible. The indices are demanded by the customers from the suppliers and are used by manufacturers as advertising. According to the number of the quality characteristics monitored, we can divide them into indices:

• Of one characteristic
• Of more quality characteristics monitored simultaneously

According to the nature of the quality characteristic, into indices:

• With normal distribution
• With a different distribution
• Of immeasurable characters

The many side effects of the process cause the actual value of the monitored characteristic to be more or less different from the desired (target-T) value. Most influences act randomly, unexpectedly (random influences – Common Causes), while others act in a certain way "regularly" or systematically (systematic influences – Special Causes). As a result of the action of random influences, the distribution of values has its laws – it is a distribution that can be described mathematically. Systematic influences cause various distribution deformations. Their effect can be recognised or defined in the noise of random influences, so we also call them definable causes.

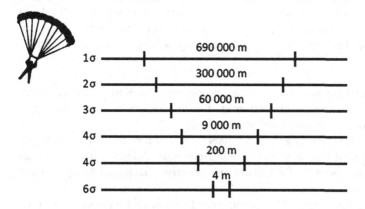

Figure 6.11 Illustration of a parachutist's jump onto a target (Töpfer, 2008)

Figure 6.12 Illustration of the car and the weight deviation (based on Töpfe, 2008)

Six Sigma application example: The goal is to train a parachutist to jump on a target so that he can jump from a plane on the target with an accuracy of 6σ. This means that at the Six Sigma level, the parachutist jumps into a square with a dimension of 4×4 meters (Figure 6.11).

Example of Six Sigma application: A car manufacturer intends to produce a car weighing 1 ton with a maximum deviation of 1σ. This means that at the Six Sigma level, a car with a deviation of 3.4 g will be produced (Figure 6.12).

6.2 When Lean meets I4.0

Lilla Hortoványi, Sándor Gyula Nagy and Tamás Stukovszky

Experts agree that the successful implementation, as well as the operation of LM, is challenging because of the enormous amount of complex data.

After an extensive review, Bittencourt and co-authors (2019) concluded that I4.0 and LM are mutually supportive, where becoming smart can support lean operation.

For example, Industry 4.0 provides the infrastructure to enhance the Lean/Six Sigma capability of an organisation both at the operational and at the enterprise level (Li, Field & Davis, 2017). At the operational level, performance and operational data metrics can be transmitted in real time through the CPS network empowering the operational team with tools such as:

1. **Electronic Kanbans:** Rather than relying on conventional Kanban cards, a production order can be automatically transmitted to the downstream process upon sensing that the desired inventory level was reached
2. **Total Productive Maintenance:** Sensors detect when components need replacing (i.e., oil filters) and send signals to the maintenance staff. Additionally, signals can be transmitted alerting the need for a maintenance activity triggered by operational hours or calendar dates
3. **Data Analysis:** The data captured in real time can be analysed for possible interruptions or wastes
4. **Virtual Value Stream Mapping:** the availability of real-time data allows a more in-depth understanding of the company's status quo and assertive re-design of lean value streams
5. **Smart Product:** can collect and use the information for analysis about repeating actions from their sensor and semantic technologies, which opens the way for the lean journey of the Kaizen

IoT and CPS play a key role in implementing lean principles, such as promoting a culture that stops problem-solving and instead focuses on problem-identification and solving (Pagliosa et al., 2019). In addition, both technologies have great flexibility and can be used in different ways to achieve higher levels of quality and productivity. According to a study undertaken by the Boston Consulting Group, manufacturers that have successfully deployed Lean Industry 4.0 can reduce conversion costs by as much as 40% in five to ten years—considerably better than the reductions captured by the best-in-class independent deployment of lean or Industry 4.0. Companies also used the integrated approach to reduce costs associated with poor quality by 20% and work-in-process inventory by 30%. Since the integrated approach allows lean management and Industry 4.0 to be mutually enabling, its improvement potential is greater than the sum of the improvements achieved by either approach independently. Mutual enablement promotes benefits beyond the typical limits of either of the two approaches (Küpper et al., 2017).

Uriarte and co-authors (2018) suggest that in the future, Industry 4.0 solutions will support companies to become lean without "striving-for-lean" efforts. Nevertheless, they found evidence that Industry 4.0 solutions can support companies in overcoming even some of the existing hurdles for Lean implementation today. In particular, LM was mainly designed for mass production, but the future is about mass customisation. The technologies of Industry 4.0 can support quicker and more responsive production system design, while also maintaining a high level of efficiency. They also warn practitioners that the implementation of technologies just by themselves will not aid any gain in productivity; rather, the critical element is a change in organisational culture. Many experts support this view with the inclusion that investment in training employees is needed (Hortoványi et al., 2020). Mrugalska and Wyrwicka (2017) have a positive view of the future, claiming that Lean 4.0 is intended to support employees in their work and not to replace employees and their creativity in solving problems.

Case illustration

The Lean Aerospace Initiative (LAI) (a partnership of academics, aircraft manufacturers, commercial airlines and the U.S. Air force) considers Lean 4.0 to be the key to driving down procurement costs and improving delivery time for both commercial and defence aerospace provision (Murman et al., 2002).

Review questions

1. What are the steps in Deming cycle?
2. What are the basic pillars of the Six Sigma concept?
3. What types of wastes are to be eliminated by LM?
4. What does the application of the Kaizen method allow?
5. What is the DMAIC model used for?

Discussion questions

1. How can I4.0 and lean philosophy create synergies together?
2. How can I4.0 overcome LM's rigidity in terms of mass production?
3. Why is it critical to keep order and organise the space on the shop floor? What are the benefits of "housekeeping" on the shop floor?
4. Explain how existing lean management can support the implementation of I4.0 technologies.

Bibliography

ABCI Consultants. (2021). *ISO 9001:2015 requirements*. Retrieved from http://iso9001.certification -requirements.com/0_3_2-plan-do-check-act-cycle.html

Benková, M. (2007). *Zabezpečovanie kvality procesov*. Košice, Technická univerzita, F-BERG. Retrieved from https://people.tuke.sk/peter.bober/srp/doc/Benkova_1-28.pdf

Bevilacqua, M., Ciarapica, F. E., De Sanctis, I., Mazzuto, G., & Paciarotti, C. (2015). A changeover time reduction through an integration of lean practices: A case study from pharmaceutical sector. *Assembly Automation, 35*(1), 22–34. https://doi.org/10.1108/AA-05-2014-035

Burieta, J. (2017). *DMAIC: Model riadenia six sigma projektu*. Retrieved from https://www.ipaslovakia.sk /clanok/dmaic-model-riadenia-six-sigma-projektu-2

Čiarnienė, R., & Vienažindienė, M. (2012). Lean manufactoring: Theory and practice. *Managment Trends 17*(2), 726–732. http://doi.org/10.5755/j01.em.17.2.2205

Chapman, C. D. (2005). Clean house with lean 5S. *Quality Progress, 38*(6), 27–32. Retrieved from https://www.ame.org/sites/default/files/qrl_docs/Clean%20House%20with%205S%20J%20Rubio _0.pdf

Cogito Software. (n.d.). *Stability analysis rules*. Retrieved from http://english.cogitosoft.com/html/ product/item.aspx?id=2972

Dickmann, P. (2008). *Schlanker Materialfluss: Mit Lean production, Kanban und innovationen*. Jersey City, NJ: Springer.

Dirgo, R. (2005). *Look forward beyond lean and six sigma: A self-perpetuating enterprise improvement method*. J. Ross.

Doanh, D. (2017a). *What is muda, mura, and muri?* Retrieved from https://theleanway.net/muda-mura -muri

Doanh, D. (2017b). *What is continuous improvement (kaizen)?* Retrieved from https://theleanway.net/ what-is-continuous-improvement

Futó, J., & Baranová, V. (2012). Index spôsobilosti: Miera kvality vstupných veličín procesu rozpojovania hornín. *ATP Journal, 6,* 1–10.

Ghori, M. M. (2015). *The 7 waste of lean six sigma.* Retrieved from http://mubashirghori.blogspot.com /2015/02/the-7-waste-of-lean.html

Hessing, T. (2014). *What is six sigma? Retriever.* Retrieved from https://sixsigmastudyguide.com/what -is-six-sigma/

Hortoványi, L., Szabó, Z. R., Nagy, S. G., & Stukovszky, T. (2020). A digitális transzformáció munkahelyekre gyakorolt hatásai–Felkészültek-e a hazai vállalatok a benne rejlő nagy lehetőségre (vagy a veszélyekre)?. *Külgazdaság, 64*(3–4), 73–96. http://doi.org/10.47630/KULG.2020.64.3-4 .73

Imai, M. (2005). *Gemba Kaizen: Řízení a zlepšování kvality na pracovišti.* Computer Press.

International Organization for Standardization. (2011). *Quantitative methods in process improvement: Six sigma – Part 1. DMAIC methodology.* Retrieved from https://www.iso.org/standard/52901.html

International Organization for Standardization. (2012). *Quantitative methods in process improvement: Six sigma – Part 2: Tools and techniques.* Retrieved from https://www.iso.org/obp/ui/#iso:std:iso:13053: -2:ed-1:v1:en

International Organization for Standardization. (2015). *Quality management systems: Fundamentals and vocabulary.* Retrieved from https://www.iso.org/standard/45481.html

Ishikawa, K. (1991). *Guide to quality control* (2nd ed.). Asian Productivity Organisation.

ISO. (2011). *ISO 19011: Guidelines for auditing management systems* (2nd ed.). Geneva, Switzerland: ISO.

Košturiak, J., & Frolík, Z. (2006). *Štíhlý a inovativní podnik.* Alfa.

Kováčová, Ľ. (2012). The development of models and methods kaizen. *Transfer inováci, 22,* 193–197. Retrieved from https://www.sjf.tuke.sk/transferinovacii/pages/archiv/transfer/22-2012/pdf/193 -197.pdf

Küpper, D. A. J. D., Heidemann, A., Ströhle, J., Spindelndreier, D., & Knizek, C. (2017). *When Lean meets Industry 4.0: The next level of operational excellence.* Boston: Boston Consulting Group, Retrieved from When Lean Meets Industry 4.0 Next Level Operational Excellence (bcg.com)

Li, G., Field, J. M., & Davis, M. M. (2017). Designing lean processes with improved service quality: An application in financial services. *Quality Management Journal, 24*(1), 6–19. http://doi.org/10.1080 /10686967.2017.11918497

Mihail, A. T., Constantin, O., & Grecu, D. (2010). Applying the kaizen method and the 5S technique in the activity of post-sale services in the knowledge-based organization. *Lecture Notes in Engineering and Computer Science, 2182,* 1–5. Retrieved from https://www.researchgate.net/publication/44260889 _Applying_the_Kaizen_Method_and_the_5S_Technique_in_the_Activity_of_Post-Sale_Services _in_the_Knowledge-Based_Organization

Murman, E., Allen, T., Bozdogan, K., Cutcher-Gershenfeld, J., McManus, H., Nightingale, D., … Widnall, S. (2002). *Lean enterprise value: Insights from MIT's Lean Aerospace Initiative.* New York: Palgrave Mcmillan.

Nenadál, J., Noskievičová, D., Petříková, R., Plura, J., & Tošenovský, J. (2008). *Moderní management jakosti: Principy, postupy a metody.* Management Press.

O'Connor, P. D. T., & Kleyner, A. (2006). *Practical reliability engineering.* Wiley.

Ohno, T. (1988). *Toyota production system: Beyond large-scale production.* Taylor & Francis.

Pagliosa, M. M., Tortorella, G. L., & Ferreira, J. C. E. (2019). Industry 4.0 and lean manufacturing: A systematic literature review and future research directions. *Journal of Manufacturing Technology Managment, 31.* http://doi.org/10.1108/JMTM-12-2018-0446

Planettogehter. (2021). *Seven types of wastes in lean manufacturing.* Retrieved from https://www .planettogether.com/blog/seven-types-of-waste-in-lean-manufacturing

Plura, J. (2001). *Plánování a neustálé zlepšování jakosti.* Computer Press.

Ramdass, K. (2015). Integrating 5S principles with process improvement: A case study. *Portland international conference on management of engineering and technology* (pp. 1908–1917). https://doi.org/10 .1109/PICMET.2015.7273045

Rohani, J. M., & Zahraee, S. M. (2015). Production line analysis via value stream mapping: A lean manufacturing process of color industry. *Procedia Manufacturing 2*(2351–9789), 6–10. http://doi.org /10.1016/j.promfg.2015.07.002

Roser, C. (2015). *Muda, mura, muri: The three evils of manufacturing.* Retrieved from https://www .allaboutlean.com/muda-mura-muri/

Sekerešová, D. (1995). *Shewhartove regulačné diagramy: Slovenská technická norma.* Retrieved from https:// arl4.library.sk/arl-spu/sk/detail-spu_us_cat-0275668-STN-ISO-8258-1995-01-0271-Shewhartove -regulacne-diagramy/

Six Sigma Daily. (2013). *DPMO to sigma level relationship.* Retrieved from https://www.sixsigmadaily .com/dpmo-to-sigma-level-relationship/

Soumya, R. P., & Shantha, V. (2015). Implementation of 5S methodology in a manufacturing industry. *International Journal of Scientific and Engineering Research, 6*(8), 225–231. Retrieved from https://www .ijser.org/researchpaper/Implementation-of-5S-Methodology-in-a-Manufacturing-Industry.pdf

Spear, S. J. (2010). *The high-velocity edge: How market leaders leverage operational excellence to beat the competition* (2nd ed.). McGraw-Hill.

Stapelberg, R., & F. (2009). *Handbook of reliability, availability, maintainability and safety in engineering design.* Springer.

Svět Produktivity. (2012). *Kaizen.* Retrieved from https://www.svetproduktivity.cz/slovnik/Kaizen .htm

Svozilová, A. (2011). *Zlepšování podnikových procesů.* Grada.

Töpfer, A. (2008). *Six sigma: Koncepce a příklady pro řízení bez chyb.* Computer Press.

Young, T. M., Lebow, P. K., Lebow, S., & Adam Taylor, A. (2020). Statistical process control and related methods for improvement of the treated-wood industries. *Forest Products Journal, 70*(2), 165– 177. https://doi.org/10.13073/FPJ-D-19-0006

7 Artificial/enhanced intelligence

Andrea Kő and Tibor Kovács

Artificial intelligence (AI) is a field of cognitive science that includes image processing, speech recognition, natural language processing, robotics, machine learning and expert systems, among other areas. Artificial intelligence (AI) was launched in the 1940s, and, with the exception of two brief periods (between 1974–1980 and 1987–1993, it somehow lost researchers' interest), it grew enormously (Yao et al., 2017; Zhang et al., 2019). The latest wave of increased interest in AI started around 2010. This period is determined by three interrelated factors (Delipetrev et al., 2020): (1) the sources of big data, including e-commerce, social media, etc., (2) the machine learning approaches and algorithms that have been dramatically improved and (3) the development of powerful computers that support the computing of big data.

This chapter provides an overview of the current state of AI technologies from industrial applications perspective as well as an illustration – a real-world case study – of an industrial AI application from the field of machine learning.

7.1 AI technologies from industrial applications view

Industrial AI (I-AI) is considered a subdomain of AI and it addresses machine learning algorithms and targets industrial applications, and it provides methodology and solutions for industrial problems. It connects the academic research community with industry practitioners (Lee et al., 2018). Machine learning (ML) is a subset of artificial intelligence, concerned with the design and development of algorithms that allow computers to evolve behaviours based on empirical data (Amaran, Sahinidis & Sharda, 2016). ML is primarily concerned with the design and development of algorithms that allow computers to "learn" from historical data to discover new patterns in the data and solve problems without being specifically programmed to do so. ML became popular in manufacturing over the past 20 years. I-AI includes the following disciplines (Lee et al., 2018): Analytics technology, big data technology, cloud or cyber technology, domain know-how and evidence.

The AI development path is not straightforward. The history of AI started in the 1940s and it experienced several periods of intense development and neglect, as presented in Figure 7.1. (Zhang et al., 2019).

Despite its rather long history, I-AI is still at the stage of infancy (Lee et al., 2018), and therefore, it is fundamental to clarify its terminology, including its definition, methodologies and frameworks for its effective utilisation in the industry.

I-AI can impact manufacturing in many ways by bringing new capabilities and new applications. ML can be used to predict quality and yield, identify ways to reduce losses and improve yields and efficiencies. Applying a continuous multivariate analysis of the

DOI: 10.4324/9781003390312-8

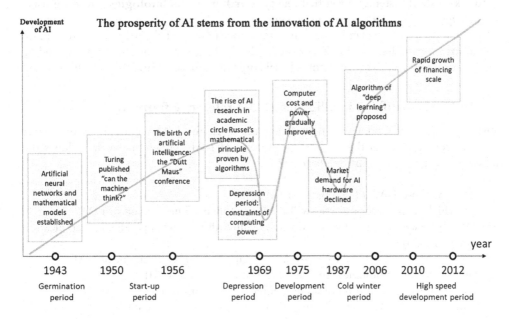

Figure 7.1 The development path of AI (based on Zhang et al., 2019)

production processes can help us better understand it and could lead to the creation of automated recommendations and alerts to prevent problems before they occur. Predictive maintenance is another important application of I-AI, which not only helps predict and prevent failures but also aids the extension of the useful life of machinery as well as reduce maintenance costs. I-AI will play a major role in the adoption of robots in manufacturing, increasing the efficiency of human–robot collaboration, ensuring the safety of personnel and optimising processes. Human–robot collaboration refers to robots helping people perform manual activities, and it involves collaborative work to achieve shared goals. I-AI will also play a role in the design phase, exploring all possible configurations of material types and production methods to find the optimal solution. Finally, I-AI will help to better understand demand patterns and to optimise inventory, staffing and energy consumption.

7.2 Industrial artificial intelligence (I-AI) – conceptual background

There is no common definition for industrial artificial intelligence. Lee et al. (2018) characterise **I-AI** as a composition of the following disciplines: Analytics technology, big data technology, cloud or cyber technology, domain know-how and evidence. Zhang et al. (2019) define I-AI as an integration of AI technology and industrial processes, where AI technology provides intelligent functions for all stages of the industrial value chain. The **industrial value chain** has five stages: customer demand, R & D design, operations management, production and processing, services and other activities. **AI technologies** can be divided into traditional and further AI categories. **Traditional AI technologies** address the following common areas: machine learning, speech understanding, voice recognition, intelligent agents, computer vision, natural language processing, neural networks, expert systems and virtual reality. **Further AI technologies** cover big data/ knowledge intelligence, swarm intelligence (Li et al., 2017), cross-media intelligence (Peng et al., 2017), hybrid enhancement intelligence (Zheng et al., 2017) and autonomous and unmanned intelligence (T. Zhang et al., 2017). I-AI has various functions, including self-control, self-adaptive, self-feedback, self-organisation, self-learning and self-decision.

7.3 Industrial artificial intelligence (I-AI) reference frameworks

Zhang et al. (2019) suggest a reference framework for I-AI technologies to answer the questions related to the application context of I-AI. This framework includes the following seven dimensions (see Figure 7.2):

1. Who will use I-AI? (The object of I-AI)
2. In which manufacturing areas will I-AI be applied? (The domain of I-AI)
3. At which stages of the industrial value chain will I-AI be applied? (The application stage of I-AI)
4. Why I-AI? Does it need to be used? (The application requirement of I-AI)
5. Which I-AI technologies are needed? (Technologies of I-AI)
6. What kinds of functions are implemented? (Functions of I-AI)
7. How will the I-AI solution integrate into the industrial value chain?

Lee et al. (2018) propose an I-AI ecosystem as a conceptual framework, which covers demands, methodologies, challenges and technologies for developing transformative AI systems for the industry (see Figure 7.3). The term "ecosystem" is the collection of technologies, products, platforms and software applications that are used in business for implementing

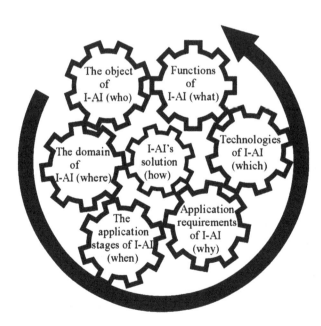

Figure 7.2 Reference architecture of I-AI (based on Zhang et al., 2019)

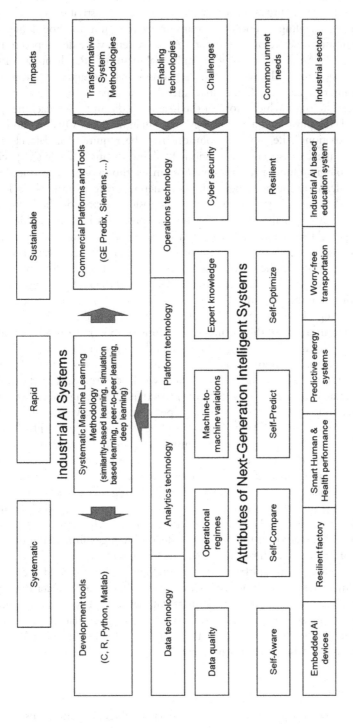

Figure 7.3 Industrial AI eco-system (based on Lee et al., 2018)

AI solutions. The term "ecosystem" is used to emphasise the importance of how these connect and interact with each other. Their framework serves as a guideline for I-AI strategy development and deployment. It is organised by the industrial sector, common unmet needs, challenges, enabling technologies, transformative system methodologies and impact within different industrial sectors. Different I-AI ecosystems were developed to target common, unmet needs. An unmet need of the industrial sector of "Resilient Factory" is exemplified by the need for "self-aware" and "self-optimised" equipment. More specifically, Computer Numerical Control (CNC) machines that make parts from metal or plastic could benefit from technologies which monitor the health condition of the machine spindle. The challenges of developing such a technology may include "Data Quality" and "Machine-to-Machine Variations", i.e., specific solutions may be required for data cleaning, signal conditioning or machine-specific calibration. Enabling technologies (e.g., specific data or analytics technologies) and Transformative System Methodologies (e.g., the development tools, machine learning methodologies and commercial platforms) may be selected in this context to develop the I-AI system that delivers a positive impact on the industrial sector.

Arinez et al. (2020) analysed I-AI systems and processes in a hierarchical way, from the processing level through the individual machine level up to the manufacturing system level. They chose this structure because plants are organised this way, both physically and functionally. At the highest level, the system-level I-AI is used for system modelling, performance analysis and decision-making. In the field of throughput performance evaluation, simulations combined with ML are one of the most important methods. In the field of decision-making, the applications are related to the scheduling and resourcing of allocations, the identification of the optimal allocations of jobs and resources with the help of ML-based methods and supervised learning and reinforcement learning. At the individual machine level, an important area of I-AI is its use in the context of human-robot collaboration (HRC). According to their framework, the relevant applications of I-AI in HRC are related to supervisory control, proactively planning robot actions, training autonomous robotic operations, monitoring operations or intervening and pursuing corrective actions among others. An example could be the application of HRC in the automotive industry. A robot could assist in adjusting the fog lights, which are hard to reach and therefore the strain on the operator would be reduced. While the robot is performing this task, the operator can perform a more ergonomic and less stressful task and, therefore, they work collaboratively. At the lowest, processing level, I-AI performs condition monitoring, analysing and recognising degradation patterns to support condition-based and predictive maintenance. Another application of I-AI is the support of manufacturing process control, the analysis of the potential effect of changes in material quality and the optimisation of processes with the aid of ML techniques.

The main challenges of industrial artificial intelligence are threefold (Lee et al., 2018): data quality, machine-to-machine interaction and cybersecurity. Data quality refers to the fact that only accurate, clean and adequate data sets can provide the required output. Smart manufacturing systems are vulnerable to cyber risks, e.g., data leakage. In machine-to-machine interaction, the challenge is that conflict between an individual AI solution and the operation of other systems can occur.

Case illustration

The following case study describes how artificial intelligence can be used to improve the performance of manufacturing equipment. The company in this example is the manufacturer of small, inexpensive electrical components for car manufacturing. The company produces millions of different components using automated equipment and dozens of similar pieces of equipment in the manufacturing plant. The performance of this equipment is critical, as the inexpensive component puts enormous pressure on manufacturing costs. Machine failures, malfunctions, breakdowns and stoppages would influence manufacturing costs negatively. Furthermore, machine failures would also result in inadequate quality, undermining the reliability of the company as a supplier and damaging the relationship with its customers.

Applying preventative equipment maintenance is therefore imperative: machine failures must be prevented cost effectively, predicting their potential occurrence and raising alarms before they happen, so that maintenance activities can be performed cost effectively. Preventative maintenance is a well-established technique, which has been applied for large and expensive components of manufacturing equipment for many years. For example, monitoring the temperature, vibration or power consumption of drive components can be effective in predicting failures. However, when the equipment has large numbers of components, traditional methods may not be feasible because they are too expensive. In this situation, it is possible to apply artificial intelligence to help in the identification of potential failures.

Artificial intelligence can process and analyse thousands of complex signals simultaneously, compare them with patterns that describe potential malfunctions and raise warnings for those. The process of implementing a predictive maintenance solution starts by installing sensors that measure those characteristics of the equipment that indicate abnormal behaviour. While traditional predictive maintenance applications most often use a single sensor, comparing its value with an empirical limit, AI methods use multiple sensors simultaneously, identifying different patterns that characterise different operational statuses (see Figure 7.4). Once the sensors are installed, signals from these sensors need to be collected, building a repository that includes signals of normal and abnormal operations. The next step of building the preventative maintenance application is to pre-process the data, to remove errors, noise and redundant parts that do not carry useful information. This is followed by classifying the signals typical for normal and abnormal operations. The amount of data that is collected for the many

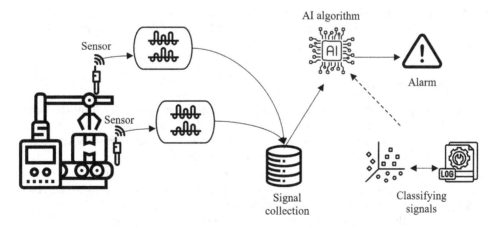

Figure 7.4 Preventative maintenance application using AI

sensors, over an extended period, makes it impossible to process and analyse it manually. Therefore, unsupervised machine learning models like clustering may be used for this step. Equipment log files may be used to understand the differences between the clusters, the equipment conditions and if malfunctions were experienced during or after the period. These clusters would ideally consist of signal patterns, which are early warning signs of malfunction. The signal collection, classification and interpretation are critical steps in the process of building preventative maintenance applications. There are potentially very few of those signals in the database that indicate a malfunction and, therefore, finding these signals and accurately classifying them is very important for building an accurate AI solution. The detailed process of classifying signals is described in Kovacs and Ko's research (Kovacs & Ko, 2020).

Once a sufficient amount of signals is collected and classified that describe the various states of the equipment, a classification AI application can be built. This classification AI application compares the live signals from the equipment and raises alarms for potential failures. The signals are used as the data set for training and validating the algorithms. There are many different algorithms available nowadays, which can accurately identify complex signals. The most efficient algorithm needs to be selected and its performance needs to be validated. The process of signal collection, classification, as well as training and validating the algorithms, does not stop with making the preventative maintenance application operational. There may be new types of signal patterns identified, which indicate new types of errors or malfunctions. This is all valuable information to make the operation more effective.

The above process may seem complicated and even expensive at first sight. The benefits of running an effective preventative maintenance system, however, can easily outweigh the cost of breakdowns, repairs, scrap due to poor quality and the penalties due to late, unreliable deliveries. Therefore, it is worth investing in the implementation of such an AI-based solution.

Review questions

1. Define industrial artificial intelligence.
2. Mention at least four I-AI technology.
3. How can I-AI impact manufacturing?
4. What are the main dimensions of the I-AI reference framework?
5. What are the main I-AI applications at the three hierarchical levels of manufacturing?
6. Compare traditional and future AI technologies.

Discussion questions

1. Visit   https://new.siemens.com/global/en/company/stories/home.html#Industry and download I-AI stories. How do they fit in an I-AI ecosystem?
2. Visit sas.com. Download at least three manufacturing customer stories. What do the various stories have in common? How do they differ?
3. Looking at the key I-AI applications of the hierarchical model proposed by Arinez et al. (2020), what could be the unmet needs for them and what would be the challenges of building successful I-AI ecosystems?
4. How could the I-AI ecosystem differ for different industrial sectors?

Acknowledgement

Funding Project No. NKFIH-869-10/2019 and its continuation in 2020 have been implemented with the support provided by the National Research, Development and Innovation Fund of Hungary, financed under the Tématerületi Kiválósági Programme funding scheme.

Bibliography

Abadi, M., Barham, P., Chen, J., Chen, Z., Davis, A., Dean, J., Devin, M., Ghemawat, S., Irving, G., Isard, M., & others. (2016). Tensorflow: A system for large-scale machine learning. 12th {USENIX} Symposium on Operating Systems Design and Implementation ({OSDI} 16), 265–283.

Amaran, S., Sahinidis, N.V., Sharda, B. & Bury, S.J. (2016). Simulation optimization: A review of algorithms and applications. *Annals of Operations Research, 240*, 351–380. doi: http://doi.org/10.1007/s10479-015-2019-x

Arinez, J. F., Chang, Q., Gao, R. X., Xu, C., & Zhang, J. (August 13, 2020). Artificial intelligence in advanced manufacturing: Current status and future outlook. *Journal of Manufacturing Science and Engineering, 142*(11), 110804. https://doi.org/10.1115/1.4047855

Bardou, O., & Sidahmed, M. (1994). Early detection of leakages in the exhaust and discharge systems of reciprocating machines by vibration analysis. *Mechanical Systems and Signal Processing, 8*(5), 551–570. https://doi.org/10.1006/mssp.1994.1039

Chollet, F., & others. (2015). *Keras*. GitHub. Retrieved from https://github.com/fchollet/keras

Delipetrev, B., Tsinarakii, C., & Kostić, U. (2020). *Historical evolution of artificial intelligence, EUR 30221*. EN, Publications Office of the European Union. https://doi.org/10.2760/801580, JRC120469

Kovacs, T., & Ko, A. (2020). Monitoring pneumatic actuators' behavior using real-world data set. *SN Computer Science, 1*(4), 196. https://doi.org/10.1007/s42979-020-00202-2

Lee, J., Davari, H., Singh, J., & Pandhare, V. (2018). Industrial artificial intelligence for industry 4.0-based manufacturing systems. *Manufacturing Letters, 18*, 20–23. https://doi.org/10.1016/j.mfglet.2018.09.002

Li, W., Wu, W., Wang, H., Cheng, X., Chen, H., Zhou, Z., & Ding, R. (2017). Crowd intelligence in AI 2.0 era. *Frontiers of Information Technology and Electronic Engineering, 18*(1), 15–43. https://doi.org/10.1631/FITEE.1601859

Peng, Y., Zhu, W., Zhao, Y., Xu, C., Huang, Q., Lu, H., Zheng, Q., Huang, T., & Gao, W. (2017). Cross-media analysis and reasoning: Advances and directions. *Frontiers of Information Technology and Electronic Engineering, 18*(1), 44–57. https://doi.org/10.1631/FITEE.1601787

Yao, X., Zhou, J., Zhang, J., & Boer, C. R. (2017). From intelligent manufacturing to smart manufacturing for industry 4.0 driven by next generation artificial intelligence and further on. *Proceedings – 2017 5th International Conference on Enterprise Systems: Industrial Digitalization by Enterprise Systems, ES 2017* (pp. 311–318). https://doi.org/10.1109/ES.2017.58

Zhang, T., Li, Q., Zhang, C. S., Liang, H., Wei, H., Li, P., Wang, T. M., Li, S., Zhu, Y. L., & Wu, C. (2017). Current trends in the development of intelligent unmanned autonomous systems. In *Frontiers of information technology and electronic engineering* (Vol. 18, Issue 1, pp. 68–85). Zhejiang University. https://doi.org/10.1631/FITEE.1601650

Zhang, X., Ming, X., Liu, Z., Yin, D., Chen, Z., & Chang, Y. (2019). A reference framework and overall planning of industrial artificial intelligence (I-AI) for new application scenarios. *International Journal of Advanced Manufacturing Technology, 101*(9–12), 2367–2389. https://doi.org/10.1007/s00170-018-3106-3

Zheng, N., Liu, Z., Ren, P., Ma, Y., Chen, S., Yu, S., Xue, J., Chen, B., & Wang, F. (2017). Hybrid-augmented intelligence: Collaboration and cognition. *Frontiers of Information Technology and Electronic Engineering, 18*(2), 153–179. https://doi.org/10.1631/FITEE.1700053

8 AI's impact on the labour market

Roland Zsolt Szabó and Bettina Boncz

Will there still be jobs left with the advancement of artificial intelligence (AI)? The press and several recent movies also address this burning question. It is burning since it touches on a sensitive social dilemma. As for the literature, there is no consensus, but researchers mostly agree that "workplace polarisation" and "technological unemployment" are the realistic consequence of the proliferation of "automation". Therefore, this chapter discusses the following two research questions: (1) how AI influences the labour market, and (2) what solutions can be found to technological unemployment.

8.1 How bright is the future?

Advances in artificial intelligence (AI) are expected to significantly reshape the labour market and more than likely change almost every job to some extent. There will be jobs that will benefit from it, but there will be jobs where human labour becomes completely unnecessary.

Scenario 1: Technological unemployment will not happen

The first scenario we identified argues that technological unemployment induced by artificial intelligence is not happening because machines will never be able to fully replace human labour. Skills like creativity, empathy, social skills or communication are and will always be human. As most jobs require one of these, full automation is not possible, only human-machine collaboration. It is also likely that the labour market will rebalance itself, or as technological progress can lower costs, companies invest more and create new workplaces while consumers have more money to articulate new needs, which bring forth new industries and products. Consequently, advocates of scenario 1 claim that technological progress and job creation are interrelated because productivity and employment have been rising together over the past decades (MacCarthy, 2014).

Scenario 2: Technological unemployment will happen

According to the second scenario, AI will be able to fully replace humans, while also saving costs, improving quality and reliability and, unfortunately, possibly causing technological unemployment. The new jobs created by technological progress are limited temporally and geographically (Peters & Jandrić, 2019).

The labour market is experiencing a phenomenon, called job polarisation. Due to technological progress, the middle sector of jobs is disappearing because their tasks are easily translated into machine language. Countries dealing with an ageing society and improving health care and diagnostics, backed up by smart technologies, will have an

DOI: 10.4324/9781003390312-9

ever-growing population who are capable and willing to work, even if the number of available workplaces remains constant. As technology is getting cheaper, after a while – even if automation will not be perfect –companies will choose to automate on a purely economic basis. Thus, billions of people worldwide are currently vulnerable to technological unemployment, and soon they will be looking for new jobs in industries that are less affected. Even if these people might try very hard, they simply will not be able to find another job, because the new job requires very different or very advanced education, skills or training (Ford, 2009). A great number of people will need to be de-skilled, re-skilled or upskilled, which, in turn, puts extra pressure on the current education system (Webster et al., 2020). This scenario urges preventive measures, smart data gathering and collaboration, and the reform of education, among others.

8.2 How to deal with technological unemployment?

Computers, automated systems, artificial intelligence and robots are replacing many jobs previously performed by humans. However, the demand for a particular job is not yet fixed in time and can change under several circumstances. For example, jobs that are deemed to be done by robots might be done again by humans due to governmental interventions of delaying or even halting the seemingly unstoppable penetration of computers (Kim et al., 2017).

The most common proposed policy response to the problem of technological unemployment is to provide some form of a **basic guaranteed income** for those who lose their jobs due to technological progress (Stevens & Marchant, 2017). This is the least preferred solution, as it is very expensive and wasteful. Working is beneficial for society because engagement in meaningful activities gives intrinsic satisfaction to individuals. People who enjoy working are happier and have higher self-esteem. Former research also proved that merit pays and benefits have a direct influence on how people perceive themselves, whether they see themselves as valued members of an organisation or society, and whether they consider themselves capable, productive and worthy (Gardner et al., 2004).

A guaranteed national income that gives recipients automatic monthly pay fails to provide an incentive to work or find a new job, learn new competencies and attend retraining programmes, and, thus, it is likely to trigger further unemployment. Most importantly, it is counterproductive. Sustained unemployment results in the loss of status, competence and self-esteem, causing severe psychological and physiological distress. A broad range of epidemiological studies demonstrates strong positive relationships between unemployment and ill health as well as mortality (Brenner & Levi, 1987).

Another way to prevent technological unemployment and protect jobs is to **mandate employment**, either directly through legislation or indirectly through labour agreements (Stevens & Marchant, 2017). Again, such governmental intervention is very expensive and risky. Although job protectionist policies may provide some short-term benefits in protecting some jobs, their long-term impact is unclear. They likely curb the desire to create new jobs in response to changing technology and patterns of demand since firms will worry about not being able to let unwanted employees go (Mortensen & Pissarides, 1999).

Another set of strategies seeks to share the available work among more workers by the reduction of weekly or monthly working hours per individual employee, for example (Stevens & Marchant, 2017). In addition, the retirement age can be set to be earlier, i.e., at a younger age. This solution assumes that people will fill their newly available time mostly with leisure activities. Some experts, however, warn us that the prospect of leisure-filled life is not appealing in reality (Vardi, 2012). Their argument is similar to the one stated earlier, namely, that work is essential to human well-being. Nevertheless, sharing available work seems to provide a fair solution for a greater number of people.

The compensation for job sharing creates another challenge because salaries and pay are supposed to be less for less work unless they are compensated by governmental subsidies. Compensation can also be levied on new taxes, especially for companies that completely replace human labour with robots. Because of the tax, companies would be motivated to keep a balance between robots and their employees, thus avoiding paying higher taxes. At the same time, robots typically perform work much more efficiently, and the increase in productivity results in higher profits, which, in turn, can compensate for the corporate surplus tax. Although it sounds logical, its implementation is not yet easy. Today, a significant portion of government revenue comes from taxing the wages of working people. However, if there are fewer people at work due to robots, the tax paid based on income will decrease, leading to a significant tax loss (Webster et al., 2020). Besides, large-scale taxation and redistribution schemes could have adverse effects on innovation (DeCanio, 2016). Therefore, protectionist policies must be designed with great consideration; otherwise, they are likely to result in losing the nation's long-term competitiveness (Stevens & Marchant, 2017).

The conclusion is that the previously mentioned solutions can be expensive and less desirable for society. Policymakers need to be aware that interventions always take place in a social context and, therefore, will have an impact on others: while intervention puts one group in a better position, it can just worsen the labour market situation of another group (Benda et al., 2019). In summary, technological unemployment is undoubtedly one of the greatest challenges of our time that requires careful consideration (Peters, 2017).

8.3 The role of education in solving technological unemployment

Researchers argue that labour market opportunities and outcomes for the lesser educated have diminished over recent decades, which makes them more vulnerable (Benda et al., 2019). For example, Frey and Osborne (2017) pointed out a structural shift in the labour market, with workers reallocating their labour supply from middle-income manufacturing to low-income service occupations because an increasing number of routine jobs are automated. In contrast, the manual tasks of service occupations are less susceptible to computerisation. At the same time, there is substantial employment growth in occupations involving cognitive tasks where skilled labour has a comparative advantage over machines. Thus, today we are witnessing the trend towards labour market polarisation, with growing employment in high-income cognitive jobs and low-income manual occupations, accompanied by a hollowing-out of middle-income routine jobs.

An increase in **educational attainment** seems to solve this problem. Looking across occupations, the college degree pays off the investment in terms of employment and wages. Consequently, by producing more graduates, some cities and even countries can gain a certain advantage over others; however, this creates a vicious circle because when the marketplace becomes flooded with college graduates, the value of their degrees necessarily drops (Peters & Jandrić, 2019). Moreover, upskilling training programmes introduced to strengthen the position of those with lower levels of education is likely to increase unemployment among those with higher education (Benda et al., 2019).

Other scholars argue that the polarisation of work is widening the gap between the layers of society (Webster et al., 2020). Given that higher education is extremely expensive in most countries, children from poor or disadvantaged families are more likely to drop out and lose their talent. In addition, there are several social barriers, such as being a member of a smaller ethnic group or being a woman, which will continue to exclude many people from higher education. It is likely to cause tremendous disenchantment and frustration, which could lead to social disruption (Marchant et al., 2014).

However, scholars agree that a fundamental shift in education is required: while the current education is based on the spirit of competition, individual achievement and intellectual rights, future education should prepare students for creative labour, peer production and collective intelligence (Peters & Jandrić, 2019). This would mean reconfiguring educational value and purpose to develop intellectual abilities that empower individuals to subordinate technology to egalitarian and sustainable goals (Means, 2017).

8.4 Worker 4.0

In Industry 4.0. context, the arrival of intelligent machines fundamentally changes labour requirements and creates a new concept: Worker 4.0 (BMAS, 2017). Worker 4.0 is not replaced by advanced technologies but rather collaborates with them (Mark et al., 2021).

The workers will fully utilise digital tools, such as big data analytics, the Internet of Things, cloud computing, autonomous and robotics systems, cyber security, augmented reality, simulation, system integration or additive manufacturing (Wai et al., 2020), which will make them able to increase their productivity. To become worker 4.0, the workforce must be trained to use these digital tools. In addition, people are required to develop new skills and abilities, which can make them capable of efficiently performing human-machine interactions during their daily work and of dealing with the ever more complex work environment (Leesakul et al., 2022) that is imposed by the rapid technological progress in the industry.

The workers who will fail to develop these skills will be susceptible to technological unemployment. Smart industry-employing companies have therefore an important role in the re-education and re-integration of workers who lack the knowledge to remain competitive in the digital world (Romero et al., 2016) so as to decrease the impact of technological unemployment on society.

The other side of the same coin is that machines need to collaborate. Experts suggest that the future direction of AI is to develop intelligent machines that will work in collaboration with humans and not compete with them (DeCanio, 2016). AI is still very far from having motives and human traits, which are beyond intelligence. Even if we invent machines that are capable of sharing emotions, their mass production is highly unrealistic. Currently, innovators aim to build specialised machines that do specific tasks that are repetitive, monotonous or dangerous (Diamond, 2020).

Nevertheless, AI today is good at the narrowly defined tasks for which it was programmed, while humans will always have both a comparative and an absolute advantage in creating and responding to genuinely novel challenges (Diamond, 2020). Nevertheless, the solution is not to protect old jobs and smash all machinery but to create new jobs (Rattner, 2014).

Review questions

1. Why technological unemployment is likely to happen?
2. Why technological unemployment will not happen?
3. What is the role of education in solving technological unemployment?

Discussion questions

1. Why can the increase in educational attainment backfire on wages?
2. Why is it important to make sure that poor and disadvantaged children can have access to higher education?

Biography

Benda, L., Koster, F., & van der Veen, R. J. (2019). Levelling the playing field? Active labour market policies, educational attainment and unemployment. *International Journal of Sociology and Social Policy*, *39*(3–4), 276–295. https://doi.org/10.1108/IJSSP-08-2018-0138

BMAS. (2017). Re-imagining work: White paper work 4.0. Retrieved from https://www.bmas.de/EN/Services/Publications/a883-white-paper.htm

Brenner, S. O., & Levi, L. (1987). Long-term unemployment among women in Sweden. *Social Science and Medicine*, *25*(2), 153–161. https://doi.org/10.1016/0277-9536(87)90383-2

DeCanio, S. J. (2016). Robots and humans – Complements or substitutes? *Journal of Macroeconomics*, *49*, 280–291.

Diamond, A. M. (2020). Robots and computers enhance us more than they replace us. *The American Economist*, *65*(1), 4–10. https://doi.org/10.1177/0569434518792674

Ford, M. R. (2009). *The lights in the tunnel: Automation, accelerating technology and the economy of the future*. Acculant Publishing.

Frey, C. B., & Osborne, M. A. (2017). The future of employment: How susceptible are jobs to computerisation? *Technological Forecasting and Social Change*, *114*, 254–280. https://doi.org/10.1016/j.techfore.2016.08.019

Gardner, D. G., Van Dyne, L., & Pierce, J. L. (2004). The effects of pay level on organization-based self-esteem and performance: A field study. *Journal of Occupational and Organizational Psychology*, *77*(3), 307–322. https://doi.org/10.1348/0963179041752646

Kim, Y. J., Kim, K., & Lee, S. K. (2017). The rise of technological unemployment and its implications on the future macroeconomic landscape. *Futures*, *87*, 1–9. https://doi.org/10.1016/j.futures.2017.01.003

Leesakul, N., Oostveen, A.-M., Eimontaite, I., Wilson, M. L., & Hyde, R. (2022). Workplace 4.0: Exploring the implications of technology adoption in digital manufacturing on a sustainable workforce. *Sustainability*, *14*(6), 3311. https://doi.org/10.3390/SU14063311

MacCarthy, M. (2014). *Time to kill the tech job-killing myth*. The Hill. Retrieved from https://thehill.com/blogs/congress-blog/technology/219224-time-to-kill-the-tech-job-killing-myth

Marchant, G. E., Stevens, Y. A., & Hennessy, J. M. (2014). Technology, unemployment & policy options: Navigating the transition to a better world. *Journal of Evolution and Technology*, *24*(1), 26–44.

Mark, B. G., Rauch, E., & Matt, D. T. (2021). Worker assistance systems in manufacturing: A review of the state of the art and future directions. *Journal of Manufacturing Systems*, *59*, 228–250. https://doi.org/10.1016/J.JMSY.2021.02.017

Means, A. J. (2017). Education for a post-work future: Automation, precarity, and stagnation. In *Education and Technological Unemployment* (pp. 245–262). Berlin, Germany: Springer.

Mortensen, D. T., & Pissarides, C. A. (1999). Unemployment responses to 'skill-biased' technology shocks: The role of labour market policy. *The Economic Journal*, *109*(455), 242–265.

Peters, M. A. (2017). Technological unemployment: Educating for the fourth industrial revolution. *Educational Philosophy and Theory, 49*(1), 1–6. https://doi.org/10.1080/00131857.2016.1177412

Peters, M. A., & Jandrić, P. (2019). Education and technological unemployment in the fourth Industrial Revolution. In *The Oxford handbook of higher education systems and university management* (pp. 1–23). Oxford University Press. https://doi.org/10.1093/oxfordhb/9780198822905.013.27

Rattner, S. (2014). Fear not the coming of the robots. *The New York Times.* Retrieved from https://www.nytimes.com/2014/06/22/opinion/sunday/steven-rattner-fear-not-the-coming-of-the-robots.html

Romero, D., Stahre, J., Wuest, T., Noran, O., Bernus, P., Fast-Berglund, Å., & Gorecky, D. (2016). *Towards an operator 4.0 typology: A human-centric perspective on the fourth industrial revolution technologies.* Proceedings of the International Conference on Computers & Industrial Engineering (pp. 1–11). Tianjin, China.

Stevens, Y. A., & Marchant, G. E. (2017). Policy solutions to technological unemployment. In *Surviving the machine age* (pp. 117–130). Palgrave Macmillan.

Vardi, M. Y. (2012, October 25). *The consequences of machine intelligence – The Atlantic.* The Atlantic. Retrieved from https://www.theatlantic.com/technology/archive/2012/10/the-consequences-of-machine-intelligence/264066/

Wai, Y. L., Joon, H. C., & Boon, T. T. (2020). *The nine pillars of technologies for industry 4.0* (Y. L. Wai, H. C. Joon, & T. T. Boon, Eds.). IET Digital Library. https://doi.org/10.1049/PBTE088E

Webster, C., Ivanov, S. H., & Ivanov, S. (2020). Robotics, artificial intelligence, and the evolving nature of work. In B. George & J. Paul (Eds.), *Digital transformation in business and society theory and cases* (pp. 127–143). Palgrave Macmillan. https://doi.org/10.1007/978-3-030-08277-2_8

Part II
Smart business transformation

9   The business model of I4.0

Zsolt Roland Szabó, Sándor Ászity and Lilla Hortoványi

Scholars have demonstrated that I4.0-related technologies impact firms' business models. It is highly likely that firms change more than one component of their business models, especially customer relationships, key resources and cost structure. Some firms may end up radically renewing their business model. The chapter introduces the phenomenon of business model innovation, its causes and its most commonly used tools, such as the Business Model Canvas and the Lean Canvas. It is important to understand that it is essential for leaders in the digital age to continually innovate their business model and the experimentation, testing and continuous learning that comes with it.

9.1 Basics and principles of the business model

Sándor Ászity

Even though the business model as a concept is very popular, it is still poorly defined in the literature. In everyday conversations, there seems to be a workable consensus on the business model, yet some definitions are found side by side, as each discipline approaches it from its particular perspective (Li, 2020).

In our working definition, the business model is the way an organisation operates (see Figure 9.1). This is the result of the founder's effort in building up a successful and sustainable business and operations to fulfil its customer demands with its value creation tools (Production System). In every case, the customer demand needs to be identified and the competitors and market actions also need to be revised from time to time (Marketing System). The competition, technical development, changes in customer demand and global circumstances make necessary product and production development (Engineering System). The organisation needs management because all the elements of the operation need to be synchronised with each other and the subsystem needs to be supported by general functions (Management and Support).

Business model innovation involves a fundamental renewal of the value proposed and delivered to customers, a significant transformation of the company's / network's processes and activities and a redefinition of revenue sources and cost structure. It is important to note that changing some elements of the business model also affects other elements, so they should also be reviewed during business model innovation (Horváth et al., 2018).

DOI: 10.4324/9781003390312-11

9.2 The business models in practice

The business model is commonly assumed to answer how the business plans to make money, in other words, be viable. A good business model provides answers to each fundamental question every manager must ask: Who is the customer? What does the customer value? How do we make money in this business? What is the underlying economic logic that explains how we can deliver value to customers at an appropriate cost? says Ovans (2015). The framework developed by Osterwalder and Pigneur (2010), the **Business Model Canvas** (BMC), is an illustrative tool for visualising not only the current business model but also taking it further by highlighting innovation opportunities (see Figure 9.2).

Its field of application is almost unlimited, be it a start-up business or a global multi-national, profit-oriented or non-profit initiative. It can be used to test completely new ideas or to innovate traditional products. The model can even be applied to one person, for example, in connection with filling a position.

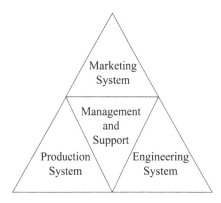

Figure 9.1 The major building blocks of the business model

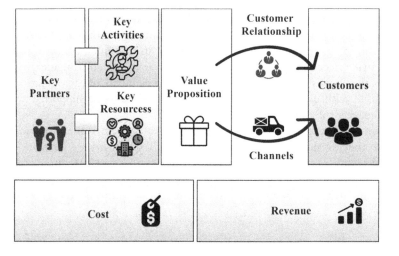

Figure 9.2 Business model canvas (based on Osterwalder & Pigneur, 2010)

BMC contains nine main building blocks from the customer side, from the infrastructural side and from the financial side. The business model describes how a model creates, delivers and captures value. The nine building blocks are grouped accordingly (Table 9.1).

The Business Model Canvas provides a perfect opportunity to visually represent ideas, whether we want to describe, understand or develop our own or another business model. It is important that the use of BMC is not a one-time activity, but that it is always continuously developed based on the latest knowledge! We can write not only specific knowledge into BMC but also assumptions that we are constantly testing. If a basic assumption turns out not to work, we need to formulate and test other assumptions until it works.

In contrast to the BMC, the Lean Canvas (LC) is a further development of the BMC and, at the same time, a business model hypothesis testing and validation tool (Maurya, 2012). In contrast to the BMC, LC offers a much more structured form for understanding customer problems and building value propositions and solutions related to them. It points out the main risks and sees their management as a continuous learning (hypothesis testing) process.

BMC and LC have five identical and four different building blocks. Among other things, the Problem section has been added to the original template, as many businesses will fail because they focus on unrealistic customer needs, wasting time and money developing inappropriate products and services. The Solution can also be identified as a new part because once a company has understood the customer problem, it is best to define a suitable solution right away. In addition, the appropriate areas must be measured during operation, which can be recorded in the Key Metrics section. The new part added fourth is Unfair Advantage, which provides a lasting source of competitive advantage for the company (Figure 9.3).

In addition to the newly added parts, among other things, the Key Activities component, which can be derived from the Solution part, has been removed. Maurya (2012) further argues that Key Resources today are getting closer and closer to Unfair Advantages, but while a Key Resource can be an Unfair Advantage, not all Unfair Advantages are Key Resources, so these two areas have been merged. In addition, Customer Relationships are well illustrated across Channels, as the author argues that sales of all products and services

Table 9.1 Nine main building blocks of Business Model Canvas

Value proposition: the set of products and services that a company offers to solve a problem for a particular consumer group.

Customer side	Infrastructure side	Financial side
Customer segments	**Key resources**	**Cost structure**
Target market	Essential tools to able to run the business model	Total expenses incurred in connection with the operation of the business model
Channels	**Key activities**	**Revenue streams**
Meeting points between the company and the customer	Set of tasks that a company must perform to successfully run its business model	The total amount of money that a company obtains from each of its target groups through value proposition
Customer relations	**Key partners**	
Maintaining further purchases, strengthening relationship with the customer in a personal or automated form	A network of members makes it a given company possible to operate	

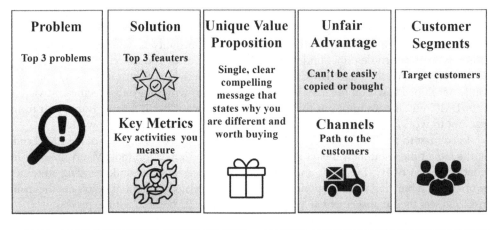

Figure 9.3 Lean Canvas (based on Maurya, 2012)

should start with direct customer relationships and then identify the right path to fit customers, Solutions and Consumer segments. Finally, the Key Partners' building block was removed, as Ash Maurya said it was important for only a few companies to build the right partnerships from the start. Completing the Lean Canvas follows an important logical line of thought that can be seen in Figure 9.3.

9.3 Digital transformation of business models

Of course, digital technologies have been a key driver of business model transformations by enabling new ways of creating and capturing value, new exchange mechanisms and transaction architectures and new boundary-spanning organisational forms (Li, 2020). The transformation is manifested in novel elements at various levels simultaneously: in the building blocks of the business model, as well as across these blocks aligning them within the new architecture of value creation in the overall value-added chain, as well as in the networking of different actors in a value-added network (Schallmo et al., 2017). The degree of the digital transformation – just as it is the case of innovations – could be regarded as incremental (marginal) as well as radical (fundamental); however, it is important to note that these are novel, non-trivial changes to the key elements of a company's business model and/or the architecture linking these elements (Prensky, 2006; Parida et al., 2019). The change in one building block usually induces changes in other blocks affecting the customers, partners and suppliers as well as competitors.

Kotarba (2018) identified two waves in which the digital transformation made an impact (see Table 9.2). The first wave is between 1980 and 2000, and it is associated with Web 1.0. The second wave is happening after 2000, and it is associated with Web 2.0.

Table 9.2 The digital transformation of certain elements of the business model over time (Kotarba, 2018)

Customer segments:

Traditional sub-segmentation based on demographics, geography, market share/size, etc.

Configurations of mutual interactions in both standard products and services, as well as transactions.

First wave

New segment-to-segment business interactions:

1. **B2C portal:** vertical or horizontal data collection
2. **B2C content delivery:** e.g. digital media sales
3. **B2C e-Commerce** such as a bookstore with online sales and offline delivery
4. **C2B** (consumer to business) e.g. clients reverse selling previously purchased goods,
5. **C2C-P2P** (consumer to consumer or person to person) market – e.g. online auction services.

Second wave

New segments are:

1. **Digital natives**
2. **Digitally excluded**
3. **Crowd**
4. **Dynamic groups**
5. **New social profiles:** YouTubers, bloggers, etc.

New segmentation strategies:

1. **Micro-segmentation** (using Big Data to further explore the unique characteristics of subpopulations).
2. **Dynamic segmentation** (e.g., using online information from real-time sensors to identify specific segmentation parameters).
3. **Behavioural segmentation** (e.g., using lifetime data to observe trends and forecast their development).

Value proposition:

Traditional factors, such as price, value, quality, bundling, cross-selling, value-added services, etc.

First wave

1. **Digital self-service:** enabling sales and aftersales activities for direct execution by clients and partners.
2. **All-in-one service point:** e.g., purchase of all financial and insurance services in one institution for simplified processing
3. **24×7 operation:** increasing the availability of self-service solutions.
4. **Value-added reseller** (VAR): scheme of enhancing original products or building them into a larger offering

Second wave

1. **Multiservice platforms** to attract not only direct customers but also other service providers, 2. **Microservices:** the set of small services with a low unit cost of usage (large scale, low price), 3. **Common customisation and hyper-personalisation:** responsiveness to detailed customer needs and preferences in the production or service delivery processes

Channels:

Channel core features:

a) owned, outsourced, or shared,

b) retail, wholesale or direct.

First wave

- Emails,
- World Wide Web,
- Online marketplaces such as Amazon.com

Second wave

1. *Apps world* – shift from the previously dominant "boxed software/license key" model to an online store with various licensing models (e.g., eternal license, freemium, etc.)
2. *Beacons* – devices that detect the presence of smart devices and are capable of push-pull information exchange in a given location
3. *Omnichannel* – evolution of the multichannel architecture by assuring the information in all channels is completely synchronised and continuous.

(Continued)

Table 9.2 Continued

Financials:

Revenues:

a) barter, sell, rent, or lease,

b) upfront fee, deferred, success fee,

c) discount systems,

d) subscription,

e) anonymous/gift card.

Costs: fixed, variable

Liquidity and cash flow

First wave	Second wave
1. **Prepaid:** creating upfront cash flows to assure product/service payment, often with automated top-ups.	1. **Freemium:** usage of products/services at the cost of interrupted service (with ads).
2. **Razor and blades:** providing a low entry cost platform and collecting revenues from supplies or maintenance (e.g., ink printers and ink cartridges).	2. **Fee-in-Free-Out:** once the provider's revenue goal is met, the service/product becomes free for others to use;
3. **Pay-as-you-go:** cash flows directly linked to the usage of the product/service, with no long-term arrangements.	3. **Pay-what-you-can:** users provide "donation" based on revenue sources (e.g., the case of Wikipedia, the online free encyclopaedia).
	4. **Pay-to-win** (unlock): the product is sold with several locked features (e.g., games)
	5. **Software-as-a-service** (SaaS); **Infrastructure-as-a-service** (IaaS): conversion of a classical software development effort/ownership into a subscription-based service.

Using the elements of BMC, Kotarba (2018) organised the major milestones of progress under these waves.

In summary, digital transformation can encourage the development of disruptive business models and offer unprecedented value-creating and value-capturing opportunities. For example, the blockchain can transform the value-capture mechanisms by enabling increased transparency among multiple actors. However, digitalisation also represents new and increased risks that are related to the implementation of business model innovation stemming from interdependencies in the ecosystem. Managers must be aware of it and learn to handle it (Parida et al., 2019).

Review questions

1. What are the most critical questions a business model must provide answers to?
2. What are the main building blocks of the Business Model Canvas?
3. What are the main building blocks of the Lean Canvas?
4. Explain, in terms of capability maturity (see chapter 3), what are the fundamental differences between wave 1 and wave 2?

Discussion questions

1. Identify based on Section I. which technologies enable the transformation of business models.
2. Explain how changing one building block in the business model may induce changes in other blocks impacting the organisation's entire value creation architecture.

Bibliography

Horváth, D., Móricz, P., & Szabó, Z. R. (2018). Üzletimodell-innováció. *Vezetéstudomány, 49*(6), 1–12.

Kotarba, M. (2018). Digital transformation of business models. *Foundations of Management, 10*, 123–142. https://doi.org/10.2478/fman-2018-0011

Li, F. (2020). The digital transformation of business models in the creative industries: A holistic framework and emerging trends. *Technovation, 10*, 92–93. https://doi.org/10.1016/j.technovation.2017.12.004

Maurya, A. (2012). *Running lean: Iterate from plan a to a plan that works.* O'Reilly.

Osterwalder, A., & Pigneur, Y. (2010). *Business model generation: A handbook for visionaries, game changers, and challengers.* Wiley & Sons.

Ovans, A. (2015). *What is a business model?* Harvard Business Review. Retrieved from https://hbr.org/2015/01/what-is-a-business-model

Parida, V., Sjödin, D., & Reim, W. (2019). Reviewing literature on digitalization, business model innovation, and sustainable industry: Past achievements and future promises. *Sustainability, 11*(2), 391.

Prensky, M. (2006). *Don't bother me Mom – I'm learning!* (1st ed.). Paragon House.

Schallmo, D., Williams, C. A., & Boardman, L. (2017). Digital transformation of business models: Best practice, enablers, and roadmap. *International Journal of Innovation Management, 21*(8), 1740014. https://doi.org/10.1142/S136391961740014

10 Marketing planning in a smart industrial environment

Barbara Jenes

Industry 4.0 is significantly transforming marketing. Marketing activities must follow changing consumer needs as a result of technological development. For example, unlike traditional marketing where customers passively consumed marketing information, today they can share online and offline feedback and opinions about a product or brand, and thus they interactively influence the marketing itself.

The purpose of this chapter is to explain the main aims and most important tools of business marketing. It introduces the fundamental difference between business-to-customer and business-to-business marketing and then describes the key tools, marketing planning methods and steps to develop a marketing strategy based on Industry 4.0 developments. It helps to understand the role of marketing within the entire scope of a company through practical examples.

10.1 Toyota's influence on marketing

In the 20th century, Japan contributed to the world with the so-called Japanese-style production approach referred to as **Just In Time** (JIT) provided by the Toyota Production System (TPS). After decades of success, manufacturers are now facing challenges posed by the rapidly changing technical environment and global production (Amasaka, 2002). In recent years, leading manufacturers in Japan have been deploying a new production strategy called "globally consistent levels of quality and simultaneous global launch". To improve quality at leading manufacturers' overseas production bases from the perspective of "global production", "a New Global Partnering Production Model, NGP-PM" – the strategic development of the "Advanced TPS" model – was also proposed. The aim is to increase global quality by generating a synergetic effect that organically connects and promotes the continual evolution of the production plants in Japan and overseas, as well as greater cooperation among production operators (Ebioka et al., 2007).

In the concept of **New JIT**, the creation of attractive and sellable products requires the implementation of a "customer satisfaction" approach. To achieve this, the entire organisation must be managed by three hardware subsystems, namely, the marketing (TMS), engineering (TDS) and production (TPS) divisions – see Figure 10.1 (Amasaka, 2002).

Within the three subsystems linked organically, TMS includes the followings (see Figure 10.2):

(a) Market creation through the gathering and use of customer information
(b) Improvement of product value by understanding the elements essential to raising merchandise value

DOI: 10.4324/9781003390312-12

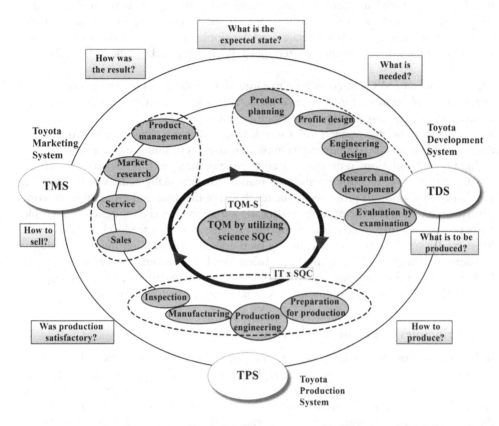

Figure 10.1 New JIT, A new principle called TQM–S at Toyota (based on Amasaka, 2002)

Figure 10.2 TMS in New JIT (Amasaka, 2002)

(c)   Establishment of hardware and software marketing systems to form ties with customers
(d)   Realisation of the necessary elements for adopting a corporate attitude (behavioural norm) of enhancing customer value and developing customer satisfaction (CS), customer delight (CD), customer retention (CR) and networks (Amasaka, 2002)

The main aim of TMS is to contribute to future development, carry out customer orientation and implement customer science in global marketing activities. These elements – although this model was developed for a global manufacturing approach – can be identified at small, medium or large business scales as well. In the following sections, we can understand the nature of business marketing and its implementation in planning and strategies.

Industry 4.0 solutions represent a gradual development in the activities of industry players. Information technology and automation fundamentally redraw manufacturing processes. Digitisation of processes facilitates their optimisation and more efficient, competitive production. The use of available data also reinterprets marketing activities: it enables more precise targeting, more efficient customer service and easier feedback and evaluation. Most marketing activities can also be digitised and automated. Continuous tracking of customers and analysis of data from B2B relationships have fundamentally redesigned marketing for major industry players, such as Toyota (car manufacturers), FMCG companies (e.g., Unilever), and telecommunication companies (e.g., Deutsche Telekom.)

10.2 Principles of business marketing

In business-to-consumer (B2C) markets companies offer their products and services to individuals (end users and consumers). In B2C marketing, the target market is the consumer using the product/service, and the goal is to increase sales to consumers. Consumers are reached through mass communication using ATL (above the line) and BTL (below the line) marketing tools. Various customer relationship management (CRM) systems have been invented to personalise (customise) communication to increase and make sales more efficient. The consumer's intention to buy is primarily driven by the satisfaction of his needs. Businesses that focus on B2C marketing observe trends closely, research their customers' purchase habits and closely monitor their competitors' tactics.

Business marketing, in some cases referred to as "B2B marketing", "Relationship marketing", "Organisational marketing" or "Industrial marketing", is the marketing practice of organisations marketing products or services to other business organisations and companies. The customer in this relationship is a (smaller or larger) business organisation and not an individual consumer. The consumer negotiates and buys in the name of a company; however, the products or services may either be similar to the mass consumer market solutions or completely different in covering high-value types of equipment or components (Hall, 2017; Hadjikhani & LaPlaca, 2013). In business marketing actions the number of stakeholders may be bigger, therefore we name it "**Relationship marketing**", as the success of actions depends on the quality of the relationship of participating stakeholders.

B2B marketing refers to the abbreviation of business-to-business marketing actions, while organisational marketing means the relationship among various business organisations.

In business marketing compared to B2C, the actions are continuing to get more complex and buyers are more sophisticated, but these are not the only differentiating areas of the field. B2B (business-to-business) marketing differs from B2C marketing in several ways (Havaldar, 2005; Bauer & Berács, 2006):

First, the number of stakeholders involved: As the name of "Relationship marketing" refers to it, in a business marketing action may be multiple departments involved and the relationship between the affected department may be crucial in the further success of negotiations. The involved departments may be operations, finance, sales and procurement, not excluding the marketing or sales team.

Second, the complexity of offerings: In a business marketing negotiation, the stakeholders expect and need more detailed and richer information about the product, supporting services or even the company itself. These different forms of data help to guide them in their decision-making process. Therefore, the process of negotiation is fulfilled with complex information throughout the whole decision-making.

Third, the buying process: In industrial decisions, the stakeholders may want to understand more about the technology and capability or other business-related services before deciding to purchase. This may lengthen the buying period and make it more iterative.

As detailed above, business marketing is product-driven in many cases; however, it must build trust-based relationships as well. According to the latest arguments – e.g., see the previously discussed New JIT model (Amasaka, 2002) – industrial or business marketing needs to incorporate new (consumer) marketing theories to be able to fully describe the current developments (Hadjikhani & LaPlaca, 2013).

The *buying process* itself is more complex and accompanies multi-stakeholders into the buying process. The aim of business marketing is always to increase pipeline and revenues and also to generate leads. The transactional factor is a large size of purchases or bids in most cases (Havaldar, 2005).

In business marketing, the markets are geographically concentrated; the buyers (or customers) are well informed and are relatively fewer; the buyer organisations or departments are highly organised and use sophisticated purchasing techniques; the purchase decisions are based on observable stages; the additional services, such as timely delivery and availability, are very important; the parties require technical expertise; and stable interpersonal relationship between buyers and sellers can be observed (Hall, 2017).

In business marketing, the buying process is based on many factors, such as agreememt on product specifications, cost-effectiveness, after-sales service and so on. The final purchasing decisions generally take a long time and involve many stakeholders from technical, commercial, operational, production and finance departments. After the initial offer (or quotation) made by the seller (in response to a written or verbal enquiry from the buyer), there are negotiations and exchange of information between the specialists and representatives from each functional area, from both the buyer and the seller companies (Hall, 2017).

However, in business marketing, in which individual customers do not negotiate with each other, personal objectives can have a major impact on the final decision-making. These personal objectives are the following: job security, promotions, higher status, salary increments and social considerations. Industrial buyers try to achieve both organisational (purchase) and personal objectives at the same time (Havaldar, 2005).

It is common practice in the agricultural sector for the largest agrochemical companies (e.g., BASF, Bayer, Monsanto, etc.) to segment their markets and reach users through B2B marketing methods. Based on segmentation, they generally distinguish among farmers, plant protection consultants and traders. Sales take place on two levels: directly at the user level and indirectly through the merchants. Within this, the relationship with merchants shows classic B2B marketing patterns: after negotiating with representatives of the company, they buy products in large batches and then resell them. Marketing with farmers is multi-layered and carries the hallmarks of Relationship Marketing: sales colleagues visit farmers and try to convince them of the effectiveness of a given product through advice and other sales techniques.

10.2.1 B2B marketing types

Segmenting the business market may lead us to find different homogenous groups of companies. The industrial business may be divided through industry classification, by region, operation variables or pure demographics (e.g., size) as well.

The aim of grouping in business marketing is to gather businesses that have similarities and therefore to target them with different B2B marketing solutions.

According to these classifications, we can differ business marketing types among micro businesses, small and medium-sized enterprises (SMEs) or large companies (Hall, 2017).

At **micro** business entities, marketing is product-driven and sales-focused in the majority of cases. They transact through the simpler buying-selling processes and perform not only rational buying but emotional buying decisions as well.

At **SME** organisations stakeholders better track their business performance and organise their marketing actions. They focus on trust-based relationships and shift towards more complex processes.

At **large companies**, we see large sizes of purchases and multi-stakeholder buying and selling processes. Mostly rational buying behaviour is determined in a more complex negotiation.

10.3 Tools and methodology in industrial marketing development

10.3.1 Business marketing planning

The basic tasks of marketing management apply to both consumer and industrial marketing. These tasks are (Hall, 2017):

1. Deciding on the target markets
2. Exploring the needs and wants (in some content: pain points) of the target markets
3. Developing products and services to meet the requirements of the target markets
4. Evolving marketing strategy and plans to reach and engage target customers better and faster than competitors.

In the industrial sector defining marketing actions requires a new approach and starts with both external and internal exploration.

B2B marketers need to invest in **market analysis** and business situation analysis of prospecting targets and partners in terms of needs, behaviours, buying process and other related aspects.

As highlighted in the New JIT (Amasaka, 2002), customer science must be implemented in the marketing systems in order to scientifically grasp customers' tastes.

Business players must also review their environment for further understanding and aspirations. Technological changes can rapidly evolve in the business landscape; therefore, marketers must be aware of the latest trends and innovations as well.

External analysis is combined of three different aspects: environmental analysis, competitor analysis and customer analysis. The internal audit focuses on the corporate's assets and operational ecosystem (Hall, 2017; Havaldar, 2005).

Environmental analysis

As we have learned in chapter 2.1. not only competitors' analyses are part of an external exploration but also environmental factors must be reviewed. The most important influencing factors, coming from external sources are distilled in the PESTEL model, which covers **political** factors such as governmental influence, can impact business confidence; **economic** factors, such as recession, can influence market demand; **social** factors can influence, e.g., the available substance of employees; new **technologies** coming to market can lead to evolving ways of production; **environmental** factors can influence the availability of minerals or sustainability concerns can influence production; **legal** aspects and new legislation can influence business management (Hall, 2017; Tóth, 2008).

Competitor analysis

Competitors can be analysed by Porter's 5 Forces, SWOT analysis. The competition analysis covers financial, operational and marketing approaches as well. It must focus on the company and its products' USPs (Unique Selling Point, which is an ownable unique benefit compared to other marketers' or their products).

Customer analysis

Industrial marketers must directly research both prospecting customers' and partners' needs; their decision-making process and criteria; and also the buying process and frequency. After analysing their existing and potential customers, they can strategically decide on whether to target them and if yes, how to fulfil their needs. In TMS "customer information" and "customer focus" pillars can improve customer value.

Internal audit

The internal audit of the company can be developed using SWOT as a first step. Following this, a marketing-focused analysis must also be done to gain insights for further marketing adjustments.

10.3.2 Developing business marketing strategy

Based on the above-mentioned analyses, marketers can develop their marketing strategies and then their marketing tool ecosystem. Developing marketing strategies means the involvement of objectives accordingly to the corporate's business goals and KPIs (key performance indicators). Strategy in companies is the foundation of business operations and organises the managers' thinking (Taylor, 2017).

Corporate strategy (see Figure 10.3): the planned approach a company has for its future business activities, or the process of deciding these plans within a company. Management decides on corporate strategy by analysing the corporation's capabilities and opportunities and by setting KPIs (key performance indicators) of planned business performance. The corporate strategy satisfies the objectives of individual departments as

Figure 10.3 Strategic ecosystem within a corporate

well as promotes overall corporate goals. We can eliminate four major types of corporate strategies: stability strategy, expansion (growth) strategy, retrenchment (renewal) strategy and a combination strategy. The corporate-level generic strategies pertain to identifying the businesses in which the company shall be engaged.

Underlining the corporate strategy, a **marketing strategy** refers to a business's overall plan for long-term sales, acquiring prospective consumers and turning them into customers of the products or services the business provides. Marketing strategy helps in developing goods and services with the best profit-making potential. It also supports an organisation to make optimum utilisation of its resources to provide a sales message to its target market.

A marketing strategy is a set of a company's marketing objectives combined into a long-term comprehensive plan; it requires comprehensive background analysis and the goals must follow a SMART (Specific, Measurable, Achievable, Results-based and Timed) approach.

Industrial marketing strategy development is based on background analysis and its main aim is to evolve the product's relevance and differentiation (also advantage) on the market. For this purpose, a commonly used method is the 4Cs analysis (see Figure 10.4).

After formulating the marketing strategy companies must develop their marketing mix toolkit.

10.3.3 Industrial marketing mix

The well-known **marketing mix** (4Ps) is a general framework for marketers to develop their marketing actions, to plan and execute their marketing activities. The marketing mix originally covers product development, the connecting price management, place selection and the promotion part of selling. In one sentence: putting the right product at the right place at the right price with the right promotion in order to increase sales and strengthen market position (Bauer & Berács, 2006).

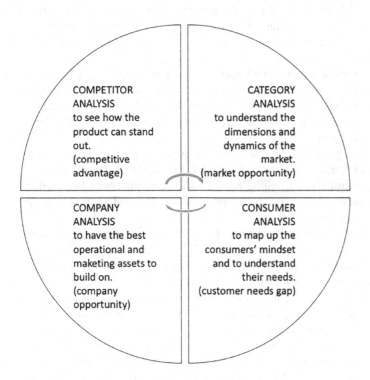

Figure 10.4 The 4Cs in strategic analysis and formulation

The purpose of the marketing mix is to capture all the key variables that need to be considered in marketing planning and implementation to meet the target audience's needs. It is also a convenient checklist for all marketers to develop and review their activities.

The 4Ps framework (however in business marketing this framework must be adjusted accordingly):

Product: originally, it is about tangible goods or intangible services that consumers require.

Price: originally, it is about the amount that a consumer is likely to pay for the product, and the determining factor behind this price is the sum of the costs of production.

Place: originally, it was about the distribution channels and places of purchase where customers can find the product

Promotion: originally, it was about different sales-boosting communication tools and channels that can generate awareness and consideration of the given product.

In business marketing, most of the above-mentioned categories are hardly applicable (Hall, 2017).

Product: in the majority of cases is tangible, high-value equipment, manufactured material, part or raw material, with additional industrial services, such as logistics, remastering etc. In business marketing, the products or services display technical complexity. Business customers place greater importance on product/service quality, delivery on time and availability of products because any delay in supply can have a significant impact on production or operations. Other influencing factors are acceptable payments, after-sales service, training (if required), spare-parts availability, repairs and maintenance capability etc.

Price: in most cases, it is the amount that a buyer organisation accepts to pay for a cost-based pricing product. In business marketing, price is one of the main factors considered in negotiations and can mainly influence the final purchasing decision. Competitive bidding, trade or dealer discounts and volume (or quantity) discounts applied on price lists are very common in this area.

Place: in most cases, the place of selling is the place of production. Companies tend to use sales force (sales and marketing people) to sell their products directly to their main clients and buyers. On the other hand, selling to small-scale customers can be based on using either distributors, dealers or agents and representatives. This selling approach can help minimise the cost of marketing.

Promotion: in industrial marketing special channels (such as expos, trade fairs, exhibitions, professional forums, etc.) are involved, and the selling is more likely to be relation-based. In industrial marketing company representatives and experts are targeted, focusing on their special needs in promotional activities (Hall, 2017).

In the New JIT, TMS is one system among the three subsystems working organically linked. TDS (Development) is in charge of the development of what is needed and what is to be produced. TPS (Production) is responsible for the "how to produce" approach, while TMS (Marketing) manages the "how to sell" approach. (Amasaka, 2002) These processes implement the actual 4P within a TQM-S system at a global company.

According to this, the first step in the marketing mix is to analyse the partners' and customers' current and future needs or create and explore new ways of fulfilment.

Following that, the optimal way of thinking is to define the cost and the price of the product or solution to analyse what the customer is willing to pay.

The next step is to deliver the offer to the buyer in various ways. The place of selling and the form of communication is dependent on many factors, such as the complexity of the business and the nature of the target company or specific target stakeholders. Multiple formats can support the negotiations, such as exhibitions, face-to-face negotiations, study tours, in-situ demonstrations, etc. The main aim is to engage the customers and generate sales.

After building the products, solutions and services accordingly, companies must review their costs and pricing in parallel and also align their channel and distribution strategy with the optimisation of communication and sales efforts.

10.3.4 STP in industrial marketing

Segmentation, targeting and positioning (STP) is a familiar strategic approach in marketing and also one of the most commonly applied marketing models in practice (Bauer & Berács, 2006). Using the STP model means following the below steps.

Segmentation of the market: to gain business, an organisation must divide potential customers into groups of entities with common characteristics and needs. This allows the company to tailor its approach to meet each group's needs cost-effectively.

There are generic approaches to segment the target markets (e.g., end-consumers).

Demographic: by personal attributes, such as age, marital status, gender, ethnicity, sexuality, education or occupation.

Geographic: by country, region, state, city or neighbourhood.

Psychographic: by risk aversion, values or lifestyle.

Behavioural: by how people use the product, how loyal they are or the benefits that they are looking for.

In an industrial environment, the segmentation of business partners is also applicable.

B2B companies can be divided into segments by the so-called demographic approach (company age, company size, market share, etc.), by geographic approach (region, location, infrastructure, etc.) or by behavioural approach (technology needs, buying behaviour, negotiation style, etc.).

Targeting prospecting segments

In the following step, the company must decide which segments to target by finding the most protective ones. There are several factors to consider in this phase.

The first one is profitability. A company must define which partner group can contribute the most to the strategic bottom line. Another point to consider is the size and potential growth of each segment. A company must evaluate which segment is large enough to address and which segment has the potential for growth. Last, the company should consider how the organisation can effectively serve its business partner.

Positioning

While the first two steps covered approaches towards customers, the third one is about competition. A company should explore why business partners will purchase its product or service. For this reason, the identification of the unique selling proposition (USP) must be done. Then drawing a positioning map can help to understand how each segment perceives the company's product and create a value proposition that clearly explains how the offering will meet this requirement better than any of the competitors' products that can also serve the company's efforts. As a result of these, positioning defines where the product (item or service) stands concerning others offering similar products and services in the marketplace as well as in the mind of the consumer. **Positioning is an important element of a marketing plan**. Product positioning is the process marketers use to determine how to best communicate their products' attributes to their target customers based on customer needs, competitive pressures, available communication channels and carefully crafted key messages.

Steps of the **positioning process**

1. Confirm the company's understanding of market dynamics
2. Identifying the company's competitive advantages
3. Choosing competitive advantages that define market "niche" or available market sectors
4. Definition of positioning strategy
5. Communication and delivery of the positioning strategy

Positioning can be understood and developed in various ways. On the one hand, it can be distilled from the product attributes, e.g., characteristics of the product or category, or, on the other hand, the types of consumers, competition, etc. All these attributes represent a different approach to developing positioning, even though all of them have the common objective of differentiating the product from the competitors. There are six commonly used positioning approaches:

1. Based on product characteristics or customer benefits
2. Based on the category
3. Based on product use or application
4. By pricing
5. Based on geographic location, culture
6. Based on the competition

In business marketing there are five typical positions to take:

1. New technologies
2. Special product offering
3. Tailor-made solutions
4. Better cost/price
5. Geographical presence

The **ecosystem of the industrial marketing** formulation is summarised in Figure 10.5.

10.4 Industrial marketing in practice

10.4.1 Evaluation of product life cycle

The life story of most successful products is a history of their passing through certain recognisable stages (Levitt, 1965).

Stage 1. **Market Development**: when a new product is first brought to market, before there is a proven demand for it, and often before it has been fully proven out technically in all respects. In this stage sales are low.

Stage 2. **Market Growth**: in the second stage demand begins to accelerate for the product and the size of the total market expands rapidly. It might also be called the "Takeoff Stage".

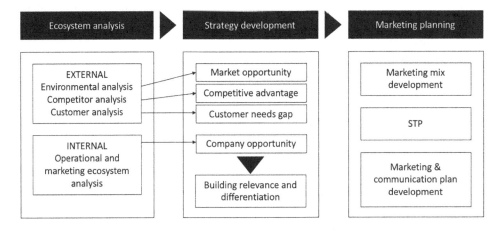

Figure 10.5 Industrial marketing formulation source (based on Hall, 2017, p. 27)

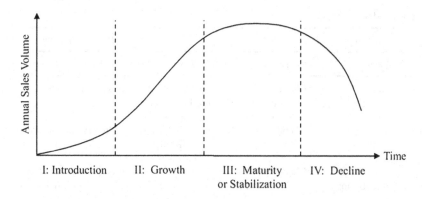

Figure 10.6 The Product Life Cycle (Levitt, 1965)

Stage 3. **Market Maturity**: demand for product levels off and grows, reaching already mass market or a bigger audience.

Stage 4. **Market Decline**: after maturity, the product begins to lose consumer appeal and sales drift downward as a consequence (see Figure 10.6).

In the **development** stage, bringing a new product to market is fraught with unknowns, uncertainties and frequently unknowable risks. This stage requires a huge amount of preliminary work and market analysis. Generally, demand has to be "created" during the product's initial market development stage through an effective "awareness-generating" strategy.

In the **growth** stage, the usual characteristic of a successful new product is a gradual rise. At some point in this rise, a marked increase in consumer demand occurs and sales take off. And at this point product and brand differentiation begin to develop as well.

In the next, **maturity** stage the company faces market saturation. This means that most companies or segments that are sales prospects will be owning or use the product. In this stage, price competition may become intense but the stabilisation of the product position is possible.

When market maturity tapers off and consequently comes to an end, the product enters the market **decline** stage. In all cases of maturity and decline, the industry is transformed. As demand declines, the overcapacity that was already apparent during the period of maturity now becomes endemic (Levitt, 1965).

In business marketing the key to successful manufacturing is not just understanding this life cycle, but also proactively managing products throughout their lifetime and applying the appropriate resources and sales and marketing strategies, depending on what stage products are at in the cycle (see Table 10.1).

10.4.2 Business marketing communication tools

In business marketing, the emphasis is on personal selling through the company's sales force. Apart from personal selling, organisations may apply advertisements (e.g., in business magazines and trade journals), or use brochures/leaflets at events and expos. To reach out to their potential partners and clients, direct mails/direct emails can be used. Participation in exhibitions or trade shows and delivering technical presentations and

Table 10.1 Managing products through the life cycle

Introduction	Product management			Product withdrawal
	/Growth	//Maturity	///Decline	
Generating awareness	Strengthen product/brand prestige	Maintaining product/brand knowledge	Repositioning Freshen product/ brand image	Avoid damaging image
Building relevance Generating try-out	Increasing number of users	Strengthen loyalty	Reserve switchers with other products	Preserve clients with extra service
Market presence for innovators	Strengthening distribution	Maintain stable distribution	Ensure key positions in key channels	Replace product in key channels
Skimming when the product is highly innovative	Market-entry pricing	Maximise profit	Price discounts	Minimise loss Withdrawal pricing

organising conferences and seminars are the elements of sales promotion activities. In recent years, digital marketing has become a new territory, by which companies can replace their traditional communication tools to some extent.

The classic B2C marketing tools are divided into two major groups: ATL ("above the line") and BTL ("below the line") tools. ATL devices are high-access devices: they include all the solutions that a company can provide for mass and cost-effective access. These are the followings: TV, radio, print ads, OOH ("out-of-home": billboards, CLP, etc.). BTL tools include POS (point of sales) materials, PR (public relations tools, direct marketing (e.g., direct mail), exhibitions and more. The latter has a more direct impact, but, at the same time, it serves smaller target groups.

B2B marketing uses only a portion of the classic ATL and BTL toolkit and to a different extent. In B2B marketing, a company sells to a company, so the personal presentation of corporate products and services is the primary goal. Accordingly, all tools for communication and sales are included: leaflets, flyers, professional presentation materials, brochures, eDM, online marketing, exhibitions, etc. Their use also varies from company to company and the proportion of tools varies from industry to industry. The changes seen in Industry 4.0 can be seen here as well: more and more digital and online and CRM solutions can be found in B2B marketing.

The most commonly used tools that comply with Industry 4.0 principles in business marketing are:

Relationship management (CRM – Customer Relationship Management): Marketing managers believe that it is difficult to reach the right decision-makers through digital marketing and social media, therefore a well-established customer relationship is more valuable than ever. These relationships are mainly generated and managed by the company's sales force and representatives. They are responsible for not only contacting prospecting new clients but also pampering existing ones. In many companies, the management of customer relationships has become an important strategic priority because loyal customers and partners are more profitable than transactional customers or new customers. CRM aims to retain valued customers by developing long-term relationships and providing excellent real-time customer service. CRM systems often integrate sales, customer service and marketing information.

Digital marketing (websites, social media, SEO, SEM, eDM): companies use digital communication channels and tools such as social media (including blogging), user communities (e.g., Facebook, LinkedIn, Twitter, intranets) and user-generated content to some extent. The literature divides these tools into owned (website), paid (social media advertisements) and earned (user-generated content, word of mouth) media.

According to professional marketers, digital marketing increases the efficiency of communications; fosters customer relationships, communications and interaction; creates awareness and helps build brands; and generates sales leads (Karjaluoto et al., 2015).

Within digital marketing, email marketing is a tool by which companies distribute newsletters and customer magazines and send invitations to seminars, trade shows and other events. Email is also widely used in person-to-person communication. The perceived effectiveness of an email may be a consequence of its similarity to face-to-face interaction in terms of exchanging customer-specific content with the added option of contact whenever it is most convenient to both parties.

Events: trade shows, trade fairs, seminars, roadshows, exhibitions, expos, study tours and other events where companies can introduce their capabilities and products. The aim of these events is to contact new partners, vendors and prospective clients and generate further discussion between the parties.

Advertisements (classic promotion tools, TV, radio, print, out-of-home, point of sales materials, leaflet): these tools help industrial marketers in communicating products and other information. These tools are used less often and with less access to business marketing.

Methods used to influence industrial customers

Sales presentation, style of negotiation, special dealings between parties, customer service. As discussed earlier, these are tools for direct contracting and selling between two companies.

The list above gives an overview of the most commonly used tools and their purposes.

Review questions

1. What is the difference between B2C and B2B markets?
2. What is the difference between B2C and B2B marketing?
3. How can B2B marketing be characterised?
4. What changes has the spread of Industry 4.0 brought to B2B marketing?
5. What are the steps of STP in industrial marketing?
6. What tools do companies use in B2B marketing?

Discussion questions

1. How will the spread of digitalisation change industrial marketing?
2. With the spread of the Industry 4.0 approach, will marketing also become fully automated?
3. Will the automation of CRM systems replace the work of the sales team?

Bibliography

Amasaka, K. (2002). "New JIT": A new management technology principle at Toyota. *International Journal of Production Economics, 80*(2), 135–144. https://doi .org /10 .1016 /S0925 -5273(02)00313-4

Bauer, A., & Berács, J. (2006). *Marketing*. Aula.

Ebioka, K., Yamaji, M., Sakai, H., & Amasaka, K. (2007). A new global partnering production model "NGP-PM" utilizing "Advanced TPS". *Journal of Business and Economics Research, 9*(5). https://doi .org/10.19030/jber.v5i9.2576

Hadjikhani, A., & LaPlaca, P. (2013). Development of B2B marketing theory. *Industrial Marketing Management, 42*(3), 294–305. https://doi.org/10.1016/j.indmarman.2013.03.011

Hall, S. (2017). *Innovative B2B marketing: New models, processes and theory*. Kogan Page.

Havaldar, K. K. (2005). *Industrial marketing: Text and cases* (2nd ed.). Tata McGraw-Hill Education.

Karjaluoto, H., Mustonen, N., & Ulkuniemi, P. (2015). The role of digital channels in industrial marketing communications. *Journal of Business and Industrial Marketing, 30*(6), 703–710. https://doi .org/10.1108/JBIM-04-2013-0092

Levitt, T. (1965). Exploit the product life cycle. *Harvard Business Review, 43*(6), 81–94.

Taylor, H. (2017). *B2B marketing strategy: Differentiate, develop and deliver lasting customer engagement*. Kogan Page.

Tóth, T. (2008). *Nemzetközi Marketing*. Akadémia.

11 Smart supply chain

Gelei Andrea

The objective of this chapter is to discuss how and why Industry 4.0 solutions might contribute to better supply chain management. The goal of supply chain management is to increase this system-level performance that is critical in today's business environment with the increasing bargaining power of customers. Hence, managers deepen their understanding of supply chains and their management challenges. Thus, first, the concepts of supply chain and how I.0 can contribute to a more effective and efficient supply chain management are considered. Both structural and process-related aspects of supply chain management are discussed. Next, the topic of supply chain performance measurement is elaborated. Then, we introduce the concept of lean and agile supply chain management and discuss different combinations of them by consciously locating the decoupling point along the supply chain. Since firms' competitiveness cannot be separated from the operation of their supply chains, both supply chain coordination and integration and the contribution of I4.0 solutions are presented.

11.1 The concept of supply chain management

The term "supply chain management" (SCM) first appeared in a printed form in the work of Oliver and Weber back in the early 1980s (1982). It clearly indicated a new era of management, since it was a definite shift from company level to more complex levels of analysis. Nowadays, it is almost commonplace that it is not companies but supply chains that compete with each other. However, at that time the term indicated a fundamental change, the recognised need for the coordinated and integrated management of several companies involved in creating customer value.

Cavinato (1992) defined the **supply chain** as a concept that consists of a group of firms that add value along product flow from raw materials to the final customer. One year later Cooper and Ellram (1993) emphasised the integration element of the concept when they defined it as a management philosophy that aims to manage the total flow of materials from the supplier to the ultimate user in an integrated way. In the early 1920s of the new millennium, Mentzer et al. (2001) defined the concept of supply chain management as a systemic and strategic coordination of business functions within a particular company and across firms cooperating in value creation. Managing such a complex supply chain has the overall **objective to improve the performance** of both the complete supply chain and its constituent firms.

This conceptualisation reflects a gradual development path that began with an effort to manage the internal business functions – such as sales, distribution and production,

DOI: 10.4324/9781003390312-13

for example – in a coordinated way. Then, functional coordination was followed by extensive coordination, creating a vertically aligned flow of value creation within the firm, along with several functions. Subsequently, this internal coordination effort was extended to independent companies. This last step of development is also called external integration. Here, not only the members of the focal firm's internal supply chain but also external supply chain partners are integrated into the concept of supply chain management.

The definition of SCM emphasises two key building blocks of any supply chain, (1) the processes, and (2) the business partners along which these processes have to be managed in an integrated way. Key **processes** cover the complex material flow (inbound logistics, production and outbound logistics), while the key **actors** are suppliers, production facilities and customers. Recent definitions follow this conceptualisation and complement it with a description of the basic management tools along which supply chain integration can be achieved. The CSCMP (Council of Supply Chain Management Professionals) defined **supply chain management** in 2016 as the planning and management of all activities involved in sourcing and procurement, conversion and all logistics activities, in coordination and collaboration with all relevant partners.

A well-known practical application of the above-introduced complex supply chain, conceptualisation is the **SCOR model** developed by the Supply Chain Council (SCC). SCC is an independent, global, non-profit organisation that was initiated in 1996 by more than 60 member companies, such as Bayer, Compaq, Procter & Gamble, Lockheed Martin, Nortel, Texas Instrument, 3M and many more. SCC developed the so-called supply chain operations reference model (SCOR) to develop and provide a cross-industry standard framework for supply chain management (www.supply-chain.org).

The model is supported by a complex software solution that integrates the supply chain management concept with performance measurement, benchmarking and business process reengineering (Huan, Sheoran & Wang, 2004). It provides a standard description of relevant business processes in a complex supply chain (Figure 11.1) and the relationships between these processes. Key processes in the SCOR model are the source, make, deliver,

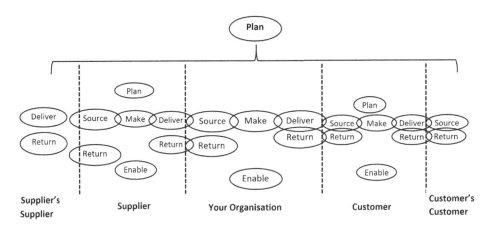

Figure 11.1 The SCOR model (based on APICS, 2017, p. 5)

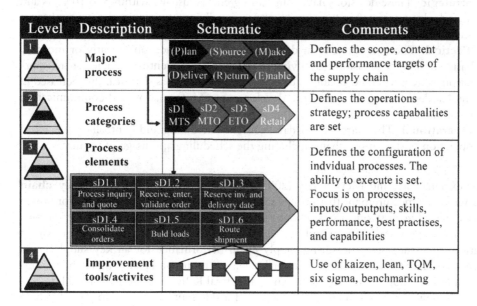

Figure 11.2 Decomposition of key processes in the SCOR model (based on APICS, 2017, p. 6)

return and plan. These processes are duplicated and have to be managed in an integrated way along the complex supply chain.

The model decomposes these key business processes in increasing levels and further divides them into process elements, tasks, and activities (Figure 11.2). The activity-level process understanding makes it possible to link performance to actual process solutions, and also best practices, and highlights improvement possibilities.

In the classic understanding, the supply chain is described as a linear chain that creates products or services and delivers them to the final consumers. However, in reality, a supply chain is usually more complex, and, instead of chains, an interlinked network of different chains is responsible for value creation. Managing these networks of chains necessitates both a process and a **system approach**, which can be accomplished only when partners of a given supply chain recognise the potential in managing their complex operation in a coordinated and integrated way, orient themselves accordingly and make aligned actions to implement the supply chain management philosophy (Mentzer et al., 2001). This is crucial; supply chain management is a joint effort of the supply chain partners to seek system-level synergies and better overall performance.

11.2 Supply chain performance

Performance measurement is the first step in any supply chain management effort. Its overall objective is to provide useful information for decision-makers that enable them to look for areas where performance is lagging, identify improvement potentials and search for solutions that facilitate value creation more effectively and efficiently.

Supply chain management is complex; several levels of decision-making might result in its aligned, integrated management. Simchi-Levi, Kaminsky and Simchi-Levi (2008) differentiated three key **decision-making levels** in supply chains:

- **Strategic**: These decisions have long-lasting effects, usually within 3 to 10 years and include decisions such as "make or buy decisions", investments in plants, warehouses and their capacities, and the creation of the logistics network
- **Tactical**: These medium-term decisions are usually made on a yearly or monthly basis and include decisions specifying production and inventory policies or transportation strategies. The timeline of tactical-level decisions has significantly decreased in the last decade, mainly due to the development of information and communication technologies
- **Operational**: These are day-to-day decisions scheduling and controlling the actual operation of the supply chain, including the scheduling and usage of resources

Gunasekaran, Patel and McGaughey (2004) developed a framework for **supply chain performance** measurement that groups supply chain performance indicators from three perspectives. The first one is the above-introduced timeframe, the second perspective distinguishes between financial and non-financial KPIs (key performance indicators). In addition, they suggested measuring supply chain performance for all key supply chain processes of the SCOR model, source, make deliver, return and plan. Sustainability considerations gain more and more importance. Potential KPIs are listed in Table 11.1.

The Supply Chain Council (2012) provided a different taxonomy for supply chain performance measures when differentiating five key sets of **process performance dimensions**:

Reliability: This performance dimension focuses on how predictable an outcome of a process is. Metrics capturing this performance dimension include on-time operation and quantity and quality aspects of sourcing, production and distribution.

Responsiveness: This process attribute is about the speed of processes, such as cycle-time or lead-time metrics.

Table 11.1 Key performance indicators for supply chain management (Gunasekaran et al., 2004, p. 345)

Core SC processes	Strategic KPIs	Tactical KPIs	Operational KPIs
Source	Supplier network agility	Supplier pricing against the market	Supplier lead time
			Supplier quality
		The efficiency of purchase order cycle time	
Make	Range of offered products and services	Capacity utilisation	Percentages of defects
			Cost per operation hour
Delivery	Delivery network complexity	Effectiveness of delivery invoicing	On-time delivery of products
		Percentage of finished goods in transit	Number of faultless deliveries
Pan	Variances against budget	Accuracy of forecasting techniques	Resource productivity
	Net profit vs productivity ratio	Planning process cycle time	Percentage of urgent delivery
	Net cash flow time	Product development cycle time	

Agility: This describes the ability to respond to unexpected changes. Both external and internal triggers of such changes have to be taken into consideration and be measured, including natural disasters, economic crises, the COVID-19 pandemic, (cyber) terrorism, a burn down of a plant or warehouses, change in customer needs and order, etc.

Costs: This dimension captures relevant cost elements on process and supply chain levels. Besides the cost of materials, all production and logistics costs must be monitored. Administration and management of coordinating internal processes and operations with external might incur significant costs as well.

Assets: Efficient asset deployment and management are important on the supply chain level too. Out- or back-sourcing decisions significantly influence overall supply chain cost. Cash-to-cash cycle time return on fixed assets, inventory levels and turns are additional elements of a complex supply chain performance measurement system.

Measuring the performance of a supply chain is not without challenges. Gunasekaran, Patel and Tirtiroglu (2001) identified several fundamental issues in this respect. First, they emphasised the need for a balanced measurement system that builds on both financial and non-financial KPIs to facilitate effective decision-making on all three levels. Second, it is important not to lose supply chain context and measure performance on the system level, instead of focusing only on specific KPIs capturing a specific aspect of supply chain operation.

Stadtler and Kilger (2008) added important issues to supply chain level performance measurement. They emphasised the need for an adequately thought-through definition of SC performance indicators. Any supply chain consists of several cooperating firms and processes. Without a clear understanding and harmonised measurement, supply chain performance management becomes fragmented. In such cases, it cannot provide system-level information for decision-makers. Capturing relevant data must also be synchronised. KPIs, with different data capture, again hinder the overall objective of performance measurement and effective and efficient decision-making. A rich information base, including performance-related data, is the basis for SCM. A lack of trust might hinder the development of a supply chain-wide information base. Thus, confidentiality and non-opportunistic behaviour in data capture and sharing have high importance.

11.3 Lean or/and agile supply chains

Despite the differences in defining supply chain management, conceptualisations agree that increased integration between supply chain partners leads to better supply chain level performance. However, several authors highlight the need for an **aligned approach.** An approach that takes specific **characteristics of the product** into account and customises management. A key product characteristic is the predictability of the future, namely, anticipated customer demand (Fisher, 1997). In this respect, two basic product types should be distinguished: **functional and innovative products**. Functional products satisfy basic needs with long life cycles. Consequently, the demand for them can be forecasted relatively easily. On the contrary, innovative products have short life cycles that decrease the predictability of future demand. Further relevant characteristics are summarised in Table 11.2.

The predictability of future demand significantly affects the cost structure of a supply chain, thus its management focus. The total supply chain cost can be divided into two general cost types: **physical cost** and **market mediation cost** (Fisher, 1997). These capture the costs of the two basic functions any supply chain should fulfil: a physical

Table 11.2 Key product characteristics of functional and innovative products (Fisher, 1997, p.107)

	Functional product	*Innovative product*
Product life cycle	Long	Short
Product variety	Low	High
Predictability	Relatively easy	
The average margin of error in the forecast at the time production is committed	10%	40% to 100%
Average stockout rate	1% to 2%	10% to 40%
Average forced end-of-season markdown as a percentage of the full price	0%	10% to 25%

and a market mediation function. The physical function is responsible for converting raw materials into components and finished goods, and then transporting these products along the supply chain. The purpose of the market mediation function is to ensure that products reaching the marketplace match consumer needs. The physical cost of a supply chain captures all the costs associated with the physical function and includes the production and logistics costs (e.g., transportation and inventory and warehouse cost) of all the products supplied by the chain and sold at a full price. The market mediation function generates the market mediation cost. This includes all the supply chain costs that result from a bad adaptation to actual customer demand, such as markdowns, the cost of surplus, unnecessary inventory or lack of inventory leading to lost sales opportunities and dissatisfied customers.

The predictable character of a functional product makes it relatively easy to match supply and demand. Thus, the supply chain of functional products is to be designed concerning the physical cost and managed with a focus on minimising physical cost. This primary focus can be achieved through a systematic approach to cost efficiency in operations (Fisher, 1997):

- Maintaining high average capacity utilisation
- Minimising inventory investment throughout the chain
- Shortening lead times as long as they do not increase the operational costs
- Selecting suppliers based on their operational performance, mainly quality and cost

The highly uncertain character of the innovative product type necessitates a different focus since the market mediation cost is dominant. The supply chain can lose a lot with bad adaptation; the management focus therefore should be on minimising the market mediation cost, and so management focus should be on (Fisher, 1997):

- Increasing responsiveness to unpredictable demand
- Deploying excess capacity buffer
- Deploying excess buffer stock when necessary
- Investing in lead time reduction aggressively
- Applying speed, flexibility and quality as primary supplier selection criteria

The previous **supply chain type** is called **physically efficient**, while the latter one is **market responsive**. Fisher suggests that misaligned supply chain management results in deteriorating performance. Sellding and Olhager (2007) tested this hypothesis empirically. As a result of extensive empirical research, they found that companies with a match between product characteristics and appropriate supply chain management solutions outperform those that miss this synchronisation. Thus, Fisher's basic supply chain typology is well established and still widely accepted (Ramdas & Spekman, 2000; Lee, 2002; Hong, Wang & Gong, 2019).

An important research stream in supply chain management combines this typology with lean and agile manufacturing concepts and discusses how agility and leanness depend on the supply chain management strategy. **Agility** means that we use market knowledge and technology to exploit profitable opportunities in a volatile market. **Leanness** means that we eliminate all the waste from our value stream (Naylor, Naim and Berry, 1999). Basically, a lean supply chain is the physically efficient one in Fisher's traditional terminology, and an agile supply chain is the market-responsive one (Naylor et al., 1999; Mason-Jones, Naylor & Towill, 2000; Nag, Han and Yao, 2014). However, these researchers introduce several complex supply chain strategies through the different positioning of the **decoupling point**. Originally, the decoupling point was conceptualised as the point in a complex system, such as a supply chain, that separates the part oriented towards customer orders (in an agile form) from the part based on forward planning (with an objective to increase efficiency and leanness; Hoekstra & Romme, 1992). This point is usually the point in a supply chain at which strategic inventory is held to buffer against variability in demand. It is associated with **postponement strategies** as well that have the objective to move product differentiation close to the end user (Cooper, 2008). Postponing the decoupling point reduces the risk of bad adaptation and the cost of market mediation. Downstream from the decoupling point products are **pull**ed by the final customer; this part of the operation is market driven. Upstream from the decoupling point the supply chain is forecast driven and has a **push** style in operation (Naylor et al., 1999).

By varying the position of the decoupling point, the following basic supply chain strategies can be interpreted (Hoekstra & Romme, 1992):

1. Buy-to-Order strategy: Appropriate for unique products with variable demand. These products contain customised parts and components. Due to the high level of uniqueness, the customer is willing to wait for the product and is prepared to accept longer lead times

2. Make-to-Order strategy: A strategy suggested for products with considerable variety and demand variability but mainly using similar input components and modules. Customers are aware of this variability; however, the time accepted for customer order fulfilment is significantly shorter

3. Assemble-to-Order strategy: This still can offer some customisation and respond to customer-specific needs but only to a limited level, mainly with respect to a varied product mix from the same product range. The actual customer service lead time must be reduced considerably

4. Make-to-Stock strategy: This applies to low-demand variation products. Only variation stemming from varied locations can be efficiently managed

5. Ship-to-Stock strategy: It stands for a standard, functional product, where not only high-volume fluctuations limit efficiency but also high variation in geographical locations

Combined supply chain strategies with the appropriate positioning of the decoupling point are also termed **"leagile" strategies** (Naylor et al., 1999). It is the strategic combination of the lean and agile paradigms in managing complex supply chains by positioning the decoupling point in order to match the need for responding to a volatile demand downstream and parallel providing cost efficiency upstream from the decoupling point (Mason-Jones et al., 2000). The objective of leagile supply chain management is to minimise system-level cost, in respect of both key supply chain cost types. The physical cost and lean management approach dominate the upstream operation, whereas the market mediating cost is the key management consideration downstream, where agility is in focus.

11.4 Supply chain management in the era of Industry 4.0

Managing any supply chain necessitates the aligned operation of internal and external network members. The former is usually called **coordination**, and the latter is the **integration** element of supply chain management (Stadler, 2015).

Without such an aligned operation, chain-level performance deteriorates, leading to the decreased overall competitiveness of all the firms involved in the supply chain. The well-known bullwhip effect indicates this problem. Effective inventory levels and orders along the supply chain are dominated by large fluctuations. The amplitude and variance of these inventories increase steadily usually with a time phase, the more one moves upstream, resulting in huge chain-level inefficiencies (Forrester, 1958). Several causes might contribute to the bullwhip effect in a supply chain. One of the key reasons is distorted demand information and the resulting lack of a coordinated and aligned operation (Figure 11.3).

Supply Chain Coordination relates to the way materials and related information flows are managed and it has three building blocks:

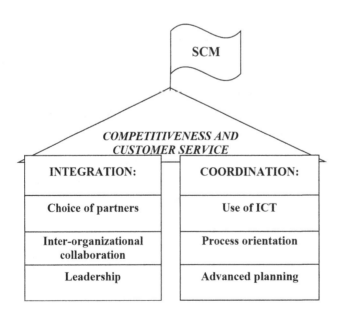

Figure 11.3 House of SCM (based on Stadler, 2015, p. 6)

- Process orientation
- Advanced planning
- Utilisation of information and communication technologies (Stadtler, 2015)

As we have already discussed, supply chain operation encompasses several closely linked operational processes from deliver, through make to return. Hundreds of decisions are made along these supply chain processes. These are largely resource planning decisions responsible for planning the different resources needed in effective and efficient execution. They have the overall objective to support decision-makers by identifying alternatives and selecting the most suitable solution.

Supply chains are highly complex. It is impossible to plan all the detailed aspects of their operation. Thus, it is necessary and useful to simplify reality to some extent and develop generalised models of it. The so-called **Supply chain planning (SCP) matrix** (Rohde, Meyr and Wagner, 2000) is a simplified model of supply chain–related resource planning tasks. This matrix has two aspects. On the one hand, it indicates the relevant **time horizons** of the planning tasks and, on the other hand, it models the key **operational areas** of the supply chain (Figure 11.4.). Advanced supply chain planning is carried out on three-time horizons: long-term, mid-term and short-term planning (Anthony, 1965):

- Long-term planning: These decisions (also called strategic planning decisions) are responsible for creating the structure of a supply chain and its operational areas. They have long-lasting effects, over several (usually from three to five) years
- Mid-term planning: Given the network structure, these tactical planning tasks are responsible for setting the guidelines and policies of operations. Rough quantities and the timing of critical material flows and associated resource needs are specified on this level. Its planning horizon ranges usually from six to 24 months; however, due to recent developments it can encompass monthly planning
- Short-term planning: The lowest planning level sets the detailed operational plan for execution and control. It can also be called operational planning. These tasks require the highest degree of detail and accuracy. The planning horizon is between a few days ()

We can bet on it that reality will deviate from the plan. It is a key management task to monitor these deviations and replan the operation if they are larger than expected.

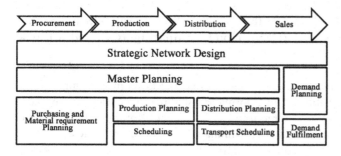

Figure 11.4 Software modules covering the SCP-Matrix (based on Meyr, Wagner & Rohde, 2015, p. 100)

Planning can never be static. It is continuously carried out dynamically on a rolling horizon basis. However, planning can also be guided by unforeseeable events (Stadtler, 2015).

Planning is an important means of cooperation within supply chain management (Meyr et al., 2015). It is accompanied by intensive information sharing and processing. We discuss two directions of these information flows here, horizontal and vertical. **Horizontal information flow** goes upstream and starts with sharing customer orders, sales forecasts and internal orders, such as for warehouse replenishment or production, for example, but also purchasing orders. Along this information flow, the chain becomes customer driven. We must note, however, that downstream information change is also intensive, including inventory-related data, information on actual and future capacity utilisation or lead times. **Vertical information flow**s downwards to coordinate resource plans, including aggregate quantities and allocated capacities, projected stock levels and due dates. Upwards information flow is also prevalent, providing upper-level planning with detailed data on actual performance, including cost, production or transport rates and capacity utilisation.

The coordination of these information flows and the complex planning tasks is accomplished by advanced planning rooted in comprehensive and efficient information sharing enabled by the use of information and communication technologies (ICTs). The core of any supply chain planning is the Advanced Planning System (APS), a special Enterprise Resource System (ERP) that is capable to support these complex planning tasks dynamically. It has several main characteristics as follows (Ivert & Johnsson, 2010):

- It integrates the resource planning of all core supply chain processes from the supplier to the customer
- In a hierarchical approach
- Based on real-time information sharing
- It includes highly sophisticated optimisation methodologies (also heuristics)
- It includes technologies of easy visualisation to foster quick and well-founded decision-making

11.5 Coordination in supply chain management and Industry 4.0

As discussed earlier in this book, an info-communication revolution is taking place in the industry that leads to a new way of operation, usually called Industry 4.0. Several pieces of research focus on how this affects supply chain coordination and its elements, information sharing, intensive communication and enhanced planning. Based on an extensive literature review, Wiedenmann and Größler (2019) discuss the positive impact of different Industry 4.0 technologies on the bullwhip effect. Specifically, the positive effects of **cyber-physical systems (CPS)**, **cloud computing (CC)** and **artificial intelligence (AI)** are presented:

- Implementing CPS can increase the visibility of material flows in the supply chain, improve information availability and information sharing and enrich the available information base. All these are prerequisites of advanced planning. Thus, applying CPS can lead to better plans and faster replanning that might result in the decrease of the bullwhip effect and a more agile operation
- CC enables real-time information sharing along the supply chain that also increases information availability and enhances information sharing, which results in decreased

information inconsistency. The flexible and scalable infrastructure and high communication safety also contribute to decreasing the negative consequences of the bullwhip effect
- AI can interpret patterns in enriched data sets, including the so-called big data. New patterns and related new interdependencies within the complex supply chain can be revealed, which might facilitate rational decision-making and be used to counteract the bullwhip effect

Ben-Daya, Hassini and Bahroun (2019) discuss the effect of the **Internet of Things (IoT)** on supply chain management in a process approach. They follow the above-discussed SCOR model and identify the role of IoT in SCM along key processes. (The "Plan" process is not discussed as a separate process. Instead, all the others include the planning aspects.):

- Source: They argue that IoT enables the virtualisation of supply chains making **tracking and tracing** easy and the control of the chain feasible. A virtual supply chain supplies huge amounts of data and allows us to perform the advanced planning and controlling of the operation – in the case of sourcing but also in the case of all the other operational processes
- Make: Companies have applied automation in their production for several decades. These traditional systems are organised in a hierarchical way using data silos. Nowadays, Industry 4.0 technologies –such as sensors, controllers, analytics software, telemetry, big data and cloud computing – provide new opportunities for smart manufacturing. Potential areas enhanced by IoT applications are the following: factory visibility, connected supply chain, production planning and scheduling and proactive maintenance
- Delivery: This key operational area includes order management, warehouse and inventory management and transportation. The majority of SCM-related IoT literature deals with transportation. The second most frequently discussed sub-process is inventorying followed by warehouse operation. Similarly, to previous processes, virtualisation is the key that generates higher **visibility**, leading to enriched databases and easier information sharing. These are the key triggers of better performance that might result from IoT applications
- Return: The first approach to gain visibility and increase the ability of "tracking and tracing" reverse logistics processes was due to Radio Frequency Identification (RFID) applications. Today IoT solutions can further increase visibility in this case as well and might contribute to better planning and executing return operations

Case illustration

It is a well-known truth that poor supply chain visibility has been choking the supply chain and logistics industry for decades. According to SupplyChainDive, 94% of businesses do not have full visibility of their supply chain and logistics operations. It is worrying. The problems that come with poor supply chain visibility gradually eat into a business's revenue, efficiency, productivity and customer experience. The question is why is it so difficult to achieve high levels of supply chain visibility? Traditional means of executing operations are one of the major reasons behind poor visibility. Legacy IT systems work in silos. This makes it extremely difficult for supply chain and logistics stakeholders to get a holistic picture of all the things that happen on the ground.

Savvy businesses are aggressively exploring and investing in cutting-edge technologies, such as machine learning, business analytics and digital control towers to enhance supply chain and logistics visibility. Machine learning algorithms empower businesses to gain predictive intelligence by scanning through historical KPI data of routes previously undertaken and 3PL providers availed. Knowledge about these KPIs empowers logistics stakeholders to gain predictive visibility. Business or cognitive analytics empowers businesses to mine and crunch data from disparate systems and gain critical business insights. It helps logistics stakeholders accurately benchmark KPIs, figure out inconsistencies in SLAs and identify financial holes and other inconsistencies in the entire process of supply chain and logistics. A digital control tower (DCT) empowers businesses to gain real-time supply chain visibility that logistics stakeholders can act upon, such as pick-up problems, route-wise performance, delivery delays, etc. for all orders on a single screen, drastically improving supply chain management.

As customer experience rapidly takes over price as a major competitive differentiator and margins keep shrinking, ensuring end-to-end visibility of supply chains and logistics operations will become imperative (FarEye, n.d.).

Coordination is a prerequisite for supply chain integration (Morash & Clinton, 1998). Therefore, after discussing supply chain coordination, we can turn our attention to SC integration.

As indicated in Figure 11.3 integration is the second building block of the House of SCM. It is considered a decisive element in increasing supply chain performance, and it is about aligning the objectives of supply chain partners in order to achieve a harmonised, effective and efficient operation. Supply chain integration builds on three interlinked parts (Stadtler, 2015):

- The choice of appropriate partners
- Organising collaboration on the network level
- Leadership

In the following, we discuss these parts, then we close this discussion by elaborating on the Industry 4.0 aspects of supply chain integration.

After a firm has decided to **outsource** a specific activity to external partners, the question arises, Who is to outsource it? The choice of partners is the starting point in any integration effort since this will specify the structure of a supply chain. The choice of partners in the supply chain management setting is not restricted to the issue of relevant evaluation criteria (e.g., cost, quality, lead time, reliability). It is much more about developing appropriate relationships. The intensification of global competition poses serious challenges for **relationship management** along the supply chain that might contribute to mutually beneficial business relationships (Lambert & Cooper, 2000).

Relationships have special importance from the integration perspective because different relationship types necessitate different management tools and techniques. At the same time, they offer alternative levels of integration benefits. Both the integration with key customers and with key suppliers are important. A close, mutually beneficial relationship with key customers can contribute to better supply chain performance through, for example, more accurate demand information that allows increased responsiveness for the focal firm and might lead to better supply chain planning, shorter lead times, less obsolete inventory and a lower level of cost. Integration with key customers has been found to influence customer satisfaction positively (Homburg & Stock, 2004). Similarly, it might affect the innovation capability of the supply chain and the time needed for new product development positively (Song & Di Benedetto, 2008). Strategic relationship management with key suppliers is expected to increase suppliers' capability to understand the requirements of the focal firm, which again might increase the adaptation capability of the supply chain. Intensive information sharing regarding products and operational processes helps the focal firm to develop better supply chain plans that might lead to shorter lead times, higher flexibility and better overall customer service. Integration with suppliers not only affects operational performance but also, similar to the integration with customers, it might positively influence the focal firm's innovation competence (Koufteros, Cheng & Lai, 2007). Integration efforts with key supply chain partners are beneficial to the focal firm and the complex supply chain as well, and they have quite similar performance consequences. Therefore, we continue our discussion in a generalised way and discuss how supply chain relationships, conceptualised as a dyadic relationship between a customer and a supplier, are managed in an integrated way.

Traditionally, we distinguish two types of supply chain relationship management models (Dyer, Cho & Chu, 1998): (1) The so-called **arm's-length model** that advocates minimum dependence and maximum bargaining power. (2) The **partnership model** is more balanced and can be characterised as mutually committed. Further distinctions are summarised in Table 11.3.

In a traditional approach, we have thought of these two relationship models as mutually exclusive. A good illustration of this is the example of car manufacturers. US corporations have previously focused on the arm's-length relationship model while managing their supplier relationships. On the contrary, in the case of Japanese corporations, the partner model was believed to be dominant. Back in the 1990s, Dyer et al. (1998) carried out an extensive study on this topic and analysed more than 450 supplier–automaker relationships in the USA, Japan and Korea. The results of this study partially confirmed this assumption. US automakers had a strong focus on the arm's-length relationship model. Korean manufacturers reflected the relationship management model that was attributed to Japanese firms or, more generally, to firms in the Far East, an almost exclusive focus on the partnership model. However, Japanese automakers – mainly Toyota – overcame the "one-size-fits-all" approach, and they reflected a more strategic approach to supplier relationship management. It was because both models have their advantages and

Table 11.3 Characteristics of the two basic supply chain relationship management models (Dyer et al., 1998, p.72)

The arm's-length model	The partnership model
• Buyer: no exclusivity to supplier	• Exclusivity towards one partner (buyer/supplier)
• Supplier: no exclusivity to buyer	• Single sourcing
• Multiple sourcing	• Long-term contracts
• Short- or medium-term contracts	• High level of dependence and risk
• Low level of dependence and risk	• High level of trust
• Low level of trust	• Intensive information sharing including sensitive
• Low level of information sharing, only basic data are shared but not the sensitive ones	information (e.g., inventory levels, cost, innovation)
• The level of relation-specific investments are balanced, mutually low	• The level of relation-specific investments is balanced and mutually high

disadvantages. The advantages of the partner model have previously been discussed. But it has drawbacks as well. A relationship applying the partner model is costly to develop and maintain. It might create a locked-in effect and make switching to other suppliers also costly. This is also true from the supplier's perspective. Similarly, the arm's-length model has both advantages and disadvantages. Suppliers in this model do not have to commit themselves to a customer. They might work with several automakers, which might generate huge order volumes and lead to scale economy and low unit cost. These relationships are easy to develop and maintain and back cost efficiency, too. See a summary of the advantages and disadvantages of both relationship models in Table 11.4.

Based on the advantages and disadvantages of both relationship management models, Japanese automakers applied a **segmented relationship management approach**. They analysed each specific supplier relationship in a strategic context, considered key attributes of the supplier's product and aligned these attributes with the advantages of the models. In case a supplier had a product that contributed to the core competence of the automaker, the partnership model was implemented to facilitate close collaboration and higher innovation performance. In case the supplier's product had rather low innovation capability, the preferred model was the arm's-length model with the key advantage of cost efficiency. In this segmented approach, the contribution of the supplier base can be maximised.

For quite a long time, managers believed that long-term competitive advantage comes from such a segmented supply base. However, competitive circumstances have changed a lot during the last decades, firms cannot aim at a pure cost leadership or differentiation strategy anymore (Porter, 1985). A new paradigm appeared, that of mass customisation, which combines traditional competitive priorities. From the perspective of supply base management, this requires the combination of the two traditional relationship management models leading to different hybrid models. Hybrid sourcing strategies are operational models that have the ambition of combining the benefits and minimising the drawbacks of both traditional relationship models. It is common in these hybrid strategies that the focal firm develops and maintains long-term relationships with usually two suppliers for a component. This **triadic set of supply chain relationships** is seen as long-lasting, generating commitment and trust between partners that foster intensive collaboration and faster innovation. At the same time, the focal firm of the triad (being in the customer's position usually) aims at triggering competitiveness between the two suppliers, too, to maintain cost efficiency.

Table 11.4 Advantages and disadvantages of the two classic supply chain relationship management models (Dyer et al., 1998)

The arm's-length model	*The partnership model*
• Suppliers can grow, and become big – high level of scale economics • Firms can learn from different partners • This is a source for incremental types of innovations • The cooperation is not costly • Innovation capability, and adaptation if necessary, is slow • Competitive priority: cost	• Mutual exclusivity and commitment • Backs the development of radical innovations • Innovations, changes and adaptations can be carried out easily and fast • Suppliers cannot grow that much – lower level of scale economics • Managing the relationship is costly • Competitive priority: customisation

Three types of such hybrid supply models have been described in the literature: "parallel sourcing" (Richardson & Roumasset, 1995), "network sourcing" (Hines, 1995) and the triadic sourcing model (Dubois & Fredriksson, 2008). All these hybrid strategies are different from the so-called dual sourcing. In a dual-sourcing situation, two independent suppliers are used to supplying the same purchased component (Van Weele, 2005). In the case of a hybrid strategy, at least two suppliers are capable of delivering the same component. Still, the buyer applies single sourcing for a specific product. Compared to the other two hybrid sourcing strategies, the triadic sourcing strategy has a speciality, because here the buyer "actively creates and encourages interdependencies between the two suppliers" (Dubois & Fredriksson, 2008, p. 170). The triad has three active, interrelated relationships in this case. Not only the two buyer-supplier relationships of the triad are interrelated but also there is a direct relationship between the two suppliers facilitated by the buyer firm. Using another terminology, this constellation is called a closed triad, where all actors interact with each other (Smith & Laage-Hellman, 1992).

The strategic segmentation approach itself represents a systemic approach to supplier relationship management. These new developments reinforce this. Instead of managing single dyadic relationships in supply chains, the management's objective should be to manage supplier relationships as a complex, interdependent system (Vickery, Jayaram, Droge, & Calantone, 2003).

Triadic sourcing models represent an important change in relationship management. Instead of managing relationships individually, on a dyadic basis, several companies systemically manage the portfolios of suppliers. Japanese automakers seem to have competitive advantages in this respect.[1] More specifically, knowledge diffusion appears to be still more efficient and fast in Toyota's network. One of the reasons for this is the **leadership** role Toyota, the focal firm, takes in managing this network.

This leading role is described by Dyer and Nebeoka (2000, p. 351) as follows. To encourage suppliers to participate and openly share knowledge, Toyota has heavily subsidised the network (with knowledge and resources) during the early stages of its formation to ensure that suppliers realise substantial benefits from participation. Suppliers are motivated to participate because they quickly learn that participating in the collective learning processes is vastly superior to trying to isolate their proprietary knowledge.

Without the leading role of the focal firm, and its associated dedication and investment, no network-level collaboration can be long-lasting and efficient. Toyota realised that these investments serve the purpose of creating a common identity among members, and the lead firm must play a key role in developing this identity. This common identity is a social capital that can effectively be used in building trust, and decreasing opportunism that might lead to an increased willingness to cooperate, and share proprietary and sensitive information facilitating knowledge sharing, joint knowledge generation and innovations. If the network can get its members to "cooperate in a social community", it will create learning opportunities far superior to firms that do not reside within such a network. In Japan, Toyota's network is known as the "Toyota Group" and Toyota openly promotes a philosophy within the Toyota Group called "coexistence and co-prosperity" (Kyoson kyoei in Japanese; Dyer & Nebeoka, 2000, p. 352).

11.6 Integration in supply chain management and Industry 4.0

As discussed before, supply chain integration is an extension of supply chain coordination. While coordination aims at aligning and managing the complex operation of the lead firm's internal network, supply chain integration focuses on external, independent partners. All the Industry 4.0 solutions concerning supply chain coordination have a role in integrating external partners into the supply chain too, since both planning and efficient process management are key between external supply chain partners as well. However, the concept of an external supply chain has special challenges as well, where Industry 4.0 solutions might help, too. The key special challenge we discuss in this Section is managing **supply chain resilience**. Supply chain resilience is the ability of the complex supply chain to return to its original / desired status after a disturbance (Christopher, 2016). Resilience is closely related to supply chain risk and risk management since the goal is to identify sources of risks, map their potential consequences and create plans for effective recovery.

Supply chains are vulnerable to many risks that can be grouped into five main **risk types** (Mason-Jones & Towill, 1998; Christopher, 2016):

- Demand risk, supply risk
- Process risk
- Environmental risk
- Control risk

Managing risks associated with demand, supply and process uncertainties has intensively been discussed in the context of coordination. Due to an increased level of outsourcing, and the intensive globalisation of supply chain operations extending over several geographical areas, the risk associated with environment and control has intensified (Butner, 2010), generating more and more severe challenges. The COVID-19 pandemic crisis is a recent example of this. To survive in today's complex environment, supply chains need to be agile, they need to develop their risk mitigation capabilities and increase their structural flexibility (Ben-Daya et al., 2019). The **visibility** of a supply chain can strongly support these capabilities because it decreases the time to respond and contributes to better adaptation. Information technology in general, and Industry 4.0 solutions in particular, might help a lot in increasing this visibility with external supply chain partners. IoT, for example, might enhance supply chain level communication by enabling the efficient communication of humans to things and by autonomously coordinating among "things" (Ben-Daya et al., 2019).

As Ellis, Morris and Santagate (2015) point out, IoT provides new levels of supply chain visibility, agility and adaptability to cope with various SCM challenges. IoT is a sensor-based technology, and these sensors operate as a medium between supply chain analysis and action "by capturing various elements of action (velocity, variability, volume, and value) and communicating these elements to analytics engines, which in turn convert this data into actionable insight" (Ellis et al., 2015, p. 9).

Even so, the availability of the necessary information is not always the bottleneck resource in decision-making. Instead, those technologies are missing that shorten the **lead times between data gathering, analysis and decision-making**. IoT allows such a reduction in these lead times. Consequently, supply chains can be more agile, responsive, resilient and risk-bearing (Ben-Daya et al., 2019).

Case illustration

In what follows, the way a car manufacturer optimised its operation efficiency in a volatile demand environment and significantly increased its production volumes without additional investment is discussed. The challenge was that the focal firm was an international car manufacturer that had to adapt to a very competitive market and uncertain environment. The production of specific engines needed to be boosted to meet increasing demand with the same capacity. The company's main challenge was to ensure that the production of assembled engines met customer demand every week over a fifty-two-week period. They needed a software solution that could anticipate the effect of bottlenecks on the whole organisation and take into account the following factors:

- Capacity variability over time
- Shared resources between products with different cycle times
- Multiple resources capable of manufacturing the same product
- Demand volatility
- Lead times
- Storage capacity

The solution was that with the aid of the Cosmo Tech Supply Chain, a realistic and exhaustive Simulation Digital Twin of the whole engine production system was deployed. The software was designed to:

- Model the focal firm's multiple production sites and complex flows (factories, product diversity, stocks, transports, etc.)
- Model real-world constraints (equipment capacity, labour shifts, lead times, etc.)
- Include all necessary data (demand, contractors' agreements, production output, bill of materials, routings, etc.)

Tens of thousands of simulations were executed to create the optimal production plan with the current supply chain configuration in less than 20 minutes (Cosmotech, n.d).

Summary

The content of the chapter has been developed in a step-by-step approach, building on the previous ones. First, key terms, such as supply chain and supply chain management, were defined. As a next step, traditional supply chain management solutions were discussed related to both the lean and the agile approach. The chapter also highlighted the importance of combining these approaches using the concept of the decoupling point. "The house of supply chain management" provides an overview of the means that contribute to better coordination and integration within the supply chain. After discussing the element of this house, we linked them to Industry 4.0 applications. The chapter includes several case examples that help the reader to understand the link between supply chain management and Industry 4.0. We close the chapter with review and discussion questions that can be used for deepening an understanding of key terms and getting an insight into their application in specific business situations.

Review questions

1. How would you describe the gradual evolution of the concept of "supply chain management"?
2. Please identify the key building elements of a supply chain. How does the SCOR model conceptualise these elements?

3. What decision-making levels can contribute to better supply chain performance? Please, characterise and compare them. Can you name some examples representing different levels of such decision-making?
4. On what levels can supply chain performance be measured? Please, name specific KPIs for all potential levels.
5. What process performance dimensions make up the taxonomy for supply chain performance measures?
6. What is the difference between coordination and integration in supply chain management?
7. What are the similarities and differences between supply chain coordination and integration? What specific building blocks do they have? How are they interlinked? Please think of "The House of SCM".

Discussion questions

1. Please provide examples of performance measurements that is (1) system-level and (2) not system-level. Which can contribute to effective supply chain management, and why?
2. How would you characterise the following products from the perspective of aligned supply chain management: stationaries and ski accessories? What type of products do they represent? What specific supply chain management solutions would you propose to use and why?
3. What is the "decoupling point" in a supply chain responsible for? What specific strategies can be developed by differently positioning this decoupling point in the supply chain?
4. How would you summarise the importance of the supply chain planning matrix? Please name a few concrete resource planning decisions and place them within the matrix.
5. Please check the case example on supply chain visibility. Where do the solutions discuss in the example fit in? Are these related to supply chain coordination or integration?
6. Please read the case example on the resilient supply chain. Why and how can simulation contribute to a more resilient supply chain operation?

Note

1 Suppliers in the car-making industry produce approx. 70% of the value of the final product, the car (Dyer and Nebeoka, 2000). Therefore, it is a sector where effective management of suppliers is particularly important. It is not a coincidence that many new relationship and integration concepts and solutions are born here, and then spread to other sectors.

Bibliography

Anthony, R. (1965). *Planning and control systems: A framework for analysis*. Harvard University.
APICS. (2017). *The SCOR model*. Retrieved from http://www.apics.org/docs/default-source/scor -training/scor-v12-0-framework-introduction.pdf?sfvrsn=2
Ben-Daya, M., Hassini, E., & Bahroun, Z. (2019). Internet of things and supply chain management: A literature review. *International Journal of Production Research*, 57(15–16), 4719–4742. https://doi.org /10.1080/00207543.2017.1402140

Butner, K. (2010). The smarter supply chain of the Future. *Strategy & Leadership, 38*(1), 22–31.

Cavinato, J. L. (1992). A total cost/value model for supply chain competitiveness. *Journal of Business Logistics, 13*(2), 285–301. Retrieved from https://www.proquest.com/openview/a33300ebb0bf08b f886e32fe5c3d4676/1?pq-origsite=gscholar&cbl=36584.

Christopher, M. (2016). *Logistics & supply chain management.* Pearson.

Cooper, M. C. (2008). Supply chain postponement and speculation strategies. *Journal of Operations Management, 26*(2), 148–163.

Cooper, M. C., & Ellram, L. M. (1993). Characteristics of supply chain management and the implications for purchasing and logistics strategy. *International Journal of Logistics Management, 4*(2), 13–24. https:// doi.org/10.1108/09574099310804957

Cosmotech. (n.d.). *Achieve production planning excellence.* Retrieved from https://cosmotech.com/ solutions/case-study-production-planning-and-control/

Council of Supply Chain Management Professionals. (2016). *CSCMP supply chain management definitions and glossary.* Retrieved from https://cscmp.org/supply-chain-management-definitions

Dubois, A., & Fredriksson, P. (2008). Cooperating and competing in supply networks: Making sense of a triadic sourcing strategy. *Journal of Purchasing and Supply Management, 14*(3), 170–171. https://doi .org/10.1016/j.pursup.2008.05.002

Dyer, J. H., Cho, D. S., & Chu, W. (1998). Strategic supplier segmentation: The next "Best practice" in supply chain management. *California Management Review, 40*(2), 57–77. https://doi.org/10.2307 /41165933

Dyer, J. H., & Nobeoka, K. (2000). Creating and managing a high-performance knowledge-sharing network: The Toyota case. *Strategic Management Journal, 21*(3), 345–367. https://doi.org/10.1002/ (SICI)1097-0266(200003)21:3<345::AID-SMJ96>3.0.CO;2-N

Ellis, S., Morris, H. D., & Santagate, J. (2015). *IoT-enabled analytic applications revolutionize supply chain planning and execution.* Retrieved from https://www.sensifyinc.com/wp-content/uploads/2016/05/ IDC-IoT-enabled-analytics-applications_final.pdf

FarEye. (n.d.). *Overcoming challenges in achieving supply chain visibility.* Retrieved from https://www .getfareye.com/insights/blog/overcoming-challenges-in-achieving-supply-chain-visibility-in-2020 ?utm_source=ad&utm_medium=google&utm_campaign=visibility&utm_term=supplyChainUK &gclid=Cj0KCQiAkZKNBhDiARIsAPsk0WijDV_NTkOGXjEo3mEbjvQ5x2WNWJj7SHZ DdeK8lbH9sdhNhsJMUaMaAjZyEALw_wcB

Fisher, M. L. (1997). What is the right supply chain for your product?. *Harvard Business Review,* (March– April), 105–116. Retrieved from https://mba.teipir.gr/files/Fisher_What_is_the_right_SC_for _your_product.pdf

Forrester, J. W. (1958). Industrial dynamics: A major breakthrough for decision makers. *Harvard Business Review, 36*(4), 37–66.

Gunasekaran, A., Patel, C., & McGaughey, R. E. (2004). A framework for supply chain performance measurement. *International Journal of Production Economics, 87*(3), 333–347. https://doi.org/10.1016/j .ijpe.2003.08.003

Gunasekaran, A., Patel, C., & Tirtiroglu, E. (2001). Performance measures and metrics in a supply chain environment. *International Journal of Operations and Production Management, 21*(1/2), 71–87. https:// doi.org/10.1108/01443570110358468

Hines, P. (1995). Network sourcing: A hybrid approach. *International Journal of Purchasing and Materials Management, 31*(1), 17–17. https://doi.org/10.1111/j.1745-493X.1995.tb00199.x

Hoekstra, S., & Romme, J. (1992). *Integrated logistics structures: Developing customer oriented goods flow.* McGraw-Hill.

Homburg, C., & Stock, R. M. (2004). The link between salespeople's job satisfaction and customer satisfaction in a business-to-business context: A dyadic analysis. *Journal of Academy of Marketing Science, 32*(2), 144–158. https://doi.org/10.1177/0092070303261415

Hong, Z., Wang, H., & Gong, Y. (2019). Green product design considering functional-product reference. *International Journal of Production Economics, 210*, 155–168. https://doi.org/10.1016/j.ijpe .2019.01.008

Huan, S. H., Sheoran, S. K., & Wang, G. (2004). A review and analysis of supply chain operations reference (SCOR) model. *Supply Chain Management: An International Journal, 9*(1), 23–29. https://doi.org/10.1108/13598540410517557

Ivert, L. K., & Jonsson, P. (2010). The potential benefits of advanced planning and scheduling systems in sales and operations planning. *Industrial Management and Data Systems, 110*(5), 659–681. https://doi.org/10.1108/02635571011044713

Koufteros, X. A., Cheng, T. C. E., & Lai, K. H. (2007). Black-box and gray box supplier integration in product development: Antecedents, consequences and the moderating role of firm size. *Journal of Operations Management, 25*(4), 847–870. https://doi.org/10.1016/j.jom.2006.10.009

Lambert, D. M., & Cooper, M. C. (2000). Issues in supply chain management. *Industrial Marketing Management, 29*(1), 65–83. https://doi.org/10.1016/S0019-8501(99)00113-3

Lee, H. (2002). Aligning supply chain strategies with product uncertainties. *California Management Review, 44*(3), 105–119. Retrieved from https://journals.sagepub.com/doi/pdf/10.2307/41166135?casa_token=HqsMDDExdNIAAAAA%3A70lmnaAyxBbfkHv7hJq995zAPfFav6u-vlckt9TYIoqflXY0w66ENn8yT7nAIXow8axb1MVTfEiX&

Mason-Jones, R., Naylor, B., & Towill, D. R. (2000). Engineering the leagile supply chain. *International Journal of Agile Management Systems, 2*(1), 54–61. https://doi.org/10.1108/14654650010312606

Mason-Jones, R., & Towill, D. R. (1998). Shrinking the supply chain uncertainty circle. *IOM Control, 24*(7), 17–22.

Mentzer, J. T., DeWitt, W., Keebler, J. S., Min, S., Nix, N. W., Smith, C. D., & Zacharia, Z. G. (2001). Defining supply chain management. *Journal of Business Logistics, 22*(2), 1–25. https://doi.org/10.1002/j.2158-1592.2001.tb00001.x

Meyr, H., Wagner, M., & Rohde, J. (2015). Structure of advanced planning systems. In H. Stadtler, C. Kilger & H. Meyr (Eds.), *Supply chain management and advanced planning: Concepts, models, software and case studies* (5th ed., pp. 99–106). Springer.

Morash, E. A., & Clinton, S. R. (1998). Supply chain integration: Customer value through collaborative closeness versus operational excellence. *Journal of Marketing Theory and Practice, 6*(4), 104–120. https://doi.org/10.1080/10696679.1998.11501814

Nag, B., Han, C., & Yao, D. Q. (2014). Mapping supply chain strategy: An industry analysis. *Journal of Manufacturing Technology Management, 25*(3), 351–370. https://doi.org/10.1108/JMTM-06-2012-0062

Naylor, J. B., Naim, M. M., & Berry, D. (1999). Leagility: Integrating the lean and agile manufacturing paradigms in the total supply chain. *International Journal of Production Economics, 62*(1–2), 107–118. https://doi.org/10.1016/S0925-5273(98)00223-0

Oliver, R. K., & Weber, M. D. (1982). *Supply-chain management: Logistics catches up with strategy.* Chapman & Hall.

Porter, M. E. (1985). *Competitive advantage: Creating and sustaining superior performance.* Free Press.

Ramdas, K., & Spekman, R. E. (2000). Chain or shackles: Understanding what drives supply-chain performance. *Interfaces, 30*(4), 3–21. https://doi.org/10.1287/inte.30.4.3.11644

Richardson, J., & Roumasset, J. (1995). Sole sourcing, competitive sourcing, parallel sourcing: Mechanisms for supplier performance. *Managerial and Decision Economics, 16*(1), 71–84. https://doi.org/10.1002/mde.4090160109

Rohde, J., Meyr, H., & Wagner, M. (2000). Die supply chain planning matrix. *PPS Management, 5*(1), 10–15.

Selldin, E., & Olhager, J. (2007). Linking products with supply chains: Testing Fisher's model. *Supply Chain Management, 12*(1), 42–51. https://doi.org/10.1108

Simchi-Levi, D., Kaminsky, P., & Simchi-Levi, E. (2008). *Designing and managing the supply chain: Concepts, strategies, and case studies.* McGraw-Hill/Irwin.

Smith, P. C., & Laage-Hellman, J. (1992). Small group analysis in industrial networks. In B. Axelsson & G. Easton (Eds.), *Industrial networks: A new view of reality* (pp. 37–61). Routledge.

Song, M., & Di Benedetto, C. A. (2008). Supplier's involvement and success of radical new product development in new ventures. *Journal of Operations Management, 26*(1), 1–22. https://doi.org/10.1016/j.jom.2007.06.001

Stadtler, H. (2015). Supply chain management: An overview. In H. Stadtler, C. Kilger & H. Meyr (Eds.), *Supply chain management and advanced planning: Concepts, models, software and case studies* (5th ed., pp. 3–28). Springer.

Stadtler, H., & Kilger, C. (2008). *Supply chain management and advanced planning: Concepts, models, software and case studies* (4th ed.). Springer.

Supply-Chain Council. (2012). *Supply-chain operations reference-model: Revision 11.0.* Retrieved from https://docs.huihoo.com/scm/supply-chain-operations-reference-model-r11.0.pdf

Van Weele, A. J. (2005). *Purchasing and supply chain management: Analysis, strategy, planning and practice* (4th ed.). Thompson Learning.

Vickery, S. K., Jayaram, J., Droge, C., & Calantone, R. (2003). The effects of an integrative supply chain strategy on customer service and financial performance: An analysis of direct versus indirect relationships. *Journal of Operations Management, 21*(5), 523–539. https://doi.org/10.1016/j.jom.2003.02.002

Wiedenmann, M., & Größler, A. (2019). The impact of digital technologies on operational causes of the bullwhip effect: A literature review. *Procedia CIRP, 81*, 552–557. https://doi.org/10.1016/j.procir.2019.03.154

12 Fintech and smart banking

Lilla Hortoványi, Sándor Gyula Nagy, Dóra Horváth and Zsolt Roland Szabó

"Fintech" refers to the supply of innovative financial services that rely on I4.0 technologies and disruptive business models typically outside the traditional financial sector. The fundamental difference between these revolutionary services is that they approach consumer problems differently and, consequently, they provide different solutions.

Compared to traditional banking services, fintech services are just as high quality, but at a lower price for organisations operating in any industry, whether large or small. First, automated financial services are cheaper and faster. Second, real-time access to robust financial data enables quick decision-making and quick intervention. Firms can gain a deeper understanding of consumer problems and integrate innovative solutions more quickly into their offerings. Third, alternative payment solutions and credit services provide better customer service. But exactly how, we will present in this chapter. Finally, the monitoring of innovative financial technologies is almost a must for all companies if they operate in the long run.

In this chapter, we introduce fintech and smart banking. To do so, we must elaborate on the application of bitcoin and blockchain technology, including its benefits and some of the associated risks. In addition, we discuss in detail two financial business models: crowdsourcing and P2P lending.

12.1 The fintech revolution

The global financial crisis of 2008, combined with greater access to information technology and wider use of mobile devices, allowed a new generation of firms to deliver financial services. These "fintech" companies operate in parallel with traditional banks; the most highly affected segments include lending, payments and cross-border transfers (Cortina & Schmukler, 2018). The scope of activity started with money transfers, peer-to-peer loans and crowdfunding gradually spreading to the newer areas of blockchain, cryptocurrencies and robo-investing[1] (Goldstein et al., 2019).

By leveraging emerging digital technologies, fintech enables, innovates and disrupts the financial services market (Gimpel et al., 2018).

Large financial service providers, in particular, banks, have been pioneers in using digital technologies. By the 1980s, financial services had become a largely digital industry, relying on electronic transactions between financial institutions, financial market participants and customers around the world (Alt et al., 2018). The digitalisation of financial services can be exemplified by the application of SWIFT for transfers, ATMs and other electronic interfaces for customers. However, this era was characterised by innovations that improved the existing structures.

DOI: 10.4324/9781003390312-14

The **fintech revolution** is unique in that much of the change is happening from outside the financial industry since the disruptors are technology firms. But what is disruptive innovation? According to Clayton M. Christensen, one of the most influential management thinkers of today, disruptive innovations make products and services more accessible and affordable, thereby making them available to a larger population. Every disruptive innovation has three pillars: (1) It is based on an **enabling technology** that makes a product or a service more affordable and accessible to a wider population. (2) It is also built on an innovative business model that provides solutions for the problems of **non-customers** (the ones who previously could not buy products or services in a given market) and **low-end consumers** (the least profitable customers). (3) Suppliers, distributors and customers all prosper from disruptive technology and, hence, they form a **coherent value network** together. In other words, the emerging market offers profits and growth potential.

Historically, there was a large gap between the financial products available to households and businesses (especially in developing countries), and they were very different. The banking sector constrained lending to households, due, in part, to high costs relative to low transaction values and difficulties in identifying and assessing the risk of potential borrowers. Opening a bank account was often denied or deemed too expensive for many low-income families or households with moderate means. As a result, a significant portion of the population was either neglected or completely underserved financially. Moreover, the physical bank branches served as a primary point of contact for customers; hence, the branch network (the number and locations) was considered to be an important source of competitive advantage, which of course made operation costs high. Finally, young customers found banking services slow and inefficient. They wanted simplified and direct experiences where they do not have to wait in line for hours to fill in forms. They did not even want to fill in the forms anymore. They did not want to hear sales talks of random products. Luckily, the fintech revolution ended this era by offering new forms of financial solutions for those traditionally neglected.

Case illustration

Fintech smartphone applications provide a solution for consumers who have low or irregular incomes and are therefore not included in the customer base of traditional banks. They are not part of the customer bases for a variety of reasons, including the fact that banks cannot make a profit from them that is high enough to be acceptable to their brand. The massive use of mobile phones has allowed great successes, such as that of M-Pesa in Kenya and ten other African countries, which have already enabled more than 30 million users to transfer money, take out loans and make deposits using mobile phones from the remotest rural areas. TransferWise allows customers to send money across borders by matching transactions with other users sending in the opposite direction, thereby avoiding the high fees associated with international transfers. In China and neighbouring countries, platforms such as WeChat have more than a billion users who perform all kinds of financial transactions using mobile phones without having opened a bank account. Another Asian non-bank finance giant is Ant Financial, the financial arm of Alibaba, a high-tech company that allows hundreds of millions of users to borrow money in just three minutes or make investments in the world's largest monetary fund. Ant Financial is already among the ten largest financial companies in the world by valuation (Noya, 2019).

The fintech revolution has offered and delivered financial services in new and more attractive non-banking channels. It substituted traditional banks and their services in new ways and consequently transformed business models and financial intermediation; furthermore, it extended consumer access outside branches and beyond normal banking business hours and achieved higher levels of personalisation based on digital sensing and big data analytics (Gozman et al., 2018).

In summary, the fintech revolution has disrupted the financial world. Without the heavy legacy of traditional banks, fintech firms have focused on solving non-consumer problems with an exceptional user experience at lower costs and, hence, they were able to appeal to "mainstream" customers and move upmarket displacing some of the long-established incumbents. For example, the fintech sector surpassed traditional banks' global share of unsecured loans in 2015 and was the leading source of personal loans in the United States in 2018 (Brown, 2020). Finally, fintech is a lucrative business with a coherent value network. Due to the ever-rising demand, the global fintech market was valued at USD7301.78 billion in 2020 and is forecasted to grow at a CAGR of 26.87% between 2021 and 2026 (Yahoo!Finance, 2021).

Millennials are particularly attracted to fintech solutions and four out of five consider obtaining their banking services from a major tech company such as Google or Apple. Large e-commerce platforms, including Amazon, eBay and Alibaba, have also begun to offer online credits to their registered users. Having access to the history of transactions, they can assess the default risks of the users and provide them with tailored offers.

In this fierce competition, survival has become technology driven. The incumbents who were able to survive recognised the power of disruption and began to transform their operations.

Case illustration

Citigroup was the first to embrace digital banking in Tokyo in 2010. The new concept offered instant account opening technology, allowing customers to open an account virtually, without the use of paper documents at their own pace. They were also one of the first banks to use video chat services for interactions with customers. Many banks followed Citigroup with their own version, hence smart banking 1.0 was in place (Lacroix, 2019).

Smart banking is different from online banking. Online banking is essentially a virtual iteration of traditional banking: the same operations take place except they do not happen in a branch office but through a mobile device or computer. In contrast, **smart banking** is about using data for personalised services. In the beginning, smart banking meant taking advantage of technology to remove transactional friction points along the customer journey. But soon, with the rise of big data analytics, AI and machine learning, smart banking began to focus on the aspects of the banking process customers would not see, namely, the supporting infrastructure that allows banks to minimise risk and better understand the financial behaviours and needs of their customers (Lacroix, 2019). This is not surprising, since data are the new currency.

To understand the disruptive power of blockchain, we introduce **bitcoin** first, which is a decentralised, **digital currency** created in January 2009. In 2008, the mysterious and pseudonymous Satoshi Nakamoto published a white paper about the code of the **cryptocurrency** (i.e., cryptography ensures it is secure). The identity of the person or persons who created the technology is still a mystery. The computer code is open source and can be downloaded and analysed by anybody.

Bitcoin is not issued or backed by any banks or governments but is mined. Generally, mining requires solving computationally difficult puzzles and miners are rewarded with some bitcoin (Frankenfield, 2021). The reward is halved every 210,000 blocks, meaning that fewer and fewer bitcoins are released into circulation. The block reward was 50 new bitcoins in 2009. On May 11, 2020, the third halving occurred, bringing the reward for each block discovery down to 6.25 bitcoins. This is bitcoin's way of creating scarcity. As of October 2021, there are about 18.85 million bitcoins already in circulation, leaving just around 2.15 million left to be released via mining rewards (Conway, 2021). Bitcoin is very popular and has triggered the launch of hundreds of other cryptocurrencies, collectively referred to as altcoins. In countries like Venezuela, Argentina or Zimbabwe, which are heavily in debt, bitcoin and other cryptocurrencies are gaining tremendous traction because they give people an option to hedge for a worst-case scenario. Cryptocurrencies enable people to save in a currency that is not dependent on a government (Ashford & Curry, 2021).

Bitcoin uses blockchain technology to record transactions in a decentralised system that is not controlled by any central authority and remains free from government interference (Paul & Sadath, 2021). While initially popularised by bitcoin, blockchain is much more than a foundation for cryptocurrency. It offers a secure way to exchange any kind of good, service or transaction (Ahram et al., 2017).

As Singhal and his co-authors (2018) explain, blockchain is essentially a data structure in the sense that it is a chain of blocks linked together. A block can mean just one single transaction or multiple transactions clubbed together. Once a transaction is recorded in a block, it remains there forever. Moreover, it is not feasible to invert or alter a transaction, because blockchain uses a hash pointer: the hash of the previous block is stored in the header of the current block. Every block points to its previous block, known as "the parent block." Every new block that gets added to the chain becomes the parent block for the next block to be added. It goes all the way to the first block that gets created in the blockchain, which is called "the genesis block." In such a design where blocks are linked back with hashes, it is practically unfeasible for someone to alter data in any block. In addition, blockchain is stored in a network of computers (also referred to as "nodes" or "miners"). Each transaction is validated individually by the nodes, which accept or reject them after checking their authenticity. Once approved, the transaction is logged forever in the existing blockchain and broadcast to other nodes (Figure 12.1).

Anyone – whether they run a Bitcoin "node" or not – can see these transactions occurring in real time. Bitcoin had around 13,768 full nodes, as of mid-November 2021, and this number is growing, making the system immutable (Cortina & Schmukler, 2018).

However, Bitcoin is not without risks. Most individuals who own and use bitcoin have not acquired their tokens through mining operations. Rather, they buy and sell bitcoin and other digital currencies on any of the popular online markets, known as bitcoin exchanges or cryptocurrency exchanges. Such transactions – like any other virtual marketplaces – are subjects of attacks by hackers, malware and operational glitches. If a thief gains access to a bitcoin owner's computer hard drive and steals their private encryption key, they could transfer the stolen bitcoins to another account. Moreover, hackers may attack bitcoin exchanges to gain access to thousands of digital wallets where Bitcoin is stored. In 2014, Mt. Gox – a bitcoin exchange in Japan – was forced to close down after millions of dollars' worth of bitcoin were stolen.

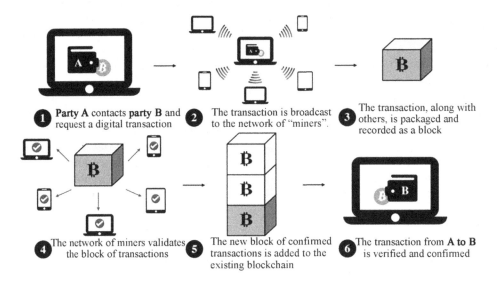

1. **Party A** contacts **party B** and request a digital transaction
2. The transaction is broadcast to the network of "miners".
3. The transaction, along with others, is packaged and recorded as a block
4. The network of miners validates the block of transactions
5. The new block of confirmed transactions is added to the existing blockchain
6. The transaction from **A** to **B** is verified and confirmed

Figure 12.1 How blockchain works (based on Cortina & Schmukler, 2018)

Case illustration

The applicability of blockchain technology is far wider than just recording bitcoin transactions. Other sectors, such as health care, media, government and construction, embraced the technology to come up with innovative solutions that are transparent and immutable thanks to the tamper-proof chain of content running a decentralised network of participating "nodes." Following are a few illustrations of the widespread applicability of blockchain technology:

MedRec provides patients with a transparent and accessible view of their medical history across different health-care providers. As patients move between providers, their data get scattered across different organisations, losing easy access to records. Currently, providers – not patients – are in control of these medical data and patients face significant hurdles in viewing their reports. MedRec was developed using the Ethereum blockchain, a system called "smart contracts" that unifies access to data across disparate providers in the hand of the patients.

Jiocoin, India's biggest conglomerate, has developed a blockchain-based supply chain logistics platform along with its own cryptocurrency, Jiocoin. The company has a massive network of entertainment offerings, including Jio Phones, JioTV, JioNet WiFi, Jio Cinema and Jio Music as well as Jio Money. Throughout the Jio ecosystem, loyalty points can be issued in Jiocoin cryptocurrency and customers can use them for purchases of food, travel, apparel and more (Marr, 2021). Some global banks started collaborating with fintech companies as vendors or partners rather than fighting against them as competitors. Such collaboration can enable the banks to extend their product range and gain access to new markets by making use of cutting-edge platforms and services (Enriques & Ringe, 2020). The former case means that the bank buys a solution from a fintech firm. The latter means deep technical integration, custom builds and co-creation, which is sold by the bank to its customers under the label "powered by" (Scott, 2021). As they reach saturation point in their native digital marketing channels, many fintechs are actively looking for partnerships to grow their business. They bring to the table their higher speed, risk tolerance and flexibility, while banks offer their customer base (Galvin et al., 2018). Thanks to the positive experience with partnerships, the range of new products and services available to users is constantly expanding.

As we have discussed earlier, the fintech revolution was disruptive to the financial sector. The technology enabled a group of individuals to act as investors and collectively provide funds for creative projects, which consequently has radically disrupted the traditional capital sources of business angels, venture capital or private equity firms (Szabó et al., 2021). The next sections discuss crowdfunding and P2P lending, the highly effective financing alternatives in detail.

12.2 Crowdfunding

Lee and Shin (2018) defined six financial technology business models: (1) crowdfunding, (2) peer-to-peer lending, (3) insurance, (4) payments, (5) wealth management and (6) capital markets. In the following, we examine four selected dimensions of the Lean Canvas of crowdfunding and peer-to-peer landing.

After the global economic crisis, the funding capacity of the banking sector decreased, and the options to finance creative projects got even more limited, which particularly heavily affected small companies and artists (Belleflamme et al., 2014; Szabó et al., 2021). In 2001, Brian Camelio, a Grammy winner musician and entrepreneur, launched a platform, ArtiShare, for artists to fund their projects with the general public, who, in return, can get access to extra materials from the artist. This was when the first crowdfunding platform was born. Its success has inspired thousands of similar websites around the world (Lacasse et al., 2016).

There are four main types of crowdfunding models: donation-based, reward-based, equity-based and lending-based (Hossain & Operaocha, 2017). The donation-based model is based on altruism. Funders support causes that are important to them, without any financial compensation (Ahlers et al., 2015). In equity-based models, investors receive equity stakes in exchange for financial support (Belleflamme et al., 2014). In reward-based projects, campaigners offer some kind of material incentives to backers based on the amount offered (Cox & Nguyen, 2018). The lending-based model is discussed separately in section 12.3 because of its importance. An overview of the analysis is in Table 12.1.

The two main segments of customers of crowdfunding platforms can be defined as campaigners and funders (backers). Campaigners include individuals (entrepreneurs), start-ups and small and medium-sized enterprises (SMEs; Kaminski et al., 2018). For start-ups and other innovative projects, financial resources may be provided by family members, friends, business angels and venture capital investors. Tenders and traditional bank loans are also possible financing options for these projects (Kuti & Madarász, 2014). SMEs often have difficulties obtaining funding, partly because of a lack of adequate value for potential investors, and partly because they cannot convince investors about their ideas (Golic, 2014). Entrepreneurs and small businesses are often unable to obtain bank loans and other traditional forms of finance because they lack the appropriate collateral or credit history (Beck et al., 2007). The money required by these small organisations is often too small for venture capital, but too much for family members, and banks may find it too expensive to finance small businesses (Cox & Nguyen, 2018).

Table 12.1 The unique value proposition of crowdfunding

Customer segments	• Campaigners: individuals, start-ups, SMEs
	• Funders
Problems	• Lack of adequate value for potential investors
	• Difficulties persuading investors
	• The money required is too low for venture capital
	• Too costly to monitor small businesses
Existing solutions	• Family and friends
	• Business angels
	• Venture capital
	• Tenders
	• Banks
Unique value proposition	• Improved access to capital
	• Obtaining funding at a much lower cost
	• Reduced barriers to market entry
	• Elimination of economic differences
	• A direct connection between campaigners and backers
	• Direct communication
	• Direct feedback on products: product development proposals
	• Reduced risk for investors
	• The possibility of building an investment portfolio across diverse projects
	• Early access to products
	• Formalised contracts

One of the biggest advantages of crowdfunding platforms is that they provide improved access to capital for entrepreneurs, start-ups and SMEs (Cox & Nguyen, 2018). The lower operational costs of online platforms mean that transaction fees are lower, enabling campaigners to obtain funding at a much lower cost (Agrawal et al., 2013). Access to financial resources from crowdfunding can significantly reduce entry barriers (Revest & Sapio, 2019). According to Agrawal et al. (2011), crowdfunding makes it possible to eliminate economic differences related to geographical distance in the financing of early-stage projects. On crowdfunding platforms, campaigners and backers can interact without a financial intermediary (Mollick, 2014). Thanks to direct communication, e.g., the reward-based model, campaigners can analyse the market potential of their developments and receive direct feedback on their products (Ellman & Hurkens, 2015). They can then use this feedback to develop their products further.

It may be advantageous for these investors to divide their investments across different projects, reducing risk and building an investment portfolio of diverse projects. Funders can also obtain early access to the products. Crowdfunding platforms ensure that contracts are always formalised (Agrawal et al., 2013).

Well-known examples of reward-based crowdfunding are Kickstarter and Indiegogo. Both platforms provide the opportunity to collect funding for a product, project or campaign, covering the unique value proposition opportunities determined in this paper. However, some differences can be identified between the two solutions in terms of the funding scheme, eligible countries, application process, maximum reward and reward levels (Indiegogo, n.d.; Kickstarter, n.d.). These can be significant discriminating factors for customers.

Crowdfunding has many of the main advantages of fintech. It fills a huge funding gap. Companies and individuals can get financial resources faster and obtain rapid feedback on whether their business idea is marketable. As a result, whole new types of innovations can emerge. Without intermediaries, a much closer relationship is created between companies and investors. By supporting fast-growing businesses, crowdfunding solutions can increase GDP and boost economic growth. They can also lead to a more competitive environment, faster information flow and higher capital allocation efficiency. When companies approach investors individually, the flow of information is limited and often less effective in obtaining funds. At the micro-level, crowdfunding can reduce costs and risks and provide more efficient services. However, criminals may use fake companies to collect money, resulting in money laundering. It is also possible for people to support fake causes or those that pose a threat to society (e.g., terrorist financing).

Case illustration

Terraplanter is a modern-life friendly product, which uses no soil – hence no dirt – to keep plants indoors with minimum effort. The innovative idea is based on a ceramic material that has just the right amount of porosity and hygroscopic tendencies to allow water to diffuse through the material and allow the plant to grow on the surface of the product. The product works as a water bank, built with a parametric design that allows plant roots to grip the surface. Moreover, the product is reusable. The crowdfunding campaign was a big hit on Kickstarter: in June 2020, 55,236 backers pledged $6.391.763 to help bring this project to life.

12.3 The peer-to-peer lending

Traditionally, lending and deposit services were core to commercial banking at both retail and wholesale levels. The fintech revolution disrupted their petrified and inflexible business model. The challenge was great because peer-to-peer lending (P2P lending) has opened up new services for many kinds of clientele (especially artists and musicians, ethnic minorities and immigrants and small business people) who failed to meet credit requirements, who were unable to offer appropriate collateral or sufficient amount of personal assets or who lacked business experience (Gomber et al., 2018). Traditional lending was also hampered by bureaucratic banking processes and complicated documentation. Mills and McCarthy (2016) pointed out that the amount of money required by a start-up or small business may also be too small for a bank or a business angel but too big for a friend or family member. In many countries, a high proportion of people do not have a bank account with a financial institution, which can also be a barrier to traditional lending. The lack of bank accounts and the increasing use of mobile phones for payment services also support the spread of fintech solutions, including P2P lending.

Online platforms allow individuals and companies to lend to each other without any other intermediary (Lee, 2016). Zopa was the first lending website, which appeared in 2005 in the United Kingdom. The biggest P2P lending webpages include the Lending Club (USA), Prosper (USA) and Ppdai (China). Several authors consider P2P lending as essentially a crowdfunding business model (e.g., Kuti & Madarász, 2014; Hossain & Operaocha, 2017). However, we have discussed it separately because of its importance and dominance. Fleming and Sorenson (2016) emphasised that P2P lending can be considered as part of a larger phenomenon, including crowdfunded debts. The Lean Canvas analysis is shown in Table 12.2.

P2P lending offers several benefits to both lenders and credit borrowers in response to these issues. One of the major advantages of P2P lending is that credit appraisal is much faster than conventional bank lending. Loan applications filed by borrowers are quickly judged on the platforms, and contracts are formalised (Agrawal et al., 2013). The companies operating the platforms are not tied to legacy banking systems and, therefore, their systems are more innovative, providing better technological conditions for both lenders and borrowers. Their operations are not usually bureaucratic, and the process of lending and documentation is much simpler and more transparent. The popularity of P2P lending is partly because of greater access to credit (e.g., larger amounts can be requested than from family members). Lenders and borrowers are directly matched in the lending platform without an intermediary or interest margin, enabling direct communication between the two parties (Balyuk 2018). There are two ways to bring the two actors together: online auction and automatic matching. In online auctions, borrowers state the amount of money they aim to borrow and the maximum interest rate they are willing to pay, and lenders indicate their minimum expected interest rate. The given minimum rate is set within a specified risk category. The auction will then take place with the platform gradually increasing the interest rate payable

Table 12.2 The unique value proposition of P2P lending

Customer segments	• Borrowers: individuals, start-ups, SMEs
	• Lenders: individuals, companies
Problems	• Lack of transparency
	• Unexpected hidden costs
	• Bureaucratic banking processes
	• Complicated documentation
	• Customers, e.g., start-ups may pose too great a risk
	• The amount of credit required may be too low (for a bank or business angel) or too high (for family and friends)
	• Unbalanced financing system
	• Lack of financing from public banks
	• Lack of bank account
Existing solutions	• Traditional bank lending
	• Business angels
	• Family, friends
Unique value proposition	• A quick assessment of loan applications
	• Formal contracts
	• No legacy systems
	• More innovative technology
	• Reduced bureaucracy
	• Simple, transparent lending process and documentation
	• Greater access to credit
	• Direct matching of lenders and borrowers
	• 24/7 platform availability
	• No prepayment penalties
	• More flexible lending
	• Higher returns
	• Reduced transaction and monitoring costs

on the amount until there are enough bids to fully cover the loan. In automatic matching, the platform links lenders and borrowers based on the interest rates set for each risk category (Tasca et al., 2016). Lenz (2016) also noted that in addition to 24/7 platform availability, many platforms have the option of the early termination of credit agreements without a prepayment penalty, allowing more flexible lending.

One of the biggest advantages for lenders is that the lower operating costs of the platform mean that they can usually get better returns on P2P lending than if they were investing in a traditional bank deposit. The transaction and monitoring costs of creditors can be reduced if platform managers develop appropriate strategies and algorithms to evaluate borrowers.

LendingClub is one of the best-known P2P lending sites. The company offers many types of lending, including personal loans, education and patient finance loans, auto refinance and small business loans. Investors can invest through a variety of channels (e.g., entire loans through purchase agreements and securitisations). The company reported that in 2018, the majority of people received their funds in as little as four days, which is much faster than traditional bank lending (LendingClub Corporation, 2018). LendingClub covers all the unique value proposition opportunities identified in this chapter but does not target SMEs as borrowers, which provides a further development opportunity.

In P2P lending, it is possible to borrow smaller amounts of money and reach previously unbanked customers (financial inclusion). However, intermediaries (e.g., banks), whose additional fees on loans contributed to the economy, are eliminated. Nonetheless, the solution has advantages for the economy, and one of the biggest benefits is that P2P lending increases the speed of money circulation. P2P lending platforms provide easier access for customers to lending services and credit costs can be reduced. However, the potential for money laundering is very high because borrowers may not be properly identified and may use false identities. In this case, the flow of money is not properly monitored and the potential for not repaying the money or committing a financial crime is both highly possible. P2P can also be a threat to banks, reducing their profitability and increasing fragility.

In summary, new online platforms – as a marketplace or peer-to-peer (P2P) lenders – provide increasing amounts of credit to consumers and small and medium enterprises (SMEs) by simply connecting the lenders with borrowers without bearing default risks. Most of the loans come from a wide range of investors (including financial institutions). These lending platforms have no retail branches and typically provide faster loan applications and smaller, shorter-term loans than banks. They also replace traditional credit scoring models with machine learning and algorithms based on big data mining to assess credit risk, which not only lowers the costs but also accelerates the approval process (Cortina & Schmukler, 2018).

Review questions

1. Why is fintech a disruptive innovation?
2. What are the differences between a physical currency (euro, dollar, etc.) and a digital currency (bitcoin, etc.)?
3. Why is blockchain immutable?
4. What are the best-known financial technology business models?
5. Why are crowdfunding business models needed by customers?
6. Why are peer-to-peer lending business models needed by customers?

Discussion questions

1. Explain how fintech has revolutionised the financial sector.
2. What features make blockchain technology applicable in the value chain, health sector or construction management?
3. Explain how blockchain works. Explain how the hash pointer can prevent tampering with data in the blockchain.
4. Discuss in small groups what the next idea could be for a kickstarter crowdfunding campaign.

Note

1 Robo-advisory service: automated investment proposals with little or no human intervention based on pre-defined parameters in accordance with the customers' investment goals, financial background and aversion to risk (Deloitte, 2015).

Bibliography

Agrawal, A. K., Catalini, C., & Goldfarb, A. (2011). *The geography of crowdfunding.* NBER WORKING PAPER SERIES. *(No. 16820).* Retrieved from w16820.pdf (nber.org)

Agrawal, A. K., Catalini, C., & Goldfarb, A. (2013). *Some simple economics of crowdfunding.* NBER WORKING PAPER SERIES. *(No. 19133).* Retrieved from w19133.pdf (nber.org)

Ahlers, G., Cumming, D. J., Guenther, C., & Schweizer, D. (2015). Signaling in equity crowdfunding. *Entrepreneurship Theory and Practice, 39*(4), 955–980.

Ahram, T., Sargolzaei, A., Sargolzaei, S., Daniels, J., & Amaba, B. (2017). Blockchain technology innovations. *Technology and Engineering Management Society Conference (TEMSCON)* (pp. 137–141). https://doi.org/10.1109/TEMSCON.2017.7998367

Alt, R., Beck, R., & Smits, M. T. (2018). FinTech and the transformation of the financial industry. *Electronic Markets, 28*(3), 235–243. https://doi.org/10.1007/S12525-018-0310-9/FIGURES/2

Ashford, K., & Curry, B. (2021, October 26). *What is bitcoin and how does it work? – Forbes advisor.* Forbes. Com. Retrieved from https://www.forbes.com/advisor/investing/what-is-bitcoin

Balyuk, T. (2018). *Financial innovation and borrowers: Evidence from peer-to-peer lending.* Issue Working Paper No. 2802220.

Beck, T., Demirguc-Kunt, A., & Peria, M. S. M. (2007). Reaching out: Access to and use of banking services across countries. *Journal of Financial Economics, 85*(1), 234–266.

Belleflamme, P., Lambert, T., & Schwienbacher, A. (2014). Crowdfunding. Tapping the right crowd. *Journal of Business Venturing, 29*(5), 585–609.

Brown, D. (2020, January 6). *Are millennials and Gen Z powering a FinTech revolution? | The edge volume 4 | Cushman & Wakefield.* Cushman and Wakefiled. Retrieved from https://www.cushmanwakefield .com/en/insights/the-edge/are-millennials-and-gen-z-powering-a-fintech-revolution

Brown, R., Maswon, S., & Rowe, A. (2018). Start-ups, entrepreneurial networks and equity crowdfunding: A processual perspective. *Industrial Marketing Management, 80*, 115–125. doi:10.1016/j. indmarman.2018.02.003

Chemmanur, T. J., & Fulghieri, P. (2014). Entrepreneurial finance and innovation: An introduction and agenda for future research. *The Review of Financial Studies, 27*(1), 1–19.

Christensen, C. M.. (n.d.). *Disruptive innovations.* Christensen Institute. Retrieved January 25, 2022, from https://www.christenseninstitute.org/disruptive-innovations/

Comming, D., & Hornuf, L. (2018). *The economics of crowdfunding: Startups, portals and investor behavior.* Palgrave Macmillan.

Conway, L. (2021). *Bitcoin halving: What you need to know.* Investopedia.Com. Retrieved from https:// www.investopedia.com/bitcoin-halving-4843769

Cortina, J. J., & Schmukler, S. L. (2018). The fintech revolution: A threat to global banking? In *Research and policy brief* (Issue 14). https://remittanceprices.worldbank.org.

Cox, J., & Nguyen, T. (2018). Does the crowd mean business? An analysis of rewards-based crowdfunding as a source of finance for start-ups and small businesses. *Journal of Small Business and Enterprise Development, 25*(1), 147–162.

Ellman, M., & Hurkens, S. (2015). *Optimal crowdfunding design.* No. 871; Barcelona GSE Working Paper Series.

Enriques, L., & Ringe, W.-G. (2020). Bank-fintech partnerships, outsourcing arrangements and the case for a mentorship regime. *Capital Markets Law Journal, 15*(4), 374–397. Retrieved from https://ssrn .com/abstract_id=3625578https://ecgi.global/content/working-papers

Flanigan, S. T. (2017). Crowdfunding and diaspora philanthropy: An integration of the literature and major concepts. *Voluntas, 28*(2), 492–509.

Fleming, L., & Sorenson, O. (2016). Financing by and for the masses: An introduction to the special issue on crowdfunding. *California Management Review, 58*(2), 5–19.

Frankenfield, J. (2021). *Bitcoin definition.* Investopedia.Com. Retrieved from https://www.investopedia .com/terms/b/bitcoin.asp

Galvin, J., Han, F., Hynes, S., Qu, J., Rajgopal, K., & Shek, A. (2018). *Synergy and disruption: Ten trends shaping fintech.* McKinsey Digital.

Gimpel, H., Rau, D., & Röglinger, M. (2018). Understanding FinTech start-ups – A taxonomy of consumer-oriented service offerings. *Electronic Markets, 28*(3), 245–264. https://doi.org/10.1007/ S12525-017-0275-0/TABLES/7

Global FinTech market report 2021: Market was valued at $7301.78 billion in 2020 – Forecast to 2026. (2021). Yahoo!Finance. Retrieved from https://finance.yahoo.com/news/global-fintech-market -report-2021-130300659.html

Goldstein, I., Jiang, W., & Karolyi, G. A. (2019). To FinTech and beyond. *The Review of Financial Studies, 32*(5), 1647–1661. https://doi.org/10.1093/RFS/HHZ025

Golic, Z. (2014). Advantages of Crodfunding as an alternative source of financing of small and medium-sized enterprises. *Proceedings of the Faculty of Economics in East Sarajevo, 8,* 39–48.

Gomber, P., Kauffman, R. J., Parker, C., & Weber, B. W. (2018). On the Fintech revolution: Interpreting the forces of innovation, disruption and transformation in financial services. *Journal of Management Information Systems, 35*(1), 220–265. Retrieved from https://ink.library.smu.edu.sg/sis_research

Gozman, D., Liebenau, J., & Mangan, J. (2018). The innovation mechanisms of Fintech start-ups: Insights from SWIFT's Innotribe competition. *Journal of Management Information Systems, 35*(1), 145–179. https://doi.org/10.1080/07421222.2018.1440768

Hossain, M., & Operaocha, G. O. (2017). Crowdfunding: Motives, definitions, typology and ethical challenges. *Entrepreneurship Research Journal, 7*(2), 1–41. https://doi.org/10.2139/ssrn.2674532

Indiegogo. (n.d.). *Official website.* Retrieved from https://www.indiegogo.com/

Kaminski, J., Hopp, C., & Tykvová, T. (2018). New technology assessment in entrepreneurial financing – Does crowdfunding predict venture capital investments? *Technological Forecasting & Social Change.* Retrieved from https://doi.org/10.1016/j.techfore.2018.11.015

Kickstarter. (n.d.). *Official website.* Retrieved from https://www.kickstarter.com/

Kuti, M., & Madarász, G. (2014). A közösségi finanszírozás. *Pénzügyi Szemle, 59*(3), 374–385.

Lacasse, R. M., Lambert, B. A., Osmani, E., Couture, C., Roy, N., Sylvain, J., & Nadeau, F. (2016). A digital tsunami: FinTech and crowdfunding. *International Scientific Conference on Digital Intelligence* (pp. 1–5).

Lacroix, J.-P. (2019). *The three phases of smart banking.* Sld.Com. Retrieved from https://www.sld.com/ blog/brand-strategy/the-future-of-banking-is-smart/

Lee, I. (2016). Fintech: Ecosystem and business models. *Advanced Science and Technology Letters, 142,* 57–62.

Lee, I., & Shin, Y. J. (2018). Fintech: Ecosystem, business models, investment decisions, and challenges. *Business Horizons, 61*(1), 35–46. https://doi.org/10.1016/j.bushor.2017.09.003

Lee, N., Sameen, H., & Cowling, M. (2015). Access to finance for innovative SMEs since the financial crisis. *Research Policy, 44*(2), 370–380.

Lee, S., & Persson, P. (2016). Financing from family and friends. *The Review of Financial Studies, 29*(9), 2341–2386.

LendingClub Corporation. (2018). *Annual report on form 10-K*. Retrieved from 10-K (sec.gov)

Lenz, R. (2016). Peer-to-Peer lending – Opportunities and risks. *European Journal of Risk and Regulation, 7*(4), 1–21.

Marr, B. (2021). *35 amazing real world examples of how blockchain is changing our world | Bernard Marr.* Bernardmarr.Com. Retrieved from https://bernardmarr.com/35-amazing-real-world-examples-of -how-blockchain-is-changing-our-world/

McBride, S., & Niblock, I. (2017). *Peer-to-peer lending investor guide. Innovating an ancient credit model.* Retrieved from Microsoft Word - P2P Lending Guide Final Edition.docx (crowdfundinsider.com)

Mills, K. G., & McCarthy, B. (2016). *The state of small business lending: Innovation and technology and the implications for regulation* (Working Paper 17-042).

Milne, A., & Parboteeah, P. (2016). *The business models and economics of peer-to-peer lending* (Issue 17).

Mollick, E. (2014). The dynamics of crowdfunding: An exploratory study. *Journal of Business Venturing, 29*(1), 1–16. https://doi.org/10.1016/j.jbusvent.2013.06.005

Nakamoto, S. (2008). *Bitcoin: A peer-to-peer electronic cash system.* Retrieved from www.bitcoin.org

Noya, E. (2019, July 30). *The fintech revolution: Who are the new competitors in banking?* Forbes.Com. Retrieved from https://www.forbes.com/sites/esade/2019/07/30/the-fintech-revolution-who-are -the-new-competitors-in-banking/?sh=4fb23bf61161

Paul, L. R., & Sadath, L. (2021). A systematic analysis on FinTech and its applications. *International Conference on Innovative Practices in Technology and Management* (ICIPTM) (pp. 1–7). https://doi.org /10.1109/ICIPTM52218.2021.9388371

Pierrakis, Y., & Collins, L. (2013). *Banking on each other. Peer-to-peer lending to business: Evidence from funding circle.* Retreived from (PDF) Banking on each other: peer-to-peer lending to business: evidence from funding circle (researchgate.net)

Revest, V., & Sapio, A. (2019). Alternative equity markets and firm creation. *Journal of Evolutionary Economics, 29*(3), 1083–1118. Retrieved from https://doi.org/10.1007/s00191-019-00618-x

Rose, S., Wentzel, D., Hopp, C., & Kaminski, J. (2018). The influence of product maturity and innovativeness of consumers' perceived uncertainty in reward-based crowdfunding. *AMA Winter Academic Conference.*

Scott, B. (2021, November 5). *Embracing fintech collaboration | ABA banking journal.* ABA Banking Journal. Retrieved from https://bankingjournal.aba.com/2021/11/embracing-fintech-collaboration/

Singhal, B., Dhameja, G., & Panda, P. S. (2018). How blockchain works. In *Beginning blockchain* (pp. 31–148). Apress. https://doi.org/10.1007/978-1-4842-3444-0_2

Szabó, R. Z. S., Szász, R., & Szedmák, B. (2021). Demand and supply sides of the crowdfunding ecosystem: The case of Kickstarter campaigns and potential Hungarian investors. *Society and Economy, 43*(2), 165–183. https://doi.org/10.1556/204.2021.00008

Tasca, P., Aste, T., Pelizzon, L., & Perony, N. (2016). *Banking beyond banks and money. A guide to banking services in the twenty-first century.* Springer.

Zhang, H., Zhao, H., Liu, Q., Xu, T., Chen, E., & Huang, X. (2018). Finding potential lenders in P2P lending: A hybrid random walk approach. *Information Sciences, 432,* 376–391. https://doi.org/10 .1016/j.ins.2017.12.017

Part III

Smart environments

13 Smart cities

Máté Szilárd Csukás and Zsolt Roland Szabó

The megatrends of population growth, climate change and digital transformation are creating a shifting global environment where the role of cities is growing. This phenomenon generates both challenges and opportunities, and it has drawn attention to the role of cities and their inhabitants. This trend has culminated in the growing popularity and influence of the smart city (SC) concept. There is no commonly agreed formal definition of this term, but it is generally accepted that it describes the deliberate and coordinated use of advanced technology, usually information and communication technology (ICT) by city governments for the benefit of the city's inhabitants and businesses. According to the European Commission, a smart city goes beyond the use of digital technologies for better resource use and fewer emissions. It means smarter urban transport networks, upgraded water supply and waste disposal facilities and more efficient ways to light and heat buildings. It also means a more interactive and responsive city administration, safer public spaces and better abilities to meet the needs of an ageing population (European Commission, n.d.).

This chapter discusses the transformation we witness in city administration and operation due to I4.0. In addition, we apply Porter's Five Forces model to analyse and evaluate smart city solutions.

13.1 Why do cities need to be smart?

Rosemann et al. (2021) emphasise that cities are **complex socio-material systems** with plenty of stakeholders, where citizens are often viewed as customers. As public systems, cities focus on the provision of a variety of essential services (e.g., transport, energy, safety, entertainment) that everyone can access (lack of exclusivity) and without competition between citizens (lack of rivalry). Goods that lack exclusivity and rivalry are called public goods.

According to experts' estimates, about 70% of the world's population will live in cities by 2050. This trend of **urbanisation** predicts an exponential increase in the complexity of the challenges cities are already facing: from traffic congestion, environmental damage, inadequate and outdated infrastructure, non-scalable health care and education systems, social disaggregation and poverty to limited resources, such as water, energy, health care and housing (Rosemann et al., 2021). The consequence of rapid and often uncontrolled urbanisation is that emissions and energy usage will continue to rise with every passing year. That is why the need for smarter urban transport networks, environment-friendly water disposal facilities and buildings with high energy efficiency is more critical than ever.

DOI: 10.4324/9781003390312-16

In 2018, it was estimated that 158 billion USD of public funding would be invested in smart city initiatives in 2022, which is almost double as compared to the forecasted 95.8 billion USD investment in 2019. Despite the potential, SC investments often failed to deliver the expected impact. The concept has been criticised for being too technocratic and neglecting essential aspects of urban development. Angelidou (2015) argued that one reason SC developments drifted away from the fundamentals is the complexity of the stakeholder ecosystem. The way cities engage with the SC concept and adopt SC solutions is complex, involving interactions between different forces and conflicting interests. These conflicts are captured by the notion of technology "push" and application "pull". Technology "push" describes the concept of the diversity of products and services, developed and marketed by vendors and supplied to the public. In contrast, application "pull" comes from local governments, which demand solutions to ensure that their city remains competitive and attractive.

Implementing a smart city initiative means not only reaching technological success but also using technology to create public value (Dameri, 2013). Yet, early efforts of smart city investments often ignored citizens' needs. The smartness of a city is achieved when the human and social capital is combined through participatory governance (Sánchez-Corcuera et al., 2019). Suppliers of technologies, such as IBM and Cisco, recognised that shortfall and provided solutions that enable **citizen engagement** and inclusivity (Trencher, 2019).

Citizens tend to have a utility-oriented view, and the "smartness" of their consumption is qualified based on the capability of the solution to eliminate citizens' former restrictions, which inhibited the consumption of a service. For example, the emergence of over-the-top solutions like WhatsApp, Viber, Skype or Zoom eradicated communication costs and therefore an economic restriction (affordability) to engage in a conversation disappeared.

Concerning citizens' participation in SC planning, researchers found that lack of trust, lack of transparency and lack of knowledge often inhibit true citizen engagement. It is critical to better understand local social dynamics, how civic participation works, who is included or excluded, who benefits and who loses, in addition to understanding the ambitions of each service provider (Webster & Leleux, 2018).

Case illustration

The development of a park took place with the involvement of the locals. Community planning brought together people from the neighbourhood, local NGOs, local government representatives and planners. They met five times. In these community plans, anyone could express their desires and needs about the park, and thus the park was designed step by step. The multifunctional community park is very popular amongst locals (Obvf.hu, 2017).

Nevertheless, a growing population means an increase in the complexity of managing cities efficiently and effectively. With the ongoing fourth industrial revolution, the solution was evident: a technologically driven, largely automated city can overcome the majority of efficiency, effectiveness and complexity-related challenges almost at once. Moreover, experts agreed that growing "smartness" will eventually mean that cities develop into more attractive places for the different segments of society. Today, smart cities offer benefits in terms of:

- Efficiency
- Citizen (stakeholder) engagement

- Quality of life
- Inclusivity
- Connectivity
- Knowledge creation and management
- Cost reduction
- Scalability and transferability
- Sustainable economic growth
- Sustainable management of natural resources

Similarly, restrictions to accessing information have disappeared with the availability of search engines.

Case illustrations

Helsinki is one of the top ten smartest cities in the world. The city set the ambitious goal to be completely carbon neutral and reduce its traffic emissions by 69% by 2035. With transitioning the entire city bus fleet to electric and expanding its Metro and electric car charging networks the implementation is on the right track. Since heating accounts for more than half of Helsinki's emissions, the city promotes the use of energy-efficient materials and solutions during renovations as well as promotes the use of renewable energy sources used in the city's buildings.

For Zurich, it all started with a streetlight project. The city introduced a series of streetlights that adapted to traffic levels using sensors, which increased their brightness or dim accordingly. The project enabled an energy saving of up to 70%. Since then, Zurich expanded its smart streetlights across the city and established a greater range of sensory technologies that can collect environmental data, measure the flow of traffic and act as a public Wi-Fi antenna.

Seoul is known for its innovativeness in helping the city's ageing population, as a safety initiative was launched in aid of senior citizens who live alone. When there is no movement detected over a certain period or if abnormal temperature, humidity or lighting are picked up by environmental sensors, relevant emergency services would be contacted immediately. Moreover, Seoul invested in a data platform creating an AI detective to flag potential crime patterns. Today, the Korean capital is also among the first cities to utilise 5G technology in mobility and transportation (Earth.org, 2021).

The first smart zebra crossing in Hungary, which detects pedestrians with various sensors and signals to motorists, operates in Debrecen. There are smart zebra crossings in seven locations in the city, and there are 30 in operation nationwide (VilágGazdaság, 2019).

13.2 Analysis of SC using Porter's Five Forces model

In the following, we present the attractiveness of SC solutions through the practical use of Porter's Five Forces model, discussed in Chapter 2. This model is an excellent tool for analysing the intensity of competition between different SC providers. The model describes the industrial structure as a determinant of profitability in the industry. It can be interpreted as a tool to determine drivers and barriers of SC developments by identifying the demand side of SC solutions (the bargaining power of SCs) and the necessary resources for the enabling environment to deploy SC solutions (bargaining power of suppliers). Before describing the model in detail, it is important to note that, in this sense, SC providers are often caught in the grip, as on the one hand, SCs are the buyers of SC solutions, but, on the other hand, they are also the providers of the enabling environment in which SC solutions operate (Figure 13.1).

The analysis of industry rivalry: The global market size is huge and growing. The expected size of the market will grow from 529.55 billion USD in 2017 to 1944.67 billion USD in 2023. This means an average annual growth rate above 20% (Orbis Research, 2018).

The reason for the rapid growth of the market is, on the one hand, the continuous expansion of the needs of existing SCs and, on the other hand, the number of new customers. As market penetration is still low, there are many opportunities for SC providers to grow and achieve higher profits.

Since the market is still in a phase of fragmentation, there are many players present, from big technology giants to start-ups with a few founders and employees. There is currently a struggle over which technology platform may be the right platform. Individual services are still difficult to compare.

Multinational SC providers (e.g., T-Systems) are trying to use their leverage on governments and municipalities and deliver their solutions in all elements of the value chain. This is, of course, sometimes carried out by subcontractors, but the behavioural pattern is similar in several cities. It is not rare that a successfully implemented SC solution by a smaller company is forcefully removed and implemented again by a large provider with political support.

Besides, a growing number of consulting companies are present in the SC solutions market, but they do not yet possess a strong market position.

Rivalry in megacities is high as the stakes are high. Global firms are building strongholds in megacities to build up technological credibility and global prestige. These projects may sacrifice short-term profits over building strong strategic positions.

Most of the megacities are located in developing markets. Besides, SC developments in Europe gain an increasing amount of public attention (Bibri & Krogstie, 2017). In the European context, smaller companies or even start-ups can offer relevant SC solutions

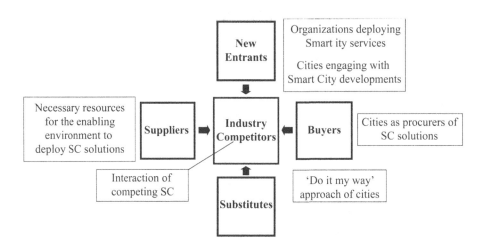

Figure 13.1 Porter's Five Forces model on smart cities (based on Csukás and Szabó, 2021, p. 9)

for cities, especially for medium-sized cities, even with limited resources and solid profit rates. Embeddedness and lobbying capabilities are also key attributes of successful growth in SC solution markets.

Moreover, a conceivable SC solution has a higher chance of adoption in a city; at the same time, there is a higher chance that other cities start copying it and competing with it. The SC concept is still relatively new, and only a few medium-sized cities have a clear SC strategy. Furthermore, even capitals are lacking knowledgeable staff for SC developments. Commonly, each city has its own SC definition and, thus, SC developments are biased because the decision-makers' perception is that they are already smart.

The analysis of the bargaining power of buyers: SC solution providers offer their products and services to municipalities. This might be a complex transaction including many actors (e.g., the government, development agencies, research institutes, etc.). In the following, we simplify the transaction to two parties, the SC solution provider and the city, and the analysis to "switching costs", "backward integration" and "buyer information about supplier products".

The lower the bargaining power of buyers, the higher the profitability of an industry segment. Switching costs are the main tool to lower the bargaining power of buyers in general, and, in particular, in the case of SC developments.

Vendor lock-in is the phenomenon in which suppliers deploy technologies to cities (e.g., broadband networks, energy grids or CCTV, etc.), which are knowledge and capital-intensive, long-lasting with low depreciation and amortisation. Once such an SC solution is selected and subsequently implemented, switching to another SC solution or a vendor would incur very high costs and risks.

Furthermore, as we pointed out earlier, the market is fragmented and there are still no standards. This results in the reliability of SC solutions being questioned. In a fast-growing market situation, developments should be rapid in order to avoid cities being locked into outdated and inefficient SC solutions. The business case of SC solutions is usually not well established and tailored to the special needs of a particular complex municipal environment. This often leads to decision-makers preferring to postpone SC projects, which, in turn, is even worse. Smaller projects could be easily adopted, which means that the benefits are also smaller or even insignificant in many cases and, therefore, they are not worth the effort on their own.

Backward integration means in this context that a city is developing its SC solution on its own. The buyer may also do the work themselves by setting up a staff or project team of local experts. One scenario is that the city establishes a publicly owned company, a foundation or an internal office in its administration to do the job.

Besides, buyer information about SC solutions is also important. Decision-makers in cities are not polymaths, they cannot be experts in every field of SC. A huge SC department is also rare, especially in the case of medium-sized cities. As of today, SC solutions are mainly technological and hard to understand, city-specific challenges are rarely referenced and there are concerns about the transparency of the added value. Eventually, technological giants focus on megacities and large and fast-growing markets, and they seldom commit resources to innovation in a smaller country or a medium-sized city (Boda, 2017). This limits the bargaining power of medium-sized cities, but it also leaves an opportunity for smaller and local SC solution providers.

Finally, the hands of decision-makers are often tied by the budgetary council, the mayor or the central government. All of them have initiatives for keeping down expenses or avoiding indebtedness, which leads to price sensitivity or budget limits to SC solutions.

For example, in Hungary local governments can be involved in debt generation only if they are permitted by the central government (Lentner, 2014). Furthermore, in the central and eastern European region, governments favour specific SC solution providers and, therefore, the choice for cities is limited.

The analysis of the bargaining power of suppliers: As we stated earlier, cities are also considered suppliers for SC solution providers because they provide the enabling environment for these solutions. Besides, organisations engaged in deploying SC solutions are technology giants or newcomers from emerging industries, where employees face complex problems that can be solved only by employing higher and more general knowledge (Boda, 2017).

Knowledgeable and specialised experts (individuals or service firms) are also required for SC development projects; consequently, capitals and central regions are in a more advantageous position than cities in the countryside, where scarce expert resources are harder to access. High-value experts are concentrated in the for-profit sector and, therefore, cities and non-profit organisations face a huge competence gap. The most valued SC experts have diverse skill sets and competencies, including business and management, engineering and sustainability-related expertise (García et al., 2015).

Another group of suppliers are the data providers for SC development. Data are required in quantity, and excellent quality, and must be up to date, accessible and reliable. Data issues are uniformly considered to be the most important hindering factor in deploying SC solutions. Decisions and initiatives based on inaccurate or missing data are extremely costly and lead to a significant disadvantage to the development of the city in the long run as well (Nagy et al., 2016).

Big data analysis is an extremely important precondition for urban development decisions; however, the area in the SC context lags in the business context (business intelligence) and is still in its infancy. Another hindering factor is that data about cities are in many cases in the hand of external owners and providers, who are usually reluctant to provide data and offer limited cooperation with many mistakes.

The threat of new entrants: The SC solutions providers' industry segment is a lucrative market with low entry barriers. Therefore, it is no surprise that from start-ups to large companies, including public and private market actors, a wide range of organisations are increasingly engaged in this industry segment. However, staying in the market is not easy either, as it is not enough to implement the first project, it is necessary to constantly develop and acquire new projects as well. This requires economies of scale, and large technology giants are advantageous in this regard.

Economies of scale are a special attribute that differentiates medium-sized cities from larger ones, especially from megacities, which are the focus of the largest and most competent multinational SC solution providers (e.g., IBM, Cisco).

Medium-sized cities are left for local and smaller providers and thus, most new entrants can be found in these cities. Profitability and the shortage of the required local knowledge and capabilities are an issue for them. If they cannot grow fast enough, they might be out of business relatively soon.

Besides, it is a double-edged sword, meaning that smaller/medium-sized cities will not get the required treatment from large suppliers and, therefore, local players or the establishment of their own SC solution providers are needed. But it has its dark side, as smaller buyers cannot access the most innovative solutions, and they have to rely on less innovative and less competent service providers.

High-end SC solutions and service quality, product differentiation and high brand awareness build customer loyalty (McNeill, 2015) which creates high barriers for new entrants that increases vendor lock-in and the profitability of the industry segment.

The threat of substitutes: There are two main substitutes for SC solution providers. The first one is when cities build their excellence centres with suitable capacities to deal with SC developments. They hire experts and specialists or found an organisation (company, foundation, project organisation, etc.) owned by the municipality and assign every single related issue to this organisation. This situation is very unlikely in the case of small and medium-sized cities presently, due to the complexity of SC developments and the shortage of experts.

In the second case, responsibilities are assigned to a local/regional development agency. These agencies provide important capacities and targets for knowledge spillovers, but they often fail to attract fitting experts and operate under reduced scope without the appropriate authorisation.

Review questions

1. How has urbanisation accelerated the need for cities to become smart?
2. Why do experts criticise early efforts of smart city developments?
3. What are the main benefits of SC solutions?
4. How would you summarise the key points of Porter's Five Forces model for SC solutions?

Discussion questions

1. Based on your expertise, what could be an attractive opportunity for you to gain from the lucrative market conditions of SC developments?
2. As a decision-maker for the city you live in, how would you boost the city's smartness?
3. Do you know local initiatives that utilised citizens' engagement? Why is it challenging to pull it together?

Bibliography

Angelidou, M. (2015). Smart cities: A conjuncture of four forces. *Cities*, *47*, 95–106. http://doi.org/10.1016/j.cities.2015.05.004

Bibri, S.E., & Krogstie, J. (2017). Smart sustainable cities of the future: An extensive interdisciplinary literature review. *Sustainable Cities and Society*, *31*, 183–212. http://doi.org/10.1016/j.scs.2017.02.016

Csukás, M. S., & Szabó, R. Z. (2021). The many faces of the smart city: Differing value propositions in the activity portfolios of nine cities. *Cities*, *112*, 1–16. http://doi.org/10.1016/j.cities.2021.103116

Dameri, R. P. (2013). Searching for smart city definition: A comprehensive proposal. *International Journal of Computers & Technology*, *11*(5), 2544–2551. https://doi.org/10.24297/ijct.v11i5.1142

Earth.org. (2021). *Top 7 smart cities in the world.* Retrieved from https://earth.org/top-7-smart-cities-in-the-world/

European Commission. (n.d.). *Smart cities.* Retrieved from https://ec.europa.eu/info/eu-regional-and-urban-development/topics/cities-and-urban-development/city-initiatives/smart-cities_en

Gil-Garcia, J. R., Pardo, T. A., & Nam, T. (2015). What makes a city smart? Identifying core components and proposing an integrative and comprehensive conceptualization. *Information Polity*, *20*(1), 61–87. http://doi.org/10.3233/IP-150354

György, B. (2017). Mi lesz a munka társadalmával, ha a munkát egyre nagyobb mértékben helyettesítik a gépek. *Munkaügyi Szemle, 60*(1), 4–10.

Lentner, C. (2014). The debt consolidation of Hungarian local governments. *Public Finance Quarterly, 59*(3), 310–325.

McNeill, D. (2015). Global firms and smart technologies: IBM and the reduction of cities. *Transactions of the Institute of British Geographers, 40*(4), 562–574. http://doi.org/10.1111/tran.12098

Nagy, Z., Szendi, D., & Tóth, G. (2016). Opportunities for adaptation of the smart city concept-a regional approach. *Theory Methodology Practice: Club Of Economics In Miskolc, 12*(2), 87–93. http://doi .org/10.18096/TMP.2016.02.08

Obvf.hu. (2017). *Mészkő utcai park*. Retrieved from https://obvf.hu/projects/meszko/

Orbis Research. (2018). *Global Smart Cities Market-Analysis of Growth: Trends and Forecasts (2018– 2023)*. Retrieved May 2018, from http://orbisresearch.com/reports/index/global-smart-cities -marketanalysis-of-growth-trends-and-forecasts-2018-2023

Rosemann, M., Becker, J., & Chasin, F. (2021). City 5.0. *Business and Information Systems Engineering, 63*(1), 71–77. https://doi.org/10.1007/S12599-020-00674-9/FIGURES/1

Sánchez-Corcuera, R., Nuñ Ez-Marcos, A., Sesma-Solance, J., Bilbao-Jayo, A., Mulero, R., Zulaika, U., Azkune, G., & Almeida, A. (2019). Smart cities survey: Technologies, application domains and challenges for the cities of the future. *International Journal of Distributed Sensor Networks, 15*(6). https:// doi.org/10.1177/1550147719853984

Trencher, G. (2019). Towards the smart city 2.0: Empirical evidence of using smartness as a tool for tackling social challenges. *Technological Forecasting and Social Change, 142*(October 2017), 117–128. https://doi.org/10.1016/j.techfore.2018.07.033

VilágGazdaság. (2019). *Már készül Debrecen smart city stratégiája*. Retrieved from https://www.vg.hu/ vilaggazdasag-magyar-gazdasag/2019/03/mar-keszul-debrecen-smart-city-strategiaja

Webster, C. W. R., & Leleux, C. (2018). Smart governance: Opportunities for technologically-mediated citizen co-production. *Information Polity, 23*(1), 95–110. https://doi.org/10.3233/IP-170065

14 Construction 4.0

Orsolya Heidenwolf and Roland Zsolt Szabó

The advent of I4.0 brought about changes in the construction industry as well. Traditionally, the construction industry was male-dominated, time-consuming and manual labour-intensive. Thanks to I4.0 this is fundamentally changing. Today for example, rather than building everything on-site using traditional methods, industry leaders gradually replace labour with smart technology to complete the work more efficiently and effectively.

The great promise of the Construction 4.0 revolution lies in the almost complete automation of the entire project life cycle. Thanks to I4.0 solutions, it is becoming possible to offer personalised, smart and connected building products. Such transformation cannot happen overnight, of course, the industry must overcome its hurdles first.

This chapter will introduce the concept of construction 4.0 to the readers in more detail.

14.1 The digitised construction value chain

According to Oesterreich and Teuteberg (2016), Building information modelling (BIM) laid the foundations for a real start to the Fourth Industrial Revolution in the construction industry, providing a new venue for multiple businesses to collaborate on digital platforms. Since construction 4.0 is still an evolving concept, and the definition of Construction 4.0 is under debate presently, this book understands it as the use of digital innovation for improving construction, the reduction of lead times and waste materials and the lowering of carbon emissions. Construction 4.0 is not limited to design and construction but also covers building operations and building afterlife management.

BIM technology created the opportunity for the traditional construction value chain (design, build, operation and rebuild or demolition) to move towards a digital platform. In the case of smart cities, operations will be expanded by optimising and integrating a built environment that can reflect people's changing needs (Centre for Digital Built Britain, 2018).

Elements such as 3D libraries, quality control, cost estimation, transparent design, visualisation, collision testing, the Common Data Environment (CDE) and environmentally friendly solutions for sustainable development are involved in the design.

In addition to innovative manufacturing solutions and expanded logistics, integrated BIM solutions, systematic data, mobile applications linking subprocesses, fault list facilitation technologies and innovative solutions are all involved in the early stages of projects (which specifically support lean construction process), along with a 4D design, which supports projects with scheduling scenarios.

DOI: 10.4324/9781003390312-17

A special role is given to the appropriate data flow between the project phases (Whyte & Lobo, 2010), which helps to ensure that building management works can be planned and monitored as well as carried out safely. These topics were addressed in detail by Gao and Pishdad-Bozorgi (2019).

Greater emphasis will also be placed on the renovation, reconstruction and demolition of buildings. New eco-friendly technologies are also appearing in recycling, life cycle analysis, demolition processes and point cloud BIM models.

The integration needed to build smart cities includes, among other things, how the built environment can improve the quality of life of city dwellers and how this information can be used to design and build economic and social infrastructures (Whyte, 2019). Technologies and services that link data flow from the design phase to integration are of paramount value. Growing data and data management facilitates the emergence of human-centred infrastructure solutions, which are also important factors for society and the environment (Engin et al., 2019). In addition, the fourth Industrial Revolution also creates many values by digitising existing assets.

This significantly segmented market faces several challenges at the project, company and technology levels. Market participants will be forced to work much more closely together than at present. Together, they need to make project-level decisions that require a high degree of change management for multiple businesses. Decisions need to be backed up by economic and strategic tools that demonstrate the effectiveness of technology transfer and provide guidance on how to implement value-added technologies in businesses. In addition to the innovative corporate culture, middle and senior management with the right IT knowledge and a skilled workforce also play an important role in creating value. Many multinational giants have already shown that firms with the right technological knowledge have significantly higher market value than their competitors, and an employee can create significantly more value in these firms (Makridakis, 2017).

14.2 Construction 4.0 technologies

In the context of Construction 4.0, the issue of data and its management is a central drive of the development of the industry. The amount, variety and speed of real-time data from sensors and other Cyber-Physical Systems (CPS) also induce further and significant innovation. Due to the strong need for collaboration in the construction industry, new solutions are needed to complement existing business platforms, such as partner-finding platforms that offer new innovative services and products that connect construction to smart factories as well as interconnect smart buildings and cities resulting in an intelligent, efficient and effective operation.

Currently, Construction 4.0 technologies can be grouped into four different clusters: (1) the various software platforms available on the market, (2) solutions that facilitate profession-specific human–computer interaction, (3) a technology layer to support digital and physical integration and (4) related sensors and devices.

The central element of digital transformation is the software platform, the main element of which is the BIM model. The combination of cloud-based collaboration and BIM creates the opportunity for additional technologies to connect to the system. The elements of the system form a data management platform throughout the project life cycle. Data flow between project phases and actors is provided by the Industry Foundation Classes (IFC) data model (Davtalab et al., 2018). This platform also acts as a common data management environment (CDE) that ensures the collaboration of project actors. Ghaffarianhoseini et al. (2017) pointed out that an integrated CDE increases the awareness of project actors' responsibility, which, in turn, increases the efficiency of processes, thereby reducing the cost of the entire project. Project-integrated CDE significantly reduces design time (Bryde et al., 2013), but proper integration also requires market players to be able to change current business models. During implementation, care must also be taken to ensure that unclearly assigned roles and responsibilities in the supply chain can lead to a lack of trust, which can also arise as an unexpected cost and logistics problem in the future.

Human–computer interaction creates the opportunity for the flow of information between humans and machines. The interaction can take place through hardware devices, image processing or even gestures. An essential element of the interaction can also be a website, a mobile application or a progressive website application (PWA). Mobile applications and on-premises devices combined with cloud solutions solve real-time project management problems; however, data security is also a challenge for many mobile application users (Conlin & Retik, 1997).

Digital and physical integration layer technologies help connect materials and objects between 3D virtual and physical space, supply chains or manufacturing solutions. These include augmented and virtual reality (Ahmed, 2019; Bassanino et al., 2014), 3D printing and projection and emerging new building materials. Many of these technologies are based on visualisation. Visualisation facilitates the discussion of complex ideas among stakeholders (Ghaffarianhoseini et al., 2017) and remote work in 3D space. VR technologies increase the role of security in design (Sacks et al., 2015), as they can display unforeseen project barriers and thus become manageable before they arise.

The associated sensors and devices allow remote and real-time data collection. These include cameras (Konstantinou et al., 2019), sensors and smart tags (RFID, BLE) as well as robotics and drones. These technologies are particularly helpful in work environments where safety and security are particularly important. Camera-based technologies support resource planning; however, there are legal issues with their application in many countries. Smart labels increase work safety and efficiency on projects through continuous tracking. While virtual simulations prevent accidents, Davila Delgado et al. (2019) suggest that, with the emergence of robotics and autonomous technologies, new occupational safety issues also arise. The use of these technologies reduces the cost of occupational safety and facilitates heavy physical work.

In addition to the combination of the listed technologies, big data analytics, machine learning and blockchain technology also appear in the entire construction value chain. Emerging technologies not only increase the efficiency of businesses but also support sustainable development and environmental protection (Carvajal-Arango et al., 2019; Lu & Lee, 2015, Ghaffarianhoseini et al., 2017).

Overall, I4.0 has several benefits to the industry, which are typically found in any other industry. These include:

1. Saving time and money by reducing error margins and increasing the speed of output
2. Raising standards and productivity by real-time close monitoring of the production
3. Improving sustainability by the elimination of waste and reduction of energy use

Additionally, there are industry-specific benefits as well:

4. Modernising the image of the industry by attracting a new generation of skilled professionals who are keen to shape our environment

5. Improving site safety and reducing chances of accidents by using augmented and virtual reality, which reduces the need for site visits as well. By recognising hazards in the environment, augmented reality devices can display real-time safety information to workers
6. Improving the quality of life since a building and the materials used in its construction and finishing have a major impact on the health and well-being of its occupants
7. Contribution to the economic growth of countries since construction is a "horizontal" industry (like the Financial Services industry), serving all industry verticals (Goconstruct.org, 2021; WEF, 2016)

Case illustrations

Skanska developed a new construction concept known as "Flying Factories", which are temporary factories set up close to construction sites; they apply "lean" manufacturing techniques to reduce construction time by up to 65% and achieve a 44% improvement in productivity relative to on-site assembly.

Broad Group China, in cooperation with ArcelorMittal, uses a system of modular building components that enables very speedy construction: a 57-storey building was built in only 19 days by moving 90% of the construction work to the factory.

BASF and Arup jointly developed an app for architects, engineers and project owners to calculate the energy savings of their designs.

Komatsu, a Japanese manufacturer of construction equipment, is developing automated bulldozers incorporating various digital systems. Drones, 3D scanners and stereo cameras gather terrain data, which is then transmitted to the bulldozers; these are equipped with intelligent machine-control systems that enable them to carry out their work autonomously and thereby speed up the pre-foundation work on construction sites, while human operators monitor the process. On mining sites, autonomous haul trucks are already in common use (WEF, 2016).

14.3 Why is digital transformation slow in construction?

There are numerous reasons why the digital transformation of the construction industry is relatively slow. In what follows, we highlight two significant barriers. First, from the perspective of construction companies, organisational, strategic and technological issues need to be considered. In this connection, it is a serious barrier that managers' and employees' level of digital knowledge is low, organisational structures are rigid and integration between companies is low. The prevalence of BIM (especially in Hungary) is low, and BIM is rarely extended to the entire value chain. The initial (slightly higher) invested work is not undertaken by the actors as it does not pay for itself; however, significant savings across the entire value chain would be achieved with proper network collaboration. The lack of trust between actors is also a problem in this regard.

Second, we discuss the issues from the perspective of the technology manufacturer or service provider. How willing is the market to embrace new technology? How fast can a technology provider grow in the market? In this respect, several new technologies are emerging, but there is a great deal of uncertainty about them and few reference projects to support the actual effectiveness of the technologies. Another possibility is that these projects are significantly different from the circumstances of the new customer. On the other hand, most new technology providers are young businesses that cannot yet meet the higher demands.

In summary, neither the demand nor the supply market can be considered mature presently. The development of Industry 4.0 means that an increasing number of professionals are appearing in the construction industry. Research institutes and consultants can help the development of Construction 4.0, an example of which is the United Kingdom. Although the supply market is currently underdeveloped, a growing number of promising technologies are emerging, and, due to the fierce market competition, an increasing number of companies are forced to implement digital transformation.

Review questions

1. Explain what the impacts of I4.0 are on the traditional construction industry.
2. Explain how new types of platforms (i.e., partner-finding) will improve efficiency and effectiveness within the industry.
3. What are the main technologies in the digitised construction value chain?

Discussion questions

1. Why is digital transformation slow in construction?
2. What are the societal and economic impacts of Construction 4.0?
3. Since the construction industry is the single largest global consumer of resources and raw materials, as well as a major proportion of solid waste generated by the industry, its modernisation is critical for a sustainable future. How does I4.0 enable the construction industry to meet this challenge?

Bibliography

Ahmed, S. (2019). A review on using opportunities of augmented reality and virtual reality in construction project management. *Organization, Technology and Management in Construction: An International Journal, 11*(1), 1839–1852. https://doi.org/10.2478/otmcj-2018-0012

Bassanino, M., Fernando, T., & Wu, K. C. (2014). Can virtual workspaces enhance team communication and collaboration in design review meetings? *Architectural Engineering and Design Management, 10*(3–4), 200–217. https://doi.org/10.1080/17452007.2013.775102

Bryde, D., Broquetas, M., & Volm, J. M. (2013). The project benefits of building information modelling (BIM). *International Journal of Project Management, 31*(7), 971–980. https://doi.org/10.1016/j.ijproman.2012.12.001

Carvajal-Arango, D., Bahamón-Jaramillo, S., Aristizábal-Monsalve, P., Vásquez-Hernández, A., & Botero, L. F. B. (2019). Relationships between lean and sustainable construction: Positive impacts of lean practices over sustainability during construction phase. *Journal of Cleaner Production, 234*, 1322–1337. https://doi.org/10.1016/j.jclepro.2019.05.216

Centre for Digital Built Britain. (2018). *Year one report towards a digital built Britain*. Retrieved from https://www.cdbb.cam.ac.uk/system/files/documents/CDBBYearOneReport2018.pdf

Conlin, J., & Retik, A. (1997). The applicability of project management software and advanced IT techniques in construction delays mitigation. *International Journal of Project Management, 15*(2), 107–120.

Davila Delgado, J. M., Oyedele, L., Ajayi, A., Akanbi, L., Akinade, O., Bilal, M., & Owolabi, H. (2019). Robotics and automated systems in construction: Understanding industry-specific challenges for adoption. *Journal of Building Engineering, 26*, 1–15. https://doi.org/10.1016/j.jobe.2019.100868

Davtalab, O., Kazemian, A., & Khoshnevis, B. (2018). Perspectives on a BIM-integrated software platform for robotic construction through contour crafting. *Automation in Construction, 89*, 13–23. https://doi.org/10.1016/j.autcon.2018.01.006

Engin, Z., van Dijk, J., Lan, T., Longley, P. A., Treleaven, P., Batty, M., & Penn, A. (2019). Data-driven urban management: Mapping the landscape. *Journal of Urban Management, 9*(2), 140–150. https://doi.org/10.1016/j.jum.2019.12.001

Gao, X., & Pishdad-Bozorgi, P. (2019). BIM-enabled facilities operation and maintenance: A review. *Advanced Engineering Informatics, 39*, 227–247. https://doi.org/10.1016/j.aei.2019.01.005

Ghaffarianhoseini, A., Tookey, J., Ghaffarianhoseini, A., Naismith, N., Azhar, S., Efimova, O., & Raahemifar, K. (2017). Building Information Modelling (BIM) uptake: Clear benefits, understanding its implementation, risks and challenges. *Renewable and Sustainable Energy Reviews, 75*, 1046–1053. https://doi.org/10.1016/j.rser.2016.11.083

GhaffarianHoseini, A., Zhang, T., Nwadigo, O., Naismith, N., Tookey, J., & Raahemifar, K. (2017). Application of nD BIM Integrated Knowledge-based Building Management System (BIM-IKBMS) for inspecting post-construction energy efficiency. *Renewable and Sustainable Energy Reviews, 72*, 935–949. https://doi.org/10.1016/j.rser.2016.12.061

Goconstruct.org. (2021). *What is construction 4.0.* Retrieved from https://www.goconstruct.org/why-choose-construction/whats-happening-in-construction/what-is-construction-40/

Kache, F., & Seuring, S. (2017). Challenges and opportunities of digital information at the intersection of big data analytics and supply chain management. *International Journal of Operations and Production Management, 37*(1), 10–36. https://doi.org/10.1108/IJOPM-02-2015-0078

Konstantinou, E., Lasenby, J., & Brilakis, I. (2019). Adaptive computer vision-based 2D tracking of workers in complex environments. *Automation in Construction, 103*, 168–184. https://doi.org/10.1016/j.autcon.2019.01.018

Lu, Q., & Lee, S. (2015). An eeBIM-based platform integrating carbon cost evaluation for sustainable building design. *Computing in Civil Engineering* (pp. 371–378).

Makridakis, S. (2017). The forthcoming Artificial Intelligence (AI) revolution: Its impact on society and firms. *Futures, 90*, 46–60. https://doi.org/10.1016/j.futures.2017.03.006

Oesterreich, T. D., & Teuteberg, F. (2016). Understanding the implications of digitisation and automation in the context of industry 4.0: A triangulation approach and elements of a research agenda for the construction industry. *Computers in Industry, 83*, 121–139. https://doi.org/10.1016/j.compind.2016.09.006

Perera, S., Nanayakkara, S., Rodrigo, M. N. N., Senaratne, S., & Weinand, R. (2020). Blockchain technology: Is it hype or real in the construction industry? *Journal of Industrial Information Integration, 17*, 100125. https://doi.org/10.1016/j.jii.2020.100125

Sacks, R., Whyte, J., Swissa, D., Raviv, G., Zhou, W., & Shapira, A. (2015). Safety by design: Dialogues between designers and builders using virtual reality. *Construction Management and Economics, 33*(1), 55–72. https://doi.org/10.1080/01446193.2015.1029504

Whyte, J. (2019). How digital information transforms project delivery models. *Project Management Journal, 50*(2), 177–194. https://doi.org/10.1177/8756972818823304

Whyte, J., & Lobo, S. (2010). Coordination and control in project-based work: Digital objects and infrastructures for delivery. *Construction Management and Economics, 28*(6), 557–567. https://doi.org/10.1080/01446193.2010.486838

World Economic Forum. (2016). *Shaping the future of construction.* Retrieved from https://www3.weforum.org/docs/WEF_Shaping_the_Future_of_Construction_full_report.pdf

15 Smart agriculture

András Gábor and Zoltán Szabó

Smart agriculture is a new trend in the utilisation of information and communication technology (ICT) in agricultural production. Sensor-based remote monitoring, data analytics, automation, mobile and cloud technologies, etc. can facilitate the digitalisation of traditional activities in agriculture and provide potential solutions for many recent problems, including the productivity of agriculture, environmental sustainability and climate change.

In short, with smart farming humanity is on the promising road to becoming highly innovative and self-reliant. For example, AI-driven machines or operated devices, such as sprinklers and fertilisers, perform their jobs more effectively but also more wisely. AI allows monitoring the plants' conditions, which, in turn, allows tailored climate control and self-watering capabilities, etc. The chapter reviews the need for smart farming and the applications of technologies in the agriculture domain.

15.1 The need for smart agriculture

In light of rapid ICT development in terms of both infrastructure and application, traditional sectors are undergoing radical transformations. The fourth Industrial Revolution has created the conditions for a higher level of **precision farming** and **smart farms**, where human presence is only required to a very limited extent (PwC, 2018).

Many paradigm shifts can be discovered in the history of capitalism. Paradigm shifts lead to industrial revolutions, which can be illustrated by the automation of the loom, the advent of steam engines and the spread of digital technology and culture. Information and communication technologies that affect many areas of our life have a decisive, though not exclusive, role in shaping the global value chain. Industry 4.0 marks an era, or rather the change of an era; it is reflected in the UN Declaration of Sustainability and an EU action plan to address the technological and competitive advantage of the United States. In this sense, Industry 4.0 covers not only the industry but all sectors of the economy. As ICT is a key element in mobilising development, and much of this is focused on digital technology. In addition to solving problems, Industry 4.0 also creates many of them. Only based on the latest developments: COVID-19 broke the global value chain, repeated lockdowns jeopardised production (Just-In-Time (JIT) delivery was not possible) and the reopening of economies shed light on saving jobs in home countries. Finally, virtual cooperation makes it urgent to regulate atypical work (especially home office) more strictly.

Even more radical changes are taking place in agriculture, and not without reason (Pierpaoli et al., 2013). FAO (Food and Agriculture of the United Nations) forecasts that 9.6 billion people will need to be fed by 2050, and, for this reason, agricultural production

DOI: 10.4324/9781003390312-18

must be increased by 70% (FAO, 2017). With current technologies, it is impossible to cope with this challenge. Emerging problems include relatively slow productivity growth, the limited availability of usable land, the growing demand for freshwater, energy demand, labour shortages and, last but not least, ecosystem sustainability, especially climate change.

Agriculture is central to some of the most daunting challenges humanity is facing. Let us start with the premise that people need to be fed. The sources of food production are limited. Although the increase in volume can be balanced by the increase in productivity, in the long run a change of eating habits and food portfolio (fried grasshopper instead of abalone or bacon) may be necessary. At the same time, increasing the volume must not lead to all cross-border exploitation of the production area, which puts the reduction of extensive cultivation at the forefront, including refraining from deforestation. Agricultural innovation is limited by the requirement to protect the health of consumers (and producers) by avoiding the use of excessive fertilisers and chemicals, promoting organic production or taking due care against genetically modified organisms (GMOs). These demands also rightly raise the need for food security, which is overshadowed by social inequalities in access to food, namely, hunger, malnutrition and food waste both regionally and globally. A further issue that needs to be addressed is that due to the global food value chain, transport and the packaging industry are both solutions and problems due to their environmental impact. Together, these formulate the requirements for the protection and maintenance of the ecosystem and biodiversity (FAO, 2017).

15.2 The concept of smart agriculture

One possible way to overcome obstacles is precision agriculture or intelligent farming.

Precision agriculture is a management strategy that gathers, processes and analyses temporal, spatial and individual data and combines the data with other information to support management decisions according to the estimated variability for improved resource use efficiency, productivity, quality, profitability and sustainability of agricultural production (International Society for Precision Agriculture, 2019, p. 1).

Similar to the industrial trends, automation can replace human activities in agriculture, too: most aspects of traditional farming are labour-intensive, with mostly repetitive and standardised tasks.

A common feature of the business processes of farming (e.g., livestock farming, arable farming and greenhouse cultivation) is that agricultural production depends on natural conditions, such as climate (day length and temperature), soil, pests, diseases and weather. ICT can contribute to the improvement of farming processes by facilitating sensing and monitoring, supporting analysis and decision-making and enhancing performance control and intervention abilities (Wolfert et al., 2017).

Precision agriculture can improve productivity with advanced **ICT solutions**, i.e., increase land yields, save or optimise water use (as water is becoming an increasingly strategic resource), improve production quality (e.g., with products and environmentally friendly production) and, in the longer term, return on such investment is expected to be positive. From a technological point of view, precision agriculture also follows the logic of the well-known structure of the information system, such as data collection, data processing and decision-making.

Digital agriculture is a broad term that describes the use of digital technologies to integrate the agricultural production value chain from the fields to the end consumers, describing the concept of digitisation in agriculture (Trendov et al., 2019). Many concepts with similar meanings can be mentioned, with overlapping content, and these terms (smart agriculture, smart farming, etc.) can be used as synonyms. By definition, **precision agriculture** signifies the managing of spatial and temporal changes to improve economic returns from the use of inputs and the reduction of environmental impact. Finally, it includes decision support systems (DSS) for total management. **Agricultural automation and robotics** refers to the process of applying the techniques of robotics, automatic control and artificial intelligence at all levels of agricultural production, including farm sticks and farm drones.

The special feature of intelligent farming at the forefront of our interest is that architecture consists of a technology portfolio and various types of ICT technologies and procedures. Neither individual technology nor architectural elements are given priority; the key is the seamless cooperation of individual elements.

The Alliance for Internet of Things Innovation (AIOTI) defines the concept of smart farming as a set of automated data management processes, including data collection, data processing and analysis tasks in agricultural production systems. Its main goal is to improve the productivity and sustainability of farming throughout the value chain by using advanced information and communication technologies, primarily **IoT technologies**. Intelligent farming should facilitate the production, sharing and reuse of animal, plant and soil metadata. This improves food safety in terms of understanding and preventing food-borne diseases – from food production to consumption – and optimises the value chain in terms of production time and quality (Gebbers & Adamchuk, 2010).

Smart farming has several potential benefits by promoting community farming, improving safety control and fraud prevention, providing cost and waste reduction opportunities, improving operational efficiency and ensuring transparency and traceability (Elijah et al., 2018). Smart technologies in agriculture can be a major source of competitive advantages: they increase productivity and facilitate better decision-making; the more efficient exploitation of operations and resources with smart technologies can also underpin new business models.

15.3 Technologies in smart farming

The technologies that underpin smart farming are still in early development, but there are many promising opportunities. The applicable technologies are at the forefront of data collection. Sensor technologies, collectively and popularly known as IoT, i.e., the Internet of Things, play a vital role. Yield estimation, the use of crop aids, goes back centuries and farmers work with the available accuracy of the estimate. Using **sensor technologies**, larger, faster and more detailed data can be collected. The unit cost of a given sensor is very low and they can be used to monitor almost all types of parameters (humidity, temperature, water level, etc.), considering the decision-making process typical of farming. Particular attention should be paid to localisation, and the use of location technologies (such as GPS) plays an important role in optimising the utilisation of agricultural machinery, among others (Stafford, 2000).

In addition to IoT, drones – unmanned aerial vehicles (UAV) – are playing an increasingly important role in agriculture. There are many variants (multirotor, fixed wing, single rotor, hybrid), and they are used for chemical application, crop estimation and pest identification and control. They are mostly equipped with cameras; it is essential to use GPS to operate them. The methods and tools of image processing are also related to this category. Here we highlight the correct interpretation and mapping of the images taken from the surface, which is dealt with in more depth by photogrammetry. The processing of images transmitted from drones is a part of the practice, but satellite-based space photography should also be mentioned more broadly here. Although drones can be understood as a robot, the family of robots is much larger; thus, a populous family of remotely controlled agricultural machines should be mentioned here (e.g., tractors, sprayers and planters). All the automated or remotely controlled tools are based on positioning, as spatial control is inconceivable without it. We can also see that by connecting different, but "single-minded," sensors, many tasks can be solved without human intervention. Improving productivity by an order of magnitude is therefore not just a dream but a reality.

A fundamental question is how the sensors communicate the data received. The **communication network, the protocols and the security** provide the next group of architectural elements. Since the wired network can be used only in a small part of agricultural production, **wireless communication** is almost mandatory; in this respect, the power consumption of Wi-Fi, and the appropriate protocols (especially due to the long distances and the varied surface) are crucial. Because the distances are quite large, **mobile communication** and mobile networks are of primary importance.

Due to a large number of data collection endpoints (sensors), fast data processing is not just a matter of processors, but special architectures and procedures help to handle large amounts of data. The sources of information are diverse, and the data formats are different. To produce satisfactory "raw material" for decision-makers at the decision-making level, not only sensor data is considered but also information available from more and more public sources, i.e., **open data**, **linked open data** and **open government data** play an important role. The combination of open data and sensor data results in diversity and variation in data collection. The technology for managing these services is known as **big data** (see Chapter 5).

The application and integration of advanced technologies lead to significant progress in agricultural practices. The Industry 4.0 trend transforms agriculture based on digital technologies, namely, sensor technologies, the Internet of Things, big data and artificial intelligence. The implementation of digital practices will also contribute to the transformation of agriculture in terms of cooperation, mobility and open innovation. The implementation of digitalised production infrastructure integrated processes, connected farms, new production equipment and connected tractors and machines will enable increased productivity, along with quality and environmental protection. Complex, improved value chains and business models can be implemented.

Technologies in livestock production, for example, provide three functions in cattle farming: monitoring of animal position and behaviour, distance feeding or herding, health management and precision traceability (Laca, 2009). Another example is the combination of machine learning applications and robots to deliver the right amount of fertiliser to the soil or connect with the automated irrigation system to provide the perfect quantity of water directly to the soil (Goap et al., 2018).

15.4 Agriculture 4.0

After reviewing the ICT infrastructure, components and applications, we discuss how Agriculture 4.0 (digital or smart agriculture) meets the sustainability criteria (the sustainability of production, economy and environment). In terms of agricultural applications, different applications in terms of crop production and animal husbandry have been and are being developed (SUNSpAce, n.d.).

In crop production (wheat or vegetable production), the basic dimensions along which applications can be reviewed are:

1. **Production and environmental relationships** (abiotic and biotic conditions and environmental parameters), air composition (O_2, CO_2, etc.), temperature, heat tolerance (drought, extreme climatic conditions), soil temperature, light conditions (number of hours per day, UV radiation) and water supply
2. **Soil nutrient supply** (fertilisation, fertiliser, composting, nitrogen, phosphate, potassium supplementation)
3. **Planting, sowing** (seed, agro-climatic conditions, choice of soil type, soil pH, water supply)
4. **Irrigation** (soil moisture content, drip irrigation, consideration of topography, choice of method appropriate to the plant type)
5. **Pests, disease control and weed control** (use of natural materials, mechanical protection, physical protection from burning, lighting and humidity, mutually reinforcing crops, traps and chemical protection)
6. **Harvesting, processing**, marketing, loss management

Typical applications that address the above-mentioned dimensions are irrigation automation, temperature, pH, humidity, carbon dioxide level control, soil nutrient replenishment (fertiliser) automation, soil moisture detection, crop monitoring and estimation.

In a greenhouse equipped with digital technology, external sensors measure the following: air temperature, relative humidity, precipitation, wind strength and wind direction, UV radiation and air pressure. Indoor sensors measure air temperature and relative humidity, UV and light intensity, CO_2 level, soil moisture, soil pH, water temperature, water electrical capacity and water pH. There are three irrigation methods to choose from: drip, steam and conventional (sprinkler) irrigation.

In animal husbandry, smart devices collect data about animals and their environment. The basic dimensions that are measured include disease prevention (or at least detection), the monitoring of weight gain and other physiological parameters of the animal and the monitoring and control of the narrower environmental parameters of animal husbandry. The basic conditions are unique identification and "customisable" solutions (in the case of many animals). Radio Frequency IDentification (RFID) is a commonly used solution for identification. Figure 15.1 shows the **automated monitoring** of weight gain, and Figure 15.2 shows the system components of data processing.

"Big data" technology can handle data collection, and pre-processing (e.g., sample creation, pattern matching, optimal sampling, etc.), but there are sophisticated and complex **data analysis** and **business intelligence** solutions to use the data required, including multiple machine learning applications (e.g., data mining, video mining, process mining; Majumdar et al., 2017).

Smart farming can be implemented on different maturity levels (represented in Figure 15.3). On the first level, the most characteristic activity is sensing. Sensing is performed by sensors, which practically measure one physical parameter, such as humidity, pH, the presence of one chemical element, etc. Drones and satellite photos are also frequent tools for sensing and monitoring. The next maturity level is reached in agriculture when (smart) farmers use the collected and processed data for decision-making and predictions, and, in general, the data support individual decisions. Smart

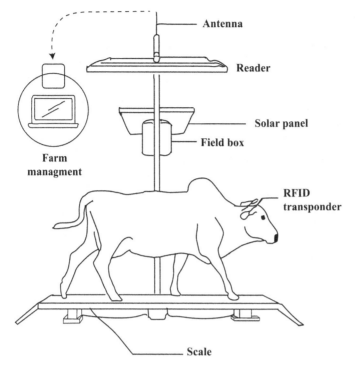

Figure 15.1 Precision livestock farming (based on Agrinteligente, n.d)

Animal Identificaton System Overview

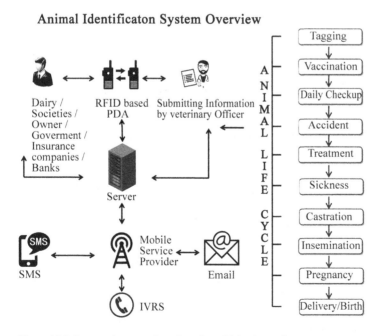

Figure 15.2 Proposed system flow (based on Bizlogics, n.d)

smart sensing
& monitoring

cloud-based
event and data
management

smart control

smart analysis
& planning

Figure 15.3 The cyber-physical management cycle of smart farming (based on Wolfert, Sørensen & Goense, 2014)

farming moves up to the third level of maturity if the collected and processed data are used for automatic or semi-automatic actions, which are often called smart control. While several IT solutions exist regarding analysis and planning, due to the large volume of real-time data collection and the processing need of the latest IT infrastructure (i.e., cloud computing and cloud solutions), implementing smart control is more challenging. **Decision models** can be traced back to four basic types:

- Descriptive models use various parameters such as soil, weather, etc. to describe spatial and temporal variability and identify risk factors to be addressed
- Analytical models use the collected data and maps related to each character to reveal the causes and indicate the necessary and feasible interventions
- Predictive models provide estimates of yields and food security using time series data sets as well as integrated soil, yield, weather and market models
- Proactive or prescriptive models use large amounts of data from intelligent farming to explore relationships under different management conditions depending on site characteristics, weather conditions and yields. These relationships can be used to adapt farming practices to local conditions

End users of Agriculture 4.0 are farmers, using applications not only from a desk but also in an often-harsh environment out in the fields (rural areas), which has a serious impact on the development of devices (weather and fault-tolerant solutions). With regard to performance and maintenance, the **cloud solution** appears to be economical and efficient presently (Park et al., 2016). Cloud technology provides **scalability** as well as keeping applications up to date, even from remote locations.

The application of Industry 4.0 technologies in agriculture is very promising, and there are many successful application cases. Farms are becoming similar to factories in the sense that they use sensors, robotics, automation and data analytics to ensure tightly controlled operations. Sensors provide farmers with important farm-related data and support farm-related operative or long-term decisions. Milking and feeding robots will save human efforts, and autonomous solutions for greenhouse lighting or irrigation will save energy and water. A good example is the CowManager system (visit: www.cowmanager.com /en-us/solution/system), which is a combination of sensors, network components and software to facilitate the work of farmers: the key component is an ear sensor that can be easily installed and provides information about the fertility, health, nutritional status and location of the herd. These data are collected by sensors, transmitted by routers and processed by an application on a smartphone or a computer. The system can be integrated into other farm management systems to facilitate the automation of ventilation, feeding and temperature control. Furthermore, it also provides early alarm signals when a cow is sick. The system helps farmers to save cost and time, and the collected information can be a valuable source of knowledge that can be used to improve the production processes of the farm.

Widespread adoption of smart farming technologies will take time, as it requires significant changes in practices and mindset, along with the modernisation of the equipment and supporting infrastructures. There are also many open issues in the standardisation of technologies, technical risks and legislation.

Review questions

1. What are the main advantages and benefits of precious agriculture?
2. What are the main smart farming technologies?
3. How can Industry 4.0 technologies be applied in agriculture? Provide a few innovative examples.

Discussion questions

1. What are the challenges that drive the development of precious agriculture?
2. What could be the prerequisites for the successful application of the smart farming concept?
3. What are the major risks and limitations of the concept?

Bibliography

Agrinteligente. (n.d.). *Precision livestock farming.* Retrieved from http://agrinteligente.com/precision -livestock-farming/

Bizlogics. (n.d.). *Proposed system flow.* Retrieved from http://www.bizlogics.co.in/animal_identification _system.html

Elijah, O., Rahman, T. A., Orikumhi, I., Leow, C. Y., & Hindia, M. N. (2018). An overview of internet of things (IoT) and data analytics in agriculture: Benefits and challenges. *IEEE Internet of Things Journal, 5*(5), 3758–3773. https://doi.org/10.1109/JIOT.2018.2844296

Food and Agriculture Organization of the United Nations. (2017). *The future of food and agriculture: Trends and challenges.* Retrieved from http://www.fao.org/3/a-i6583e.pdf

Gebbers, R., & Adamchuk, V. I. (2010). Precision agriculture and food security. *Science, 327*(5967), 828–831. https://doi.org/10.1126/science.1183899

Goap, A., Sharma, D., Shukla, A. K., & Rama, K. C. (2018). An IoT based smart irrigation management system using machine learning and open source technologies. *Computers and Electronics in Agriculture*, *155*, 41–49. https://doi.org/10.1016/j.compag.2018.09.040

International Society for Precision Agriculture. (2019). *ISPA forms official definition of 'precision agriculture'*. Retrieved from https://www.precisionag.com/market-watch/ispa-forms-official-definition-of -precision-agriculture/

Laca, E. A. (2009). Precision livestock production: Tools and concepts. *Revista Brasileira de Zootecnia*, *38*, 123–132. https://doi.org/10.1590/S1516-35982009001300014

Majumdar, J., Naraseeyappa, S., & Ankalaki, S. (2017). Analysis of agriculture data using data mining techniques: Application of big data. *Journal of Big Data*, *4*(1). https://doi.org/10.1186/s40537-017 -0077-4

Park, H., Lee, E., Park, D., Eun, J., & Kim, S. (2016). PaaS offering for the big data analysis of each individual APC. *International conference on information and communication technology convergence*, Jeju, Korea.

Pierpaoli, E., Carli, G., Pignatti, E., & Canavari, M. (2013). Drivers of precision agriculture technologies adoption: A literature review. *Procedia Technology*, *8*, 61–69. https://doi.org/10.1016/j.protcy.2013 .11.010

PwC. (2018). *Digitalizáció az agrárszektorban: Életképek a jövő okosfarmjáról*. Retrieved from https://www .pwc.com/hu/hu/kiadvanyok/assets/pdf/digitalizacio_az_agrarszektorban.pdf

Stafford, J. V. (2000). Implementing precision agriculture in the 21st century. *Journal of Agricultural and Engineering Research*, *76*(3), 267–275. https://doi.org/10.1006/jaer.2000.0577

SUNSpACe. (n.d.). *Sustainable development smart agriculture capacity*. Retrieved from http://sunspace.farm /wp-content/uploads/2021/09/D11_siteweb.pdf

Trendov, N. M., Varas, S., & Zeng, M. (2019). Digital technologies in agriculture and rural areas. Retrieved from https://www.fao.org/3/ca4887en/ca4887en.pdf

Wolfert, J., Sørensen, C. G., & Goense, D. (2014). A future internet collaboration platform for safe and healthy food from farm to fork. *Annual SRII global conference* (pp. 266–273), San Jose, CA.

Wolfert, S., Ge, L., Verdouw, C., & Bogaardt, M. J. (2017). Big data in smart farming: A review. *Agricultural Systems*, *153*, 69–80. https://doi.org/10.1016/j.agsy.2017.01.023

16 Society 5.0

Ilona Cserháti

We learned from the previous chapters that thanks to digitisation, many parts of our lives are in transition. The term "information society" refers to the computerised and automated control mechanisms within a society where several systems work in parallel and collect data, process it and then apply the results for a better quality of life. However, Society 5.0 takes it further: instead of having all systems work within a limited range, such as setting room temperature, supplying energy or ensuring that trains run on time, Society 5.0 will have an integrated system in place throughout society. It enables organisations to optimise the entire process of sustainable living in the local environment (Potočan et al., 2021).

This chapter introduces some elements of the social consequences of the digitisation process on the life of employees and families and the possible solutions to the expected social issues are discussed, i.e., how Society 5.0 can solve those problems. In addition, the chapter discusses some important elements of the societal impacts of the digitisation process of Industry 4.0 on employees and families and then looks at how Society 5.0 can respond to these issues and help address the global challenges humanity is facing.

16.1 Industry 4.0 and its social consequences

Several great inventions of the industrial revolutions (from the invention of tractors to assembly lines, cloud computing and robots) were designed to replace human labour. Yet, participation rates are higher than ever across Europe and the United States. It seems that even the fantastic labour-saving inventions of Industry 4.0 did not make human labour redundant.

It is a difficult task to accurately predict the effects of automation on the labour market, as these effects can obviously vary considerably across countries, sectors and employment groups. Research has estimated the expected rate of job losses by occupation predominantly, rather than by sector. One of the best-known studies ranked 700 occupations by automation probability. The surprising result was that 47% of employment was associated with high-risk occupations in the United States in 2010.

Several papers were published subsequently that indicated that the per cent of jobs at risk was significantly overestimated (Arntz et al., 2016). The authors of this study relied on a similar methodology to assess 21 OECD countries, but also considered that automation displaces tasks and not an occupation. They found that high-risk employment in the United States was only 9% instead of 47%, and in the OECD countries, it may range between 6% and 12%. Pouliakas (2018) used the European Skills and Jobs Survey to analyse the share of high-risk occupations in the 28 EU member states using logistic regression. He found that

DOI: 10.4324/9781003390312-19

about 14% of adult workers in the EU face a very high risk of automation. According to PWC (2018) research, up to 30% of jobs could potentially be at high risk of automation in the United Kingdom by the early 2030s, which is lower than in the United States (38%) or in Germany (35%), but higher than in Japan (21%). The risks appear the highest in sectors such as transportation and storage (56%), manufacturing (46%) and wholesale and retail (44%), but lower in sectors like health and social work (17%).

According to a piece of research by PWC (2018), up to 30% of jobs in the United Kingdom could be at risk from automation by the early 2030s, compared to a slightly higher figure of 35% in Germany and a significantly lower 21% in Japan. The risk is the highest in transport and storage (56%), manufacturing (46%) and trade (44%), while it is lowest (17%) in sectors that require much less human involvement (e.g., health and social work). They claim that the automation process will affect different industries in different ways over time. On the employee side, the high automation risk rate is mainly differentiated by employees' level of skills. Low- and medium-educated workers are expected to have higher automation rates than those with higher education. In the first phase, automation is expected to be higher for jobs that can be performed by workers with intermediate education, followed by the automation of services that have been performed by workers with low education. The results of a quantitative analysis of the Russian labour market also show that the increasing inequalities (income gap by gender, age, education level and sector) can be considered one of the global threats associated with the fourth Industrial Revolution (Koropets et al., 2022).

This shows that technological progress can eliminate jobs. However, according to Autor (2015), what is true for one product or one industry can never be true for the whole economy.

Many products on which we spend a lot of money today did not even exist a few decades ago. As automation and digitisation free up our time, we can invent new products and services that can create new types of consumption and new forms of jobs. Thus, the real challenge is not that we are running out of jobs, but whether the structure of the future labour supply will meet the demand for the new jobs that are being created (Frey & Osborne, 2013).

Cedefop – one of the EU's decentralised agencies – has recognised the importance of the quantitative forecasting of the new skills needed. These forecasts form the basis for the development of European Vocational Education and Training (VET) policies to avoid skill mismatches in Europe.

The latest skill forecast (Cedefop, Eurofound, 2018) provides labour market demand and supply projections until 2030 based on the current Europop demographic forecast and macroeconomic projections of DG ECFIN. According to their results, in addition to sectoral changes, employment trends are increasingly driven by changes in occupational patterns within the sectors, driven by technological change. An interesting result (Table 16.1.) is that both high- and low-skilled occupation ratios are expected to increase, while demand for medium-skilled occupations is projected to decline proportionally.

Accordingly, skill polarisation within the labour market is expected to continue. Income inequalities are expected to increase and the depth of poverty may also rise as a direct effect of the labour market polarisation process (Cserháti & Pirisi, 2020). Cserháti and Takács (2019) analysed potential job losses due to automation and its negative impact on the poverty gap in Hungary. Nedelkoska and Quintini (2018) found that only the development of new skills and training can be effective tools to avoid the unpleasant social consequences of Industry 4.0.

Table 16.1 Projected change by broad occupation, 2011-30 (EU-28+3) (Cedefop, 2018, p.46)

Occupations	2011	2030	%point change
Legislators, senior officials and managers	6.2	6.8	**0.6**
Professionals	17	18.7	**1.7**
Technicians and associate professionals	15.8	17.8	**2**
Clerks	10.7	9.4	*-1.3*
Service workers and shop and market sales workers	17	16.8	*-0.2*
Skilled agricultural and fishery workers	4.3	3.2	*-1.1*
Craft and related trades workers	12.3	10.2	*-2.1*
Plant and machine operators and assemblers	7.3	6.8	*-0.5*
Elementary occupations	9.5	10.4	**0.9**
All occupations and % change	100	100	8.4%

All this leads to a summary of the direct socio-economic impacts of Industry 4.0:

• Productivity increases, income and wealth accumulation accelerate
• Labour demand will be highly transformed, requiring new types of skills and competencies
• The labour market continues to polarise, with jobs that can be filled with secondary education being the most likely to disappear

Therefore, (without government intervention) inequality would rise, leaving the unemployed poorer. The polarisation of employment would reduce the size of the middle class and threaten to turn us into a more stratified society. Therefore, the key issue here is the quality of our institutions, especially our education system, which enables us to make the results of our technological prosperity available to all.

Society 5.0 articulates this vision, highlighting the role of education, lifelong learning, and the extraordinary role of the government in both regulating access to community services for all and redistributing accelerated income and wealth to ensure inclusive growth and prosperity.

16.2 People-centric and super smart

The concept of Society 5.0 was implemented by the Japan Business Federation, also referred to as Keidanren, whose mission is to contribute to sustainable development and the improvement of the quality of life on a national level. On a macroeconomic level, Society 5.0 was proposed in the Fifth Science and Technology Basic Plan and was approved by the Japanese government in 2016 (Government of Japan, 2016).

Society 5.0 is defined as "a human-centred society that balances economic advancement with the resolution of social problems by a system that highly integrates cyberspace and physical space" (Keidanren, 2016, p. 5) and it also provides all "the necessary goods and services to the people who need them at the required time and in just the right amount" (Government of Japan, 2016, p. 1); a society that is "able to respond precisely to a wide variety of social needs" (Government of Japan, 2016, p. 1); "a society in which all kinds of people can readily obtain high-quality services" (Government of Japan, 2016, p. 1).

According to Fukuyama (2018), the goal of Society 5.0 aims to enable the transformation into a human-centred society in which both economic development and the resolution of societal challenges are achieved, and people can enjoy a high quality of life that is fully active and comfortable. It is a society that attends to the various needs of people, regardless of region, age, sex, language, etc. by providing necessary items and services. Society 5.0 can also provide solutions to several global challenges, such as the ageing population, declining birth rate, population decrease and climate change.

Society 5.0 – development of economy and human society

To fully understand the essence of Society 5.0, it is worth putting social development in a historical perspective. The evolution of human society has been characterised by a gradual liberation from constraints.

Mankind started as a hunting society (Society 1.0). Next, from 13.000 BCE we lived in an agricultural society. To do this, it was necessary to acquire the ability to produce food, which freed society from starvation (Society 2.0). In the industrial society (Society 3.0), productive capacity was developed and mobility was increased. The introduction of mass production and the invention of the steam engine made these possible. Achievements of the First and Second Industrial Revolutions supported this development.

The next stage of social development (Society 4.0) was observed during the 19th and 20th centuries. This phase was characterised by the development of digitalisation, telecommunications, information processing and access to Internet-based services, which increased the level of freedom. The Third and Fourth Industrial Revolutions supported this process with the invention of the computer and the Internet, and later with a complex digital transformation (Figure 16.1).

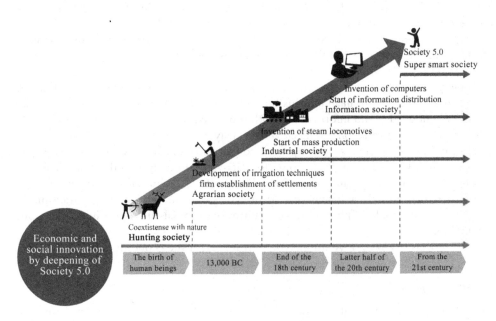

Figure 16.1 Evolution of human societies, leading to Society 5.0 (based on Fukuyama, 2018)

Table 16.2 A comparison of the development of human society based on European and Japanese initiatives (Deguchi et al., 2020)

	Industry 4.0 (Germany)	Society 5.0 (Japan)
Design	High-Tech Strategy 2020 Action Plan for Germany (2011) Recommendation for implementing the strategic initiative INDUSTRIE 4.0 (2013)	Fifth Science and Technology Basic Plan (2016) Comprehensive Strategy on Science, Technology, and Innovation for 2017 (2017) Sixth Science and Technology Basic Plan (2021)
Objectives, scope	Smart factories Focuses on manufacturing	Super smart society Society as a whole
Key phrases	Cyber-physical systems (CPS) Internet of Things (IoT) Mass customisation	High-level convergence of cyberspace and physical space Balancing economic development with the resolution of social issues

Characteristics of European (Industry 4.0) and Japanese initiatives (Society 5.0)

Industry 4.0 aims to revolutionise industrial production through higher productivity levels, implementing new business models and new production systems. The technological advances of Industry 4.0 will allow people to improve their quality of life, increase their life satisfaction and have a better work–life balance.

According to Pereira et al. (2020), humanity will have significantly more freedom to decide what kind of society it wants to create. Society 5.0 places a particular emphasis on putting people at the centre of innovation and automation (Table 16.2), using the advanced technology of Industry 4.0 for the benefit of humanity, facilitating the interconnection between people and systems through artificial intelligence in both real and in cyberspace (Deguchi et al., 2020). In a smart society, the well-being of people, the performance of the economy and the efficiency of institutions can all be improved through the thoughtful use of digital technology.

Society 5.0 will be creative, digital and sustainable. According to the Cabinet Office of the Japanese government, in an information society (Society 4.0), there is a cross-sectional sharing of knowledge and information. With too much information, it is sometimes difficult to find the information you need and to analyse it.

Society 5.0 will achieve a high degree of convergence between cyberspace and physical space. People are no longer searching for data and information in the cloud: data are automatically collected (using Internet of Things (IoT) technologies and sensor info) and analysed by artificial intelligence (AI) in cyberspace, and the results are transmitted directly back to people in physical space in forms of proposals and operating instructions (Figure 16.2).

This process opens up revolutionary opportunities for the economy and society.

Measuring smartness

How can we measure the state of actual "smartness" of an economy and determine the main components of a smart society? In 2017, the Fletcher School at Tufts University and

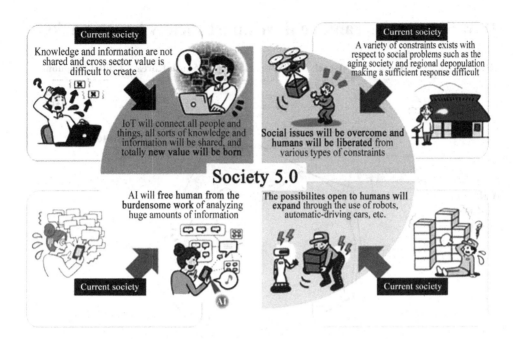

Figure 16.2 Achieving Society 5.0 (based on Cabinet office, n.d)

Microsoft Digital launched an initiative to explore this issue (Chakravorti & Chaturvedi, 2017). The performance of the D5 (the five most digitalised) countries (Estonia, Israel, New Zealand, South Korea and the United Kingdom) was monitored. Data were collected in three main areas: citizens and their well-being, the state of the economy and institutions. The aim was to establish a benchmark for smart societies. The main components were:

- *Citizens and their well-being*: Environment and quality of life, inclusiveness, talent and the human condition and talent development
- *Economy*: Global connectedness, economic robustness, entrepreneurship and innovation
- *Institutions*: Freedom, trust, safety and security and public services

Each country received a score along each indicator. The line connecting the scores of each country for the 12 components is the "footprint of smart society" (Figure 16.3).

The D5 countries with the world's most advanced digital governments can help define a global benchmark for a smart society.

When we would like to assess the "smartness" of a city, the Smart City Index (developed by the International Institute for Management Development) can be used. The index quantifies residents' perceptions of the existing infrastructure and the available technology applications and services in five key areas: health and safety, mobility, activities, opportunities and governance. In 2021 Singapore (1st), Zurich (2nd) and Oslo (3rd) proved to be the top three smart cities in the world. Budapest ranked 97th out of 118 cities surveyed by IMD.

How 5 countries rank against smart society benchmarks

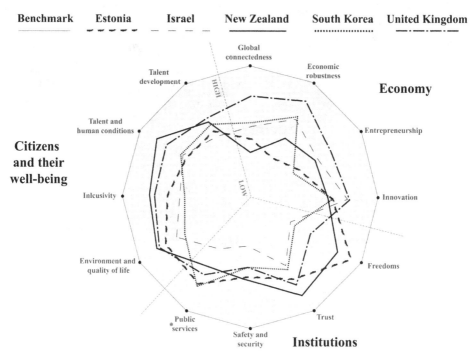

Figure 16.3 The footprint of smart society, D5 countries (based on the Fletcher School at Tufts University, n.d.)

Main societal challenges to be solved by Society 5.0 and the sustainable development goals

Society 5.0 and the UN Sustainable Development Goals share a common vision and a common direction for the necessary development patterns. In my view, there are six priority areas where Society 5.0 can help address key societal challenges. Therefore, I would enhance the development opportunities along the 17 UN Sustainable Development Goals and these six dimensions.

Basic needs

- "End poverty in all its forms everywhere" (UN, 2018, SDG goal 1)
- "End hunger, achieve food security, and improved nutrition and promote sustainable agriculture" (UN, 2018, SDG goal 2)

Artificial intelligence, agricultural robots and autonomous drones will help agricultural production. Productivity will increase sharply, and new technologies will be used to optimise food production and minimise food loss. Therefore, hunger and absolute poverty will be eradicated from our planet.

Climate change, sustainable living

- "Ensure availability and sustainable management of water and sanitation for all" (UN, 2018, SDG goal 6)
- "Ensure access to affordable, reliable, sustainable and modern energy for all" (UN, 2018, SDG goal 7)
- "Ensure sustainable consumption and production patterns" (UN, 2018, SDG goal 12)
- "Take urgent action to climate change and its impacts" (UN, 2018, SDG goal 13)
- "Conserve and sustainably use the oceans, sea, and marine resources for sustainable development" (UN, 2018, SDG goal 14)
- "Protect, restore, and promote the sustainable use of terrestrial ecosystems, sustainably manage forests, combat desertification, halt and reserve land degradation, and halt biodiversity loss" (UN, 2018, SDG goal 15)

Together, new technologies and responsible consumer behaviour can create opportunities to minimise the negative environmental impacts of economic activity and preserve rich terrestrial and aquatic biodiversity.

Innovative, inclusive labour market

- "Promote sustained, inclusive, and sustainable economic growth, full and productive employment, and decent work for all" (UN, 2018, SDG goal 8)
- "Build resilient infrastructure, promote inclusive and sustainable industrialization, and foster innovation" (UN, 2018, SDG goal 9)

Robots will do the "non-decent" kinds of work for us, while humans will be able to engage in visionary and creative activities, which produce a variety of new forms of value. Even small businesses can have access to all the information and technology they need, allowing them to broaden the innovation process.

Education, health and work–life balance

- "Ensure healthy living and promote well-being for all at all ages" (UN, 2018, SDG goal 3)
- "Ensure inclusive and equitable quality education and promote lifelong learning opportunities for all" (UN, 2018, SDG goal 4)

Society 5.0 puts a strong emphasis on high-quality education for all, which is accessible to all, as the basis for high productivity development. Lifelong learning can help to avoid skill mismatches on the macroeconomic level. A high level of productivity allows us to reduce the necessary working time and achieve a healthy work–life balance. A healthier lifestyle, alongside molecular biology and personalised medicine, will ensure a longer, healthier life for all members of society.

Inequality, inclusive growth

- "Achieve gender equality and empower all women and girls" (UN, 2018, SDG goal 5)
- "Reduce inequality within and among countries" (UN, 2018, SDG goal 10)

These issues are mainly the responsibility of governments. A fair redistribution system of expanding wealth can be achieved by providing an adequate tax-transfer system and equal opportunities for all (with special regard to early-age education).

Safety, justice, partnership

- "Make cities and human settlements inclusive, safe, resilient, and sustainable" (UN, 2018, SDG goal 11)
- "Promote peaceful and inclusive societies for sustainable development, provide access to justice for all and build effective, accountable, and inclusive institutions at all levels" (UN, 2018, SDG goal 16)
- "Strengthen the means of implementation and revitalise global partnerships for sustainable development" (UN, 2018, SDG goal 17)

Public services are also changing. Central and local governments will use digitisation-based systems to guarantee our security. It is essential to ensure equal access to justice for all – only modern, accountable institutions can ensure the independent functioning of public institutions, which is the cornerstone of Society 5.0. International cooperation can help the new model to spread outside Japan.

All in all, Society 5.0 is a Japanese vision, but its implementation could be a solution to important societal issues that need to be addressed for humanity. The realisation of Society 5.0 could provide solutions to many global socio-environmental challenges as well. It would be beneficial if humanity could use the wealth and prosperity generated by the digitisation process to build a sustainable, peaceful and prosperous society.

Review questions

1. What are the main social consequences of Industry 4.0?
2. How would you define Society 5.0?
3. What kind of societal challenges could be solved by making Society 5.0 a reality?

Discussion questions

1. What kind of life would you like to live in the circumstances of "perfect freedom"?
2. What type of education should be required in Society 5.0?
3. What kind of inequalities could still exist in Society 5.0?

Bibliography

Arntz, M., Gregory, T., & Zierahn, U. (2016). *The risk of automation for jobs in OECD countries.* OECD Social, Employment and Migration Working Papers, 189. https://doi.org/10.1787/1815199X

Autor, D. H. (2015). Why are there still so many jobs? The history and future of workplace automation. *The Journal of Economic Perspectives, 29*(3), 3–30. https://doi.org/10.1257/jep.29.3.3

Cedefop, Eurofound. (2018). *Skills forecast: Trends and challenges to 2030.* Retrieved from https://www.cedefop.europa.eu/en/publications/3077

Chakravorti, B., & Chaturvedi, R. S. (2017). *The "smart society" of the future doesn't look like science fiction.* Retrieved from The "Smart Society" of the Future Doesn't Look Like Science Fiction (hbr.org) (

Cserháti, I., & Pirisi, K. (2020). Industry 4.0 and some social consequences: Impact assessment by microsimulation for Hungary. *Society and Economy, 42*(2), 105–123.

Cserháti, I., & Takács, T. (2019). Potential job losses due to automation and its impact on poverty gap in Hungary. *Journal of WSEAS Transactions on Business and Economics, 16*, 47–53.

Deguchi, A., Hirai, C., Matsuoka, H., Nakano, T., Oshima, K., Tai, M., & Tani, S. (2020). What is society 5.0. In *Society 5.0: A people-centric super-smart society* (pp. 1–23). Tokyo, Japan: SpringerOpen.

Frey, C., & Osborne, M. (2013). *The future of employment: How susceptible are jobs to computerisation*. Retrieved from https://www.oxfordmartin.ox.ac.uk/downloads/academic/The_Future_of_Employment.pdf

Fukuyama, M. (2018). Society 5.0: Aiming for a new human-centered society. *Japan Spotlight, 1*, 47–50.

Government of Japan. (2016). *5th science, technology, and innovation basic plan*. Retrieved from https://5x5 .wirelesswatch.jp/docs/S5-plan.pdf

Government of Japan. (2021). *6th science, technology, and innovation basic plan*. Retrieved from https:// www8.cao.go.jp/cstp/english/sti_basic_plan.pdf

Japan Business Federation (Keidanren). (2016). *Toward Realization of the New Economy and Society: Reform of the Economy and Society by the Deepening of "Society 5.0"*. Keidanren, Tokyo

Keidanren. (2018). *Society 5.0: Co-creating the future*. Retrieved from https://www.keidanren.or.jp/en/ policy/2018/095_booklet.pdf

Koropets, O., Melnikova, A., & Fedorova, A. (2022). Studying risk factors for the low incomes of the industry 4.0 employees. In D. B. Solovev, V. V. Savaley, A. T. Bekker & V. I. Petukhov (Eds.), *Smart innovation, systems and technologies. Proceeding of the International Science and Technology Conference*. Springer. https://doi.org/10.1007/978-981-16-8829-4_70

Nedelkoska, L., & Quintini, G. (2018). *Automation, skills use and training*. OECD Social, Employment and Migration Working Papers, 202. https://doi.org/10.1787/2e2f4eea-en

Pereira, A. G., Lima, T. M., & Charrua-Santos, F. (2020). Industry 4.0 and society 5.0: Opportunities and threats. *International Journal of Recent Technology and Engineering, 8*(5), 3305–3308. https://doi.org /10.35940/ijrte.D8764.018520

Potočan, V., Mulej, M., & Nedelko, Z. (2021). Society 5.0: Balancing of industry 4.0, economic advancement and social problems. *Kybernetes, 50*(3), 794–811. https://doi.org/10.1108/K-12-2019 -0858

Pouliakas, K. (2018). *Automation risk in the EU labour market A skill-needs approach*. Retrieved from https:// www.cedefop.europa.eu/files/automation_risk_in_the_eu_labour_market.pdf

PwC. (2018). *Will robots really steal our jobs? An international analysis of the potential longterm impact of automation*. Retrieved from https://www.pwc.com/hu/hu/kiadvanyok/assets/pdf/impact_of_ automation_on_jobs.pdf

United Nation. (2018). *Sustainable development goals*. Retrieved from https://sdgs.un.org/goals

Wang, H., Tong, L., Takeuchi, R., & George, G. (2016). Corporate social responsibility: An overview and new research directions. *Academy of Management Journal, 59*(2), 534–544. https://doi.org/10 .5465/amj.2016

Index

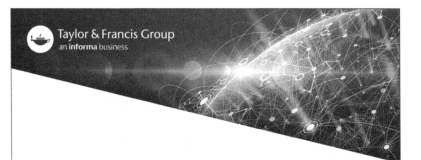

Printed in the United States
by Baker & Taylor Publisher Services